180 Creative Ideas

for **Getting Students Involved,** **Engaged,** and **Excited**

Other Teacher Resources from *The Teacher's Calendar*

The Teacher's Calendar
The Teacher's Calendar of Famous Birthdays

180 Creative Ideas

for Getting Students Involved, Engaged, and Excited

The Editors of McGraw-Hill
with Luisa Gerasimo and Sally Walker

Contemporary Books

Chicago New York San Francisco Lisbon London Madrid Mexico City
Milan New Delhi San Juan Seoul Singapore Sydney Toronto

Library of Congress Cataloging-in-Publication Data

180 creative ideas for getting students involved, engaged, and excited / the
    editors of McGraw-Hill with Luisa Gerasimo and Sally Walker.
        p.   cm.
    Includes index.
    ISBN 0-07-141229-8
    1. Creative activities and seat work.   2. Student activities—United States.
I. Title: One hundred eighty creative ideas for getting students involved, engaged,
and excited.   II. Gerasimo, Luisa.   III. Walker, Sally M.   IV. McGraw-Hill
Companies.

LB1027.25.A12   2004
371.3—dc21   2003048588

1 2 3 4 5 6 7 8 9 0   DOC/DOC   2 1 0 9 8 7 6 5 4 3

ISBN 0-07-141229-8

Interior design by Think Design Group

Contents

v

Contents

IDEAS FOR October

Contents

Contents

IDEAS FOR January

IDEAS FOR February

Contents

IDEAS FOR March

Contents

Contents

IDEAS FOR **June and July**

Appendix

Index

Introduction

With so much clamoring for students' attention, it can be a battle to have them "tune in" to the lesson at hand—or to you. With *180 Creative Ideas for Getting Students Involved, Engaged, and Excited*, we've tried to offer inspirational resources in a range of subject areas for you, the teacher, for each day of the typical school year (and some ideas for summer school).

Some of these 180 ideas have appeared as "Curriculum Connections" in *The Teacher's Calendar*, an annual reference listing interesting holidays, events, anniversaries, and more that would be of interest in your classroom. We've selected the best of these "Curriculum Connections" from the last five years and added lots of other ideas to create this new book—that can be used year after year.

180 Creative Ideas for Getting Students Involved, Engaged, and Excited is organized by the school year, from August to July. Most of these ideas are coordinated with a particular day of the year: perhaps a section on David "Davy" Crockett around the time of his birthday (August 3), or a section about Thanksgiving in late November, or information about how to figure out distance to the horizon on Weather Observer's Day (May 5). Many months have special designations: October is International Dinosaur Month, February is Black History Month, March is Women's History Month, and April is Mathematics Education Month. We've offered ways to bring these special months into the classroom.

The range of subject areas is broad: everything from classroom life and etiquette to mathematics and language arts to science and nature. To make navigating easier among these 180 ideas, we've added icons to each one signaling the subject matter covered. Here is a complete list:

Classroom Life and Etiquette

Fine Arts

Fun and Games

Geography and Social Studies

Health and Fitness

History

Holidays

Language Arts

Mathematics

Nature

Science and Technology

So here are ideas for poetry sessions, making crystals, learning local history, understanding historical figures and events, and much, much more! It is our hope that you and your class will have fun with these, learn a lot, and spend an eventful school year.

180 Creative Ideas

for Getting Students Involved, Engaged, and Excited

IDEAS FOR
August

1

Setting Classroom Goals

Get your school year off on the right track. September is National School Success Month, which focuses on helping students and parents be aware of the importance of academic work. Observing this theme can serve a twofold purpose: first, it can be used to create a sense of cohesion among new classmates; second, it can help provide a yardstick by which students can measure social and academic progress.

After beginning-of-the-year introductions are out of the way, ask students to help you list the pluses and minuses they experienced in class *as a class* last year. What actions and/or emotions were productive and created a sense of unity in their respective rooms? What detracted from this?

For homework, ask students to talk with family members and friends about their experiences in school. Have each student write a list of five helpful and five detrimental actions for achieving a successful classroom. Make lists that include all comments. Form groups of four or five students and brainstorm ways that helpful actions can be implemented in the classroom. (This divides the class initially, but some students will speak more freely if not faced with a large group.)

Come back together as a class and discuss the suggestions. Together, make a general list of five classroom goals for academic and social success in your classroom. An example might be to use "study buddies," students who quiz each other on multiplication facts or language usage. A sign-up sheet entitled "I Could Use a Helping Hand" could be posted. After a student signs up, a student proficient in the task could offer to help out by quizzing or discussion. A necessary corollary to this is removing any social stigma in admitting the need for some extra help. The focus should always be on attaining classroom success.

Highlight goals with a student-generated bulletin board for the first few weeks of school. Hold a weekly goal assessment meeting for the first two months. After that, make it a monthly task if all seems to be flowing smoothly.

$$2$$

Launch the School Year with Space Milestones

August has seen many successful space "firsts," including the transmission of the first picture of Earth from space (August 7, 1959), the first flight of Earth organisms into space (August 19, 1960), the launch of *Voyager 2* (August 20, 1977), and the launch of the space shuttle *Discovery* (August 30, 1984). And just as a space program launches rockets to explore and achieve scientific goals, a classroom can be viewed as a launching pad for academic goals.

As you discuss classroom goals (Idea 1), you can use the theme of space milestones to help. Brainstorming sessions about the new year's lessons can identify students' expectations about the topics they will be learning. Use their list of expectations to generate a "launching pad" list of classroom academic goals. Be sure to incorporate goals you must fulfill for district requirements. A launchpad bulletin board can serve as a constantly changing showcase for student work that shows attainment of a goal, regardless of its size.

Goals can include many kinds of "firsts": writing the letters of the alphabet, doing a math problem correctly, using scissors properly, producing a final draft of a composition, accomplishing reading goals, documenting science class observations, and so on. Students can celebrate many firsts, big and small, and recognize milestone achievements of classmates. More goal activities later in the book will help your students keep focused on their flight into the future.

Art projects will get your student-generated bulletin board off to a quick start. Encourage kindergarten and primary students to draw a picture of something they would like to do in class this year. Time permitting, ask them to tell the class about their drawing—a good icebreaker activity. Upper elementary and middle school students may write a paragraph, draw a picture, or write a poem or a rap about what they want to accomplish during the school year. Small group discussions could explore ways some of the goals might be achieved.

3

Switch Hands Day

During the early days of the school year, children are getting used to new faces and tasks. Have a "Switch Hands Day" as a way to break the ice. Ask your students to put themselves in another person's place. Today, all left- and right-handers should swap handedness for short periods of time. This can be a real classroom challenge, as well as an opportunity for children to learn to tolerate differences.

At recess, set up a row of trash cans. Divide students into squads. Have a relay race where students toss balls into the can nearest their line. All balls must be thrown with the "new" hand. Once the ball is in the can, the student can retrieve it and pass it to the next person in line. Don't make the distance too far—it's a lot harder than it sounds. Remember to open the door with your "other" hand on the way back inside.

During writing, announce, "Pencils down, switch hands. The next three sentences (five words for primary students) must be written with your other hand." Point out how difficult it is to see the written words as the students are writing with their left hand. Right-handers don't cover the words with their hand as they write; left-handers are forced to. Afterward, ask students to identify letters that were easy and hard to make. Let them rewrite the same words using their "normal" hand and compare them.

In science, talk about the brain and which area determines left- and right-handedness. As a math assignment, count how many students are really left-handed. Compare the percentage in your class with that estimated for the general population (about 10 percent).

Point out small differences that we don't normally consider, such as using right- and left-handed scissors. Turning screws may be difficult for lefties. Have right-handed students button their clothing with their left hand. Is it harder? Poll left-handed students and see how many have adapted and use their right hand for things like opening doors or picking up food with a fork. Many people are left- or right-eyed as well. Ask students which eye they look through a camera or telescope with. Is it on the same side as the hand they write with?

Above all, encourage students to notice that when they use the "other" hand, they often have to slow down and be more patient. Getting angry and frustrated doesn't make the job easier. That's a helpful observation for all students to note and remember, especially when working with younger siblings or people who may not have the same ability levels they do.

Davy Crockett

Birth, August 3, 1786

When we think of the rough-and-ready frontiersman in United States history, names such as Daniel Boone, Jim Bowie, and Davy Crockett spring quickly to mind. David "Davy" Crockett was born in Greene County, Tennessee, on August 3, 1786. His father ran a tavern after the family moved to Jefferson County. As a child, Davy was not fond of schooling and often played hooky.

For years, Crockett worked as an army scout and fought in the Creek Indian War, in the area that is now Florida and Alabama. He went on to a political career, holding several local elected positions, followed by a term in the Tennessee legislature from 1821 to 1824, and three terms in the U.S. House of Representatives. In 1835, after losing a reelection bid for Congress, Crockett headed out to Texas, which was then embroiled in a conflict seeking independence from Mexico. In February of the following year, he joined forces with a group of men at the Alamo, a fort in San Antonio. When the Alamo was overrun by Mexican troops on March 6, 1836, Crockett was killed during the fighting.

Davy Crockett and his many wilderness exploits became the starting point of many of America's best-loved tall tales. Everything he did, from hunting to swimming to talking, became larger-than-life each time the stories were retold. His motto was "Be always sure you're right—then go ahead!"

Introduce your students to this colorful historical figure through picture books, told as tall tales, written and illustrated for children: *The Narrow Escapes of Davy Crockett*, by Ariane Dewey (out of print, but available in library collections, ages eight to ten), and *Davy Crockett Saves the World*, by Rosalyn Schanzer (HarperCollins, 0-688-16691-0, ages six to twelve). In the first book, readers discover Crockett's hunting trials and wilderness escapades. The second story recounts how he saves the world from Halley's Comet. Both are action-filled stories that fit perfectly into Tall Tale units. Perhaps students would enjoy writing their own tall tales.

Biographies about Crockett have been written for several grade levels. *A Picture Book of Davy Crockett*, by David Adler (Holiday House, 0-8234-1343-8, ages six to nine), will appeal to primary students. *Davy Crockett: Young Rifleman*, by Aileen Parks (Simon and Schuster, 0-02-041840-X, ages eight to twelve), is one of the entries in Simon and Schuster's Young Americans series.

For social studies units on U.S. frontier history, *Voices of the Alamo*, by Sherry Garland (Scholastic, 0-590-98833-6, ages seven to ten), gives a fictionalized multicultural reflection on the battle over the Alamo. The battle is told from the viewpoints of several different participants.

(5)

National Mustard Day

August 3

If you are in school during the hot days of August, you might be looking for a totally silly break. National Mustard Day (August 3) is just the trick. This well-loved condiment, which comes in varying shades of yellow and brown, is almost as American as apple pie—at least when you're talking hot dogs.

Mustard begins life as a leafy green plant. Its seeds are very tough and can lie dormant under certain conditions for perhaps a hundred years! Prior to the development of seed heads, its leaves are edible and can be purchased in the produce section of many supermarkets. If you live someplace with farms nearby, you may have seen lush fields of small yellow flowers in the early part of summer. If so, it was probably mustard growing wild or as a crop. Perhaps you can arrange for a time in the school cafeteria to cook up a small batch of mustard greens and let everyone have a taste. The greens are loaded with vitamins A, B, and C. Afterward, vote on their taste as compared to lettuce and spinach. What do your students prefer? Don't be surprised if they don't care for the taste, it is rather strong. However, mustard greens are prized by many people around the world, including those with such disparate cooking traditions as the Greeks and many Asian cultures.

There are two kinds of mustard plants. Black mustard is the king, growing to a height of almost six feet. White mustard is smaller and only reaches two to three feet. The Latin botanical name for mustard's family is Cruciferae, a large family of plants that includes a number of edibles such as cabbage, watercress, and turnip.

Mustard in its condiment form, as a powder and as a suspension, is made from the seeds of the plant. Today, supermarkets carry a wide selection of mustards flavored with anything from horseradish to raspberries to honey. Solicit donations and hold a mustard tasting in your class. Diced tidbits of hot dogs, cheese, or crackers serve well as dippers. Bring in a dozen boiled eggs, have kids peel and chop them up. Divide the mix into two bowls. Add mayonnaise to moisten. Add powdered mustard to taste (about a teaspoon should suffice, but you will need to taste as powdered mustard varies so much) to one of the bowls and leave the other one plain. Ask students to compare batches. Which do they prefer?

Mustard was once used medicinally in something called a *plaster*. If students have read any historical books (based in a time before the mid–nineteen hundreds) they may have wondered what that meant. A plaster or poultice is a soft mass of moist herbs or ground meal applied to a cloth and then to the skin. Mustard was used to draw out toxins, increase circulation, and heat the body. There is an expression, "cut the mustard," which most kids will not know. "Cut the mustard" means being able to do something in a youthful or vigorous manner. It's usually used in a phrase such as "Do you think she will be able to cut the mustard?"

In a more serious vein, a nice discussion starter is the parable of the mustard seed found in the Bible in Matthew 13:31, or another mustard-seed comparison found in Matthew 17:20.

Your class will find mustard easy to grow, so if you have a sunny window, some cups, a little dirt, and a few seeds perhaps you could make it a class project.

6

Youth and the World

United Nations International Youth Day, August 12

International Youth Day, sponsored by the United Nations, offers teachers a great opportunity to focus on global issues and how today's youth can have an impact on them.

To get a better understanding of how important youth are to the growth and survival of families and thus communities all over the world, you may wish to assign research projects that look at a typical day in a foreign child's life. Your children may be surprised by how much children contribute to family survival. Very young children care for babies, haul water (sometimes for miles on foot), care for gardens, fields, and farm animals, tend family stores, or even work at factories to make money to help out. Ask students to contrast and compare the child they picked to the role they play at home. What contributions do kids make here?

You may find that you have students interested in duplicating the work of the United Nations within their own communities. A good reference book for youngsters interested in changing the world is *It's Our World, Too!*, by Phillip Hoose (Little, Brown and Co., 0-316-37245-5, out of print, ages nine to twelve). It includes information on young activists who have made a positive impact. The questions below can be used to spark a brainstorming session on opportunities for local activism, or as topics for essays.

- What is a human right?
- What can young people do in their own communities to help ensure justice, human dignity, and the well-being of all people?
- Why is it so important to be able to read and write?
- How is the way our country treats our youth different from, or the same as, treatment of people in other countries? (This question can lead to discussion on issues of poverty, child labor,

arranged marriages, or the hope parents worldwide have for their children.)

- What do your parents/guardians wish for your future? What do your teachers and other workers at your school hope for your future? (Children could write what they think adults wish and then ask them to learn if they are right.)
- How do we get to know youth from other countries? (Answers may include school, the Internet, travel, pen pals, foreign exchange programs, sister cities programs, and so forth.)
- Why is it a good idea for young people from different countries to get to know one another?
- Do you think it is possible for people to live on one planet and not have wars? Why or why not?
- What do you think it would take to stop fighting and wars? What can we do in our own lives/neighborhoods/schools?
- Do young people have a role in creating a peaceful and fair future, or do you have to be a grown-up to make a difference? Why?

7

Volcano Investigators

Eruption of Mount Vesuvius, August 24, 79 A.D.

". . . black and horrible clouds, broken by sinuous shapes of flaming winds, were opening with long tongues of fire . . ." When southern Italy's Mount Vesuvius erupted in 79 A.D., Pliny the Younger, a Roman teenager at the time, wrote accounts to the historian Tacitus, describing the eruption of this huge volcano and how it affected the area. Pliny the Younger was one of the fortunate people who escaped the fiery hot cloud that engulfed the city of Pompeii (his uncle, Pliny the Elder, did not). Many of the town's residents were suffocated and killed by poisonous gas and gritty ash in the air. The nearby city of Herculaneum was buried by lava flows and mud as deeply as one hundred feet.

In the intervening years people have excavated the cities numerous times. Some of the excavators were robbers, who stole valuable artifacts. These cities are protected by the government and responsible archaeological excavations have been conducted in both cities. (The television show "NOVA" has produced a video entitled "Deadly Shadow of Vesuvius," and the National Geographic Society has one entitled "In the Shadow of Vesuvius." Check your local public library for copies. Both can be easily located on the Internet.)

An interesting science project would be to divide the students into three groups of "volcano investigators." One group will discover information about pyroclastic flows. These are the deadly, rapidly moving flows of ash. More than twenty-eight thousand people were killed by a pyroclastic flow from Mt. Pelée in Martinique in 1902.

The second group can discover information about two types of lava flows called *pahoehoe* and *aa*. These are the slow-moving lava flows found in Hawaii.

The third group should find information about *lahars*. These are devastating mud flows that are triggered by volcanic eruptions. The *lahar* triggered by the 1985 Nevado del Ruíz eruption in Colombia buried the city of Armero and killed more than twenty-five thousand people.

Each group can present its findings so the class can compare and contrast the various flows. Many students are surprised to learn volcanoes aren't just lava flows. Discuss the hazards associated with each flow and whether evacuation plans for threatened cities are realistic in terms of implementation.

Nonfiction books about volcanoes include: *Why Do Volcanoes Blow Their Tops?*, by Melvin Berger and Gilda Berger (Scholastic, 0-439-09580-8, grades 2 to 4); *Shaping the Earth*, by Dorothy Hinshaw Patent (Houghton Mifflin, 0-395-85691-4, grades 5 and up), and *Volcanoes: Earth's Inner Fire*, by Sally M. Walker (Carolrhoda, 0-8761-4812-7, grades 4 to 7).

Books about Mt. Vesuvius include: *Pompeii . . . Buried Alive*, by Edith Kunhardt (Random House, 0-394-88866-9, grades K to 3); *In Search of Pompeii*, by Giovanni Caselli (Peter Bedrick, 0-87226-545-5, grades 5 and up); and *The Buried City of Pompeii*, by Shelley Tanaka (Hyperion, 0-7868-0285-5, grades 3 to 7). Mary Pope Osborne's novel *Vacation Under the Volcano* (Random House, 0-679-89050-5, grades 2 to 5) is one of the Magic Tree House adventures for younger readers.

Novels featuring volcanoes include: *Rage of Fire*, by Gloria Skurzynski (National Geographic, 0-7922-7035-5, grades 4 to 8), which takes place in Hawaii, and *The Volcano Disaster*, by Peg Kehret (Pocket, 0-671-00968-0, grades 4 to 7). This novel is a Mount St. Helens time-travel adventure.

(8)

Mock Newbery: Make Literature a School-Year Habit

Get the school year off to a rousing start by focusing on the best of recently published children's literature. Do this by holding a Mock Newbery Award competition in your classroom. This activity must be started during the first few weeks of school. Students will need the following three months to read the list of Mock Newbery candidate books.

John Newbery (1731–1767), an Englishman, is a famous historical figure in children's literature. The owner of a London bookstore, Newbery was the first person to publish and sell books for children. The Newbery Medal is sponsored each year by the Association for Library Service to Children division of the American Library Association in honor of his contributions. Announced in January or February, the annual medal is given to the author of the book that a selection committee deems the most distinguished contribution to children's literature published during the preceding year. Only authors who are U.S. citizens or residents are eligible for the Newbery Medal, which was established in 1922.

The best way to establish a Mock Newbery list is to contact the children's literature specialist in a local bookstore or the youth services librarian at your public library. He or she should be very up to date on new book titles. Each book you look at for this year's Mock Newbery should have the current year's copyright date. Work with your contact to develop a list of ten to fifteen books—more if you're really energetic. (Some bookstores may already have a Mock Newbery partnership with local schools—and a ready list. See if there's one in your area.) Include one or two nonfiction titles and a poetry book. Approach your learning center director, principal, or PTO for funds to buy at least one copy of each book. They can all be added into the school's collection by mid-January.

To get the award selection process underway, do a "book talk" on each title with the students. Perhaps the bookstore representative would be willing to do this. Or, ask willing students to read and do a book talk on the titles to their classmates. Then, let students sign out and read the books. Every student will have a vote; the only rule is that they must read at least a certain number of the books on the list (you decide: seven to ten of the offered books—or more?). Students who have read the same book can get together, discuss it, and decide if they want it to go on to the next round. They should focus on plot, theme, use of language, character development, etc. When a group decides to support a book, the group members must pitch its merits to their classmates during the next selection committee meeting (this should be the whole class, always).

Plan on holding several selection committee meetings. At the end of each meeting, hold a vote. Books with the lowest votes are off the list. Your goal is to gradually whittle the list down to two or three books in December. Then, the supporters of those books must really work to get others to read their book, so a final winner can be chosen. Select one medal recipient and two honor books. Hang signs in the hallway announcing your results. Enthusiastic students might be persuaded to give a short commercial for the winners at a school assembly.

Compare your finalists to those chosen by the American Library Association selection committee (listed on the ALA's website at ala.org/alsc/newbery.html). Do your students concur with the committee's choice of medal winner and honor books?

9

I Have a Dream

March on Washington, August 28, 1963

On August 28, 1963, Dr. Martin Luther King Jr. made his famous "I Have a Dream" speech during the March on Washington, a civil rights rally attended by more than 250,000 people. Although many people recognize the speech title, only some are familiar with its powerful, stirring text expressing hope for the future. *I Have a Dream*, by Dr. Martin Luther King Jr. (Scholastic, 0-590-20516-1, all ages), presents the text of the speech, plus illustrations by fifteen African American artists who have won a Coretta Scott King Award or honor book designation for their work. This excellent book provides a thought-provoking way for students to study the speech, and gives numerous starting points for classroom discussion on topics such as civil rights, the meaning of equality, race relations, and how we can turn a social dream into a reality.

Questions that arise from discussion groups can be used to generate student letters to government representatives. Other books that explore the theme of civil rights include: *I Am Rosa Parks*, by Rosa Parks and Jim Haskins (Penguin, 0-8037-1206-5, grades K to 3); *Dear Dr. King: Letters from Today's Children to Dr. Martin Luther King, Jr.*, edited by Jan Colbert and Ann McMillan Harms (Hyperion, 0-7868-0417-3, grades 4 to 7); and *Richard Wright and the Library Card*, by William Miller (Publishers Group West, 1-8800-0057-1, grades 3 to 8).

Schools with computer audio capabilities can access an audio version of Dr. King's speech at historychannel.com/gspeech/archive.html. Some students may have heard portions of this speech, but few will have heard more than a very short clip. Parts of the speech are very appealing to children as Dr. King talks about his own children and the future he imagines for them.

10

Celebrate Your State Fair

Most states hold a big annual gathering sometime between July and early September. Exhibits, contests, demonstrations, commercial booths, food, rides, concerts, and lots more all come together for a week or so. Your state may be having its state fair right now. If not, no matter, you can still have some good old-fashioned fun with fairs. Break students into teams and start by creating a classroom poll. Each team should create a questionnaire that will ask other students, parents, and friends about their memories of going to the state fair. Each team should come up with at least three questions, and a place to record the age, sex, and answer for each person questioned.

Take some time to let students warm up by practicing on one another. Make copies of the team surveys for students to use at home and return the next day to class. Ask each child to talk to at least three people (other than their classmates). This should give you enough material to pull together a "Fair Time Memories" booklet or bulletin board. Is there a big difference between what older folks recall and loved versus what the children in your class seem to enjoy? Has the fair changed a lot or very little in the years between the oldest person's memories and the youngest? Do women and men like the same parts of the fair, or do they have different favorites?

Have students illustrate the memory book with art depicting things you might see at the fair. Food, animals, people, rides, and demonstrations can be depicted in collage, paint, crayon, or any other media, but need to be small enough to fit in your booklet or on your board. The border of the book or board can be made to look like a white picket fence, corn dogs, or other fair-related theme.

Ask students to think of the food they eat at the fair. Does your fair give away free (or cheap) glasses of milk? Does the honey demonstrator let you taste honey? What foods do you like to purchase while there? Many fairs feature foods on sticks. Why do you think this interesting manner of serving food came to be? Have the class think of all the things that could be served on a stick. Make a big list. One Midwest state featured these hot new deep-fried items-on-a-stick in the past few years: alligator, hamburger with cheese on the inside, macaroni and cheese, and even candy bars. Every year they seem to dream up a new food item to batter, deep fry, and serve on a stick. Can your class come up with some winners? Vote on the best three foods and create art to illustrate.

(11)

Gizmos and Gadgets

National Inventor's Month, August

The old adage "Necessity is the mother of all invention" is especially appropriate for National Inventors Month, celebrated every August. And there's nothing like a new gadget, gizmo, machine, or invention for grabbing public interest.

Some of the simplest of all inventions are the ones we use every day—they're so simple we don't even regard them as inventions, or even machines. What would we do without screws, levers, inclined planes, wheels and axles and pulleys? Work a lot harder, that's for sure! Simple machines is one of the science curriculum units in most elementary and middle schools.

Because of their importance, it's important that children understand the underlying physics or mechanics principles of how these machines work. A clear understanding of simple machines enables students to implement their use and makes doing work easier. A creative writing project might revolve around scripting a play that tells a story of how prehistoric peoples may have discovered these machines. Posters advertising the newfangled machines could complement the performances, which would be effective in a reader's theater format. It might be fun to create a poster display featuring landmark inventions. Compare early inventions with the very complex inventions we have today. Notice how many modern inventions rely on electrical power.

In October 1999, the Arts & Entertainment TV cable channel polled a number of people in an effort to determine the most influential people of the millennium. Johannes Gutenberg, the inventor of the printing press, was number one. Another writing project might be a fantasy of what life today would be like if the printing press had not been invented.

As a classroom project, students could list all the machines they can think of that are part of their world. Look around the school, the neighborhood, and their homes. Combine the lists and vote on which machines are most useful, which ones are most frequently used, the silliest, etc. Graph the results on an inventions chart. Discuss what kinds of devices they would like to see invented, and what kinds of future inventions might revolutionize their lives.

Turn your students into inventors with artwork and writing projects. You may want to make up an Invention Criteria sheet to steer the activity toward practical, rather than fanciful, inventions. If your students explore this subject in depth, they can make prototypes of their inventions. A collection of inventions could become an Invention Fair.

Students should be encouraged to produce supportive documentation for inventions, including assembly instructions, owners' manuals, or warranties. Encourage students to bring in examples of such documentation from home. Together, you can discuss the advantages of the booklets (safety and use) and the drawbacks (too long or too hard to understand).

The Early Bird Physics series, published by Lerner Books, has several titles for grades 2 through 5 that focus on simple machines, how they are used, and what underlying principles make each machine work. Titles include *Work* (0-8225-2211-X), *Levers* (0-8225-2212-8), *Screws* (0-8225-2216-0), *Inclined Planes and Wedges* (0-8225-2215-2), *Wheels and Axles* (0-8225-2213-6), and *Pulleys* (0-8225-2214-4). All are written by Sally M. Walker and Roseann Feldmann and are also available in hardback.

Two publishers have created a series of books featuring inventions. Simon and Schuster's Inventions series discusses items commonly found in every home. One title is *The Clock*, by Trent Duffy (0-689-82814-4, ages twelve and up). *Telephones*, by Elaine Alphin (1-57505-432-9, ages seven to eleven), is an example from the Household History series from Carolrhoda Books. Irons, eyeglasses, toasters, and vacuum cleaners are some of the other inventions featured in the series.

What You Never Knew About Tubs, Toilets, and Showers, by Patricia Lauber (Simon and Schuster, 0-689-82420-3, ages seven to eleven), is a funny look at personal hygiene and the inventions that make bathing easier. *Girls Think of Everything*, by Catherine Thimmesh (Houghton Mifflin, 0-395-93744-2, ages twelve and up), features inventions that were thought of and designed by women. *Gizmos and Gadgets*, by Jill Hauser (Williamson, 1-8855-9326-0, ages twelve and up), provides hands-on suggestions for creating fun inventions.

Related books that students will enjoy are: *Accidents May Happen: 50 Inventions Discovered by Mistake*, by Charlotte Jones (Bantam, 0-385-32240-2, grades 2 to 8); *Brainstorm! The Stories of Twenty American Kid Inventors*, by Tom Tucker (Farrar, Straus and Giroux, 0-374-40928-5, grades 3 to 8); and *Inventors*, by Martin W. Sandler (HarperCollins, 0-06-024923-4, grades 4 and up).

(12)

The Microscopic World

National Inventor's Month, August

Some inventions have changed the course of science history. One amazing invention was made in the 1590s when Zacharias Janssen, a Dutch inventor, put together the first microscope. Prior to that, people had known about the magnifying power of glass lenses; people had been wearing eyeglasses since the thirteenth or fourteenth century. But Janssen's invention allowed human eyes to view extremely small objects clearly.

Antonie van Leeuwenhoek invented a stronger single-lens microscope in the 1670s that could magnify objects 270 times their actual size. In 1674, van Leeuwenhoek concluded that the tiny moving objects he saw with his lens were animals—a startling new thought to the scientific community of his time!

In 1931, Ernst Ruska and other scientists from Germany built the first electron microscope. This amazingly powerful microscope has let scientists examine particles that without it would be beyond our understanding.

If you don't have a microscope in your classroom, see if you can borrow one for a few days from another school—possibly the high school. Objects such as hair, paper, soil, vegetables, and flowers are fascinating to see and observe.

The Microscope Book, by Shar Levine and Leslie Johnstone (Sterling, 0-8069-4898-1, ages ten and up), is an excellent step-by-step guide for classroom microscope use. It contains a wealth of experiments and activities, all with an eye toward inquiry-based learning and discovery.

Encourage students to make detailed drawings of what they see through the microscope. Color the pictures and hang them around the classroom as a display of scientific art.

There are several books that will further extend student interest and involvement in the microscopic world. *Out of Sight*, by Seymour Simon (1-5871-7011-6, North Star, ages seven and up), will grab student interest immediately. Simon goes beyond images taken through microscopes and uses photos taken via stop-action and satellite imagery also. *Yikes! Your Body Up Close*, by Mike Janulewicz (0-689-81520-4, Simon and Schuster, ages seven to twelve), and *Yuck!*, by Robert Snedden (0-689-80676-0, Simon and Schuster, ages seven to twelve), explore objects that are fascinating and gross. *Sea Soup: Zooplankton*, by Mary Cerullo (0-8844-8219-7, Tilbury, ages eight and up), has wonderful photomicrographs of the tiny creatures that form the base of the oceanic food chain. A teacher's guide is available as a separate purchase.

As a corollary to microscopes, some students might want to further research the development of lenses for eyeglasses and contact lenses. If they do, they will run into Benjamin Franklin, who developed bifocal glasses.

(13)

Creative Fun with Puppets

Puppets have entertained and delighted audiences for hundreds of years. One of the most famous puppets is Punch, from the Punch and Judy shows that originated in the latter half of the seventeenth century. Today, almost everyone recognizes the faces of Miss Piggy and Kermit, Muppets created by Jim Henson.

Kids who love to draw will be happy to know Henson's best characters started from crazy little doodles. A fun way to get kids' creative juices flowing is to brainstorm a list of attributes for a puppet character. This activity could help reinforce what "adjective" and "adverb" mean. Make a couple of columns on your board and let the class describe a puppet. You may end up with quite a list.

Have students record ideas from the board for their personal creation. On a page with the adjectives or adverbs they chose—fluffy, funny, fast, jerky, wild, smart, ornery, orange, tall—they can begin to sketch out ideas for what the puppet would look like, and perhaps make up a name. If you have any books that show how puppets are put together older students can plan out the "engineering" aspects of their creation. They may need to add strings, levers, springs, clamps, or other small machines to make their idea moveable. Can they draw the "guts" behind the outer part of their character?

Students can have lots of fun with puppets. Have them write their own short productions or adapt selections from favorite fairy tales or picture books. If your students are learning a new language, they could write simple puppets shows that use the language in several conversational settings.

Constructing a puppet theater doesn't have to be a major undertaking. The quickest puppet "stages" can be made by turning a table on its side or by tying a rope between two chairs and hanging a sheet over it. Students may enjoy making a more elaborate stage from cardboard.

Preschoolers and kindergartners love to tell "puppet" stories with simple felt cutouts placed on flannel-covered boards. Sometimes this is easier than using regular puppets since it doesn't require much manual dexterity.

Puppets are easy to make with materials that can be found in the classroom or at home. Stick or rod puppets can be constructed with paper and a twig. Cut into fanciful shapes, they can be simple or quite elaborate. Put them behind a sheet and backlight them for shadow presentations and they are even more dramatic.

Use gloves or old socks to construct hand puppets. Attach string, yarn, buttons, paper, and other materials to create facial features and clothing.

Marionettes take a bit more work, but older students enjoy constructing them and the challenge of operating them. After the first drawings and workings are created you will perhaps want to move to actually making the puppet. This could require found objects and lots of art supplies. Be sure to have lots of glue, duct or strapping and masking tape, string, felt, feathers, paint, stiff paper, small lids or buttons for eyes, clean cans and bottles, and various cardboard scraps on hand. Children can be asked to collect items from home. Old gloves are very handy for forming puppets' hands. A very complete and educational book for the "how-to" of puppet making, *The Puppet Cookbook*, is available from the Minnesota-based Heart of the Beast Puppet and Mask Theater (0-967-6776-0-2).

Completed puppets can even be used to stage a play written by your class! Or, if nothing else, be sure to make a colorful display for the rest of the school to enjoy in a hall or library display box.

Literature connections include: *What's It Like to Be a Puppeteer?*, by Susan Poskanzer (Troll, 0-8167-1433-9, grades 1 to 3); *Creative Paper Plate Puppetry*, by Elaine Cole and David Cole (Children's Outreach, 1-883426-18-9, grades 1 to 2); and *Puppet Shows Made Easy*, by Nancy Renfro (Nancy Renfro Studios, 0-931044-13-8, grades 2 to 12).

IDEAS FOR
September

---

(14)

Observing Children's Good Manners Month

Get the school year off to a good start. September is Children's Good Manners Month. Devote some time to reviewing what kinds of behavior show good manners. Just a simple "please" or "thank you" can make a big difference in how someone perceives his or her peers.

Get parents involved. Have students discuss with their parents or guardians the kinds of rules and behaviors that were encouraged in their families as they were growing up. Grandparents, who may have been raised in the "children should be seen and not heard" days, may offer the students some interesting perspectives. Ask children to note the behaviors of characters they regularly see on TV. How do they talk and act to the other people on the show? Do they demonstrate the way the student would like to be spoken to or treated? Many television shows provide plenty of fodder for discussions about rude behavior.

Brainstorm lists of nice and rude behaviors. Students could write a short story that relates the consequences of a particular bad-manner behavior. You might want to borrow old issues of *Highlights* magazine from the library. The regular feature "Goofus and Gallant" provides examples of bad and good manners. (While Gallant is sometimes too good to be true, students will get the message.) Develop your own classroom characters who reflect good and bad classroom manners. They can also exhibit their behaviors in the lunchroom and on the playground at recess. Perhaps your class can make posters of their characters and hang them in the hallways as reminders to other students.

Table Manners, by Chris Raschka and Vladimir Radunsky (Candlewick, 0-7636-1453-X, ages seven and up), discusses how people should behave at the table. Crazy illustrations and silly situations stress the importance of good table manners. *How My Parents Learned to Eat*, by Ina Friedman (Houghton Mifflin, 0-395-44235-4, ages seven to nine), is a lovely multicultural story about different eating utensils and the difficulties that arise when culture clashes occur. Older readers will enjoy the Mrs. Piggle-Wiggle books by Betty Macdonald. They've been around for ages, but they still hold lots of chuckles and will get kids thinking about behavior. You might want to try them as a read-aloud.

There are also a number of books available that contain suggestions and activities to foster good manners. A zany, but accurate, look at inappropriate behavior can be found in *David Goes to School*, by David Shannon (Scholastic, 0-590-48087-1, preschool to grade 2). Take a look at *Social Smarts: Manners for Today's Kids*, by Elizabeth James (Houghton Mifflin, 0-395-81312-3, ages nine to twelve), *Manners Made Easy: A Workbook for Student, Parent and Teacher*, by June Moore (Broadman, 0-8054-3770-3, ages seven to eleven), and *Manners Matter: Activities to Teach Young People Social Skills*, by Debbie Pincus-Ward (McGraw-Hill, 0-866-53688-4, ages eight to twelve). These all contain information about developing and encouraging good manners.

Teachers will find many manners tips in *The Gift of Good Manners: A Parent's Guide to Raising Respectful, Kind, Considerate Children*, by Peggy Post and Cindy Post Senning, Ed D. (Harper Resource, 0-06-018549-X), who are third-generation family members of manners maven Emily Post. This is a book you may want to refer parents to when they need help with issues of politeness at home. It is very much a "how-to" book with chapters for each age group and many concrete suggestions for dealing with daily conundrums. Another reference can be found online at goodmanners.com, which offers charts and certificates, books, booklets, and even sells a teacher's manual for a good manners curriculum.

15

Appreciation for a Job Well Done

During Children's Good Manners Month have fun while students encourage each other to "do a good job." There's nothing like a pat on the back to brighten up a person's day. Talk with your students about how you feel when someone lets you know your work has been appreciated. Ask them how they feel when they are told that something they did was good. Explain that you and they are going to spread those kinds of feelings around the school this week.

Let the students design a short form along these lines: "The students in Mr./Mrs./Ms. _____ class noticed that _____ did a good job _____. We really appreciated it and want to give you a round of applause and a great big *thank-you*."

Encourage students to notice the kinds of jobs people around them are doing well. For example, how clean the school halls are in the morning, that lunch was ready for them in the cafeteria, library books were on the shelves, Ms. _____'s class was quiet and well behaved during assembly, or the bus driver drove carefully. Students will likely come up with additional examples. Fill in the "good job" doer's name and job and deliver the note via school mailbox, or let two or three students hand deliver them along with a verbal thank-you.

In the classroom, students can help each other do a good job in many ways. They might work in pairs or threes and help each other with math. They can listen to each other read aloud. They can read and make positive and constructive comments on each other's writing.

You might set up a "Good Job" list on the blackboard. Have categories like Lining Up, Walking Quietly in the Hall, Good Behavior at Assembly, and Tidy Room at the End of the Day. Reward each class's good job with a star. Set a goal of five stars per category. No extrinsic awards for "winning"—just the satisfaction of a job well done.

Remind students that they can compliment family members on their good jobs, too. Mom and Dad appreciate compliments now and then!

16

Tickling the Ivories

National Piano Month, September

September is also designated National Piano Month, so why not make a tuneful start to the new school year? The piano is one of America's most popular instruments. And while some children take piano lessons, few ever get the opportunity to look inside a piano and see how it makes sound.

Arrange with the music teacher to hold a brief "open piano" instructional session. During this time he or she can open the piano and show the children the frame inside and explain how metal strings are stretched and attached to the frame. The strings vary in length and thickness, which changes the tone's pitch. Long, thick strings are low-pitched, while short, thin, tight strings produce high pitches.

The keys on the piano keyboard are connected to levers (good opportunity for a teachable moment on simple machines). When a keyboard key is depressed, a lever moves a padded hammer, which strikes one of the metal strings and produces a musical note.

Children also love to hear the sound differences when the piano's foot pedals are used. The damper pedal lets the notes ring on, like a bell, by allowing the strings to vibrate freely. The soft pedal lightens and mutes the notes.

The music teacher could also explain the different kinds of pianos: upright, grand, player, and electronic. For a historical approach, perhaps he or she could discuss the clavichord and harpsichord, two of the piano's forerunners.

Use piano music by well-known composers and/or pianists as background music for art or during other appropriate times. All styles of piano music, from jazz to classical, include pieces that range in mood and tone. Play a wide selection during the month and see how student tastes vary.

One week consider playing classical music. Famous classical composers who wrote for the piano include Chopin, Beethoven, Mozart, and Robert and Clara Schumann. More modern pianists known for composing or performing classical pieces are Rachmaninoff, Dame Myra Hess, Daniel Barenboim, and Van Cliburn.

Another week could showcase experimental composers for the piano, such as Charles Ives. Play Ives's Piano Sonata no. 2. Its four movements were named in honor of some of America's literary giants: Thoreau, the Alcotts, Emerson, and Hawthorne. What a lovely way to let music complement the language arts curriculum.

For a perky, upbeat week, choose the ragtime piano pieces composed by Scott Joplin. Most children recognize the theme from the movie *The Sting*—Joplin's "The Entertainer"—and his "Maple Leaf Rag" is also very popular. It is impossible to sit still while listening to Joplin's fast, bouncy rags, and they definitely brighten up the atmosphere. In tune with the lighter vein, see if your library has a video of Victor Borge. Borge gained heights of fame as an accomplished pianist and comedian. His sketch on punctuation will leave middle school and older students in stitches and ready to play with audible punctuation of their own.

Perhaps you could feature jazz piano during the fourth week. Art Tatum, Bill Evans, and Dave Brubeck have recorded many pieces. Or choose the works of James P. Johnson, who invented stride piano. Boogie-woogie, another form of jazz piano, has an infectious beat that leaves fingers snapping and toes tapping.

(17)

Henry David Thoreau

Ends Two-Year Stay at Walden, September 6, 1847

Henry David Thoreau, born in Concord, Massachusetts, July 12, 1817, is perhaps best remembered for his book *Walden*. Thoreau lived at Walden Pond from July 4, 1845, to September 6, 1847. He built his own house near the pond and kept a detailed record of his thoughts and the variations in nature he observed. He felt deeply connected to nature, and the theme of *Walden* is man living in harmony with the natural world.

Thoreau liked to get close to the land and its living creatures. He reveled in taking the time to explore his surroundings: "Heaven is under our feet as well as over our heads." In today's speedy world, the art of sitting quietly or taking the time to enjoy an experience is slowly becoming lost.

Henry Hikes to Fitchburg, by D. B. Johnson (Houghton Mifflin, 0-395-96867-4, all ages), is a wonderful fictionalized version of a twenty-five-mile hike Thoreau made to Fitchburg, Massachusetts. In the story, Henry and his friend (both depicted as bears) must travel to a distant town. Henry chooses to hike. His journey involves adventure, exploring nature, wading in streams, and picking berries. Henry's friend chooses to ride the train. He works to earn the money for his ticket. Both reach the destination, but with vastly differing experiences along the way. Neither is right or wrong—their journeys are just different.

Students might enjoy describing how they would plan a journey "from here to there," and what activities would appeal to them during the trip.

Thoreau is also remembered for his essay "Civil Disobedience." Many of today's social activists who advocate passive resistance have read this essay. There are nice curriculum ties to be found between Thoreau and later reformers such as Mohandas Gandhi and Martin

Luther King Jr., who also advocated and practiced the philosophy of passive resistance.

Older readers could read excerpts from the essay and discuss what they think is important in regard to civil responsibilities. One issue might be a citizen's voting record. Many people don't bother to vote. Students could debate whether that is a responsible choice or not.

Other books for young readers about Thoreau and his writings include *New Suns Will Arise: From the Diaries of Henry David Thoreau*, selected by John Dugdale (Hyperion, 0-7868-0839-0, ages twelve and up), and *Henry David Thoreau: In Step with Nature*, by Elizabeth Ring (Millbrook, 1-56294-795-8, ages eight to eleven). In libraries, look for *Into the Deep Forest with Henry David Thoreau*, by Jim Murphy (ages twelve and up), and *A Man Named Thoreau*, by Robert Burleigh (ages eight and up).

For older students and adults, Elizabeth Witherell has edited a volume called *Thoreau: Collected Essays and Poems* (Library of America, 1-88301-195-7). A large number of Thoreau's poems and twenty-seven of his essays appear in this handy book, making it a treasure trove for classroom use. It might prove useful if you would like to read a selection to the class.

---

(18)

Two Women Folk Painters

Grandma Moses, Birth, September 7, 1860; Clementine Hunter, Birth, 1886

Anna Mary Robertson was born on September 7, 1860, in Washington County, New York. Anna married Thomas Moses, a farmer, when she was seventeen. They had ten children; five died in infancy. She did not start painting until 1938, when she was seventy-eight years old. Grandma Moses, as she became known, never had an art lesson and was completely self-taught. She began by embroidering pictures on canvas. She turned to painting when her fingers, crippled by arthritis, made holding embroidery needles too difficult. Although embroidery was her first artistic medium, she proved to be a talented painter as well.

Moses is known for the clean, simple lines of her artwork, which displays scenes she remembered from daily life in the rural setting where she grew up. Her work is very popular and can often be found reprinted on calendars and note cards. Examples of her art can be found on the Web at artcyclopedia.com/artists/moses_grandma.html. Grandma Moses died on December 13, 1961. She was 101 years old.

Clementine Hunter was also a folk artist. She was the first self-taught African American artist to receive nationwide attention in the media. Called Tebé by her family and friends, Hunter was born near the southern end of Louisiana's Cane River in 1886 (actual date unknown). Her life story reflects a rich cultural diversity. One of her grandmothers was a black Native American. Some of her family members were Creoles. Hunter spoke French and didn't learn English until she married her husband Emmanuel in 1924. She had seven children; two died as babies. She lived on Melrose Plantation for more than seventy-five years, where she and her family worked as manual laborers. Her jobs included picking cotton and pecans.

Hunter began painting in the 1930s. Like Grandma Moses, Clementine Hunter enjoyed needlework. She also liked sketching. Hunter used bright colors to depict life as she experienced it in the rural south. Her simple folk art style brims with life as it reflects the daily routines and rituals she saw. Clementine Hunter died on January 1, 1988. She was 101 years old.

Introduce both artists to your students. Talk about how their lives may have been similar and different. Discuss how their paintings are alike and how they differ. Although both women began painting later in life, it's likely they were artistically inclined as children. Have students paint a scene depicting their own lives. Hang all the art in a celebration of Grandma Moses and Clementine Hunter.

Literature connections: *The Grandma Moses Night Before Christmas*, by Clement Moore, illustrated by Grandma Moses (Random House, 0-679-91526-5, all ages); *Grandma Moses*, by Zibby O'Neal (Puffin, 0-14-032220-5, grades 4 to 8); *Talking with Tebé: Clementine Hunter, Memory Artist*, edited by Mary Lyons (Houghton Mifflin, 0-395-72031-1, grades 4 to 8). There are adult books about Moses and one on Hunter as well, and both artists are included in several folk art books.

#

Jesse Owens

Birth, September 12, 1913

Jesse Owens was born on a farm in Alabama, on September 12, 1913. His name was James Cleveland, and his family called him J.C. He had seven brothers and sisters, and his parents were sharecroppers. J.C. became known as Jesse after the family moved to Cleveland, Ohio. When a teacher asked his name, Jesse replied "J.C." His teacher, unused to hearing a Southern accent, mistakenly thought he said "Jesse." Too shy to correct her, J.C. simply became "Jesse."

Jesse grew up with little material wealth, but his life was rich with love and the many activities his family enjoyed doing together. One activity Owens's father enjoyed was the foot races often held after church on Sunday. He was the fastest man in the area. Little did he know that one day his son would become the fastest man in the world and win four gold medals in the 1936 Olympic Games in Berlin, Germany.

After his track career ended, Jesse Owens traveled all over the world, giving speeches and talking about his athletic accomplishments. Owens was elected to the Track and Field Hall of Fame in 1974. In 1979, President Jimmy Carter awarded him the Living Legends Award. Owens died of cancer on March 31, 1980.

Why not honor Jesse Owens's memory with a one hundred–meter dash and long jump contest during physical education? Before holding the event, let one or two students go to the learning center and find out what Owens's Olympic and world record times and lengths were. Outside, measure off one hundred meters, and in a sandy area (or grassy spot) make a line for a takeoff point for long jumps. If your space is limited, you can hold a fifty-meter dash and halve Owens's one hundred–meter time.

Since gym time is limited, divide the class into thirds and let everyone participate in a qualifying heat. Borrow a stopwatch from the gym teacher and time the top six winners individually (two winners from each heat).

Let interested students compete in the long jump. Nonjumpers can serve as takeoff board monitors, measurers, the cheering crowd, etc. In math class, compare the class's results with Owens's. How many times faster/farther did he run or jump? Older students can check newspaper sport sections to see who today's fast runners are. Who holds world records today?

Lutz Long was Germany's champion long jumper in 1936. He ignored Adolf Hitler's racist policies and offered tips and the hand of friendship to Owens. Older students could discuss how difficult and brave it was for Lutz to disregard an unfair policy and be a "good neighbor." Students might discuss ways they could extend a hand of friendship to students of all ethnic and religious backgrounds in school.

Biographies about Owens include: *Jesse Owens*, by Jane Sutcliffe (1-57505-487-6, Lerner, ages five to eight); *Jesse Owens: Olympic Star*, by Patricia and Frederick McKissack (0-8949-0312-8, Enslow, ages six to nine); and *Jesse Owens: Track and Field Legend*, by Judith Pinkerton Josephson (0-8949-0812-X, Enslow, ages twelve and up).

Clara Schumann

Birth, September 13, 1819

September 13 is a day to celebrate a special female pianist for National Piano Month. This day could be a way to help your students understand the way women were limited by societal expectations in the not-so-distant past. Clara, born in 1819, was the daughter of Marianne and Frederick Wieck (pronounced "Veek"). Frederick was well known in the German music community as a teacher and the owner of a piano store. Quiet, shy Clara Wieck seldom spoke when she was a very young child. In fact, she did not speak at all until she was four years old. As a result, some people believed she was deaf or possibly mentally handicapped.

Clara always loved to watch her father play the piano. She often imitated the movement of his hands as he played. Her father decided she could begin lessons when she was five years old. Clara quickly demonstrated that she possessed an innate musical ability and was highly talented. Frederick decided he would raise Clara to be a musical virtuoso. An apt pupil, Clara was eager to please her demanding father. Once she began playing the piano, she also began speaking, although hesitantly.

By the time Clara was nine years old she had debuted as a piano prodigy. At eleven, she made her first European concert tour. This was highly unusual for a woman, let alone a girl. At that time women were not encouraged to perform in public or become professionals.

Clara's brilliance as a concert pianist stunned audiences. In 1840, very much against her father's wishes, she married Robert Schumann, a composer and longtime friend. Clara Schumann also began composing music for the piano, voice, and other instruments. She composed twenty-three opuses and countless piano songs, but was not really accepted by the musical world. In her diary she wrote: "I once believed that I possessed creative talent, but I have given up this idea; a woman must not desire to compose—there has never yet been one able to do it. Should I expect to be the one?" Instead Clara Schumann became the main interpreter of her increasingly famous husband's music. He wrote and mostly she played.

She continued performing and did some composing, even as she raised her children. The house full of children influenced both parents' music. Robert wrote a group of pieces for the piano called "Kinderszenen," which featured the theme of childhood. He also wrote lullabies and an album of piano music for children learning to play piano. Robert had a history of mental illness, which gradually worsened. He died in 1856, and Clara became the sole provider for her family.

As an adult, Clara Schumann had many friends in the music world. She was particularly close to Johannes Brahms. Together, they published and made famous some of Robert Schumann's compositions.

Until recently, Clara Schumann's work had not received widespread attention. Within the past few years, however, greater attention is being paid to her compositions and her pieces are beginning to be published and performed publicly. It is important for teachers to help students understand that people who are justly deserving of our attention are often overlooked in their lifetimes and sometimes never rediscovered. Write the quote from Clara Schumann on the board and ask students to think about what she meant. Do you think she should have given up her desire to become a composer? Do they think a woman composer might face difficulty today? Why? Why not?

Introduce your students to the joy of classical music and this extraordinary woman. Use her music, and that of her contemporaries, as a soft backdrop during quiet reading time, art class, writing periods, or whenever the mood strikes. Although we have no recordings of her brilliant playing, recordings of music she composed are widely available, as are recordings of music composed by Robert Schumann and Johannes Brahms. Look in your library's collection.

Two excellent biographies for young readers are: *Clara Schumann: Piano Virtuoso*, by Susanna Reich (Clarion, 0-395-89119-1, grades 5 and up), and *Her Piano Sang: A Story About Clara Schumann*, by Barbara Allman (Carolrhoda, 1-57505-012-9, grades 3 to 6).

(21)

Better Nutrition for a Healthier You

National Five-a-Day Month, September

The order "Eat your vegetables!" makes many children hide peas under a napkin or smuggle food to the dog. However, research shows it's important for us to eat plenty of vegetables and fruits to stay healthy and reduce the risk of disease. National Five-a-Day efforts help you increase awareness of the role fruits and vegetables play in a balanced diet. They form part of the foundation of the U.S. Department of Agriculture's food pyramid.

The week before you start this unit, ask your students to keep a daily chart of all the food they eat during the week. Don't let them know the theme of the approaching week. At week's end have students list the number of vegetables and fruits they've eaten, individually and as a class. The results can be charted and graphed as part of the math curriculum. Then, talk about having a "Healthier You Week." Ask students to keep track of the new week's meals. Graph and compare results with the previous week's. Discuss vegetable likes and dislikes. A classroom book of recipes can make eating fruits and vegetables more fun. Young children can clean vegetables like broccoli, celery, and carrots and serve them with a dip as a snack.

You may want to consider inviting a nutritionist to visit your class. If students are given a clear explanation of the relationship between improved diet and better performance (in athletics, for instance) they may be more likely to form new habits. A grocer or farmer, if available in your area, may offer an interesting perspective on the safe care and management of fresh fruits and vegetables. Learn about how vegetables are grown in this country and others. There are many more varieties of veggies and fruits than we usually see in the grocery store. If possible, take a field trip to a local farmer's market or health food store to buy some uncommon varieties of apple or potato, for example. Let students compare these to the usual red delicious or Idaho baker.

Do your students know what the term *organic* means? There are new rules that define the term in the United States so that one set of standards now applies in all states. Modern agriculture is dependent on many kinds of chemical pesticides and herbicides. This can increase yields for growers in the short term, but also has a negative impact on the environment: killing songbirds, for instance. Because the chemicals used in keeping weeds and pests down can stay on foods and wash into rivers and underground aquifers, they also take a long-term toll on our health.

Chemical residues require us to pay attention to how we eat. While the skin of an apple is quite nutritious, it also retains a higher concentration of the chemical sprays used by growers. This is why we often peel our fruits. Organic fruits, on the other hand, can be washed and eaten with the peels on, if you like. If organic and/or locally grown produce is available in your area, do a taste test. Can students taste a difference? How about a locally grown tomato and one from thousands of miles away? Do any of the students grow food in family gardens? Ask for samples so students can try produce that is really fresh. This experience has been known to create a change of heart in many a child who claims, "I hate vegetables!"

Several books for young readers offer information on this and related topics: *The Edible Pyramid: Good Eating Every Day*, by Loreen Leedy (Holiday House, 0-8234-1126-5, grades K to 3); *The Food Pyramid*, by Joan Kalbacken (Children's Press, 0-516-20756-3, grades 2 to 4); *Cool as a Cucumber, Hot as a Pepper: Fruit Vegetables*, by Meredith Hughes (Lerner, 0-8225-2832-0, grades 5 to 7); *Stinky and Stringy: Stem and Bulb Vegetables*, by Meredith Hughes (Lerner, 0-8225-2833-9, grades 5 to 7); *Where Food Comes From*, by Dorothy Hinshaw Patent (Holiday House, 0-8234-0877-9, grades 1 to 5); and *Oliver's Fruit Salad*, by Vivian French (Orchard Books, 0-531-30087-0, preschool to grade 2). A recipe book for children with easy-to-follow recipes that keep healthy eating at the fore is Mollie Katzen's *Honest Pretzels: And 64 Other Amazing Recipes for Cooks Ages 8 and Up* (Tricycle Press, 1-883672-88-0).

For more information on the U.S. Department of Agriculture's Food Pyramid and a printable pyramid, go to nal.usda.gov/fnic/Fpyr/pyramid.html on the Web.

22

Exploring Hispanic Heritage

National Hispanic Heritage Month, September 15–October 15

Invite your class to a monthlong fiesta celebrating the diverse Hispanic cultures whose heritage has enriched the United States in countless ways. The majority of Hispanic Americans came from Cuba, Puerto Rico, Mexico, and Central and South America. Students can list and discuss where Hispanic influences can be found in the United States. Place names are an obvious starting point, but we also enjoy many foods from Hispanic cultures in general and from Latin America in particular.

The New York Public Library Amazing Hispanic American History: A Book of Answers for Kids, by George Ochoa (Wiley, 0-471-19204-X, grades 4 and up), is filled with trivia that will provoke discussion. You and your students can also observe this month by learning some Spanish. Simple phrases like *hola, adiós, Cómo está?*, and Spanish names for colors and common objects used in the classroom are good choices. Hispanic students in your class could lead the lessons. Check your local radio stations for a Spanish station you can turn on periodically.

A food fair is a tasty way to explore Hispanic heritage. Many cookbooks contain recipes from different regions and expose students to food other than fast-food tacos. Students can also make a piñata to top off the day's activities. Recordings of Mexican mariachi and Afro-Cuban music are found in most library collections. Your students will enjoy these rhythms and might try learning a dance or two. The cha-cha, tango, and rumba are Latin American dances.

Writers of children's literature with a Hispanic focus include Arthur Dorros, Gary Soto, Omar Castañeda, Nicholasa Mohr, Lulu Delacre, Vincent Martinez, and Lori M. Carlson. Isabel Schon's *The Best of the Latino Heritage: A Guide to the Best Juvenile Books About Latino People and Cultures* (Scarecrow, 0-8108-3221-6) lists books about Spanish-speakers in other countries and Latinos in the United States. The teacher with Spanish-speaking students will want to consult Schon's *Recommended Books in Spanish for Children and Young Adults* (Rowman & Littlefield, 0-8108-3937-7). Finally, Schon's website at the Center for the Study of Books in Spanish for Children and Adolescents at California State University, San Marcos (csusm.edu /csb/english) is a comprehensive guide.

There are many athletes of Hispanic heritage, such as baseball's Sammy Sosa, horse racing's Angel Cordero, and golf's Nancy Lopez. Your students could search the sports pages and bring in articles about other Hispanic athletes.

For a classroom debate, the topic of bilingual education is often in the news. Again, newspapers are a good source of information.

The Day of the Dead, which is celebrated from October 31 through November 2, is widely observed in Mexican American communities. For an excellent article that includes book and Web sources and teaching approaches, see "Skeletons and Marigolds: Días de los Muertos," by Jeanette Larson and Carolina Martínez in the September 1998 issue of *Book Links* magazine.

(23)

Birds, Butterflies, and Budding Young Naturalists

Fall Migration Time, September Through November

Children tend to have a good eye for naturalistic detail, and that type of observation is important to encourage as it is a skill needed in many academic and career pursuits. This time of year is a good time to find insects and birds getting ready to migrate. Houghton Mifflin has recently adapted several of Peterson's famous guides for young naturalists just starting out on their own explorations. A field trip could consist of a nature walk around the school grounds or just watching birds through the window, but if you can, get your class into the bigger classroom of the great outdoors several times a season to record what they observe. A disposable camera or two and the children's drawings and journals can make a great display to compare seasonal changes.

Although it takes planning and elbow grease, many schools are finding that a garden on school grounds returns the effort triple-fold. Students enjoy the hands-on aspect of scientific investigation, as well as the mathematical and artistic input that are necessary for an attractive garden. Start with a small garden, preferably with raised beds, as weeding is time-consuming and can be overwhelming.

The monarch butterfly (*Danaus plexippus*) of North America begins an amazing migration of up to three thousand miles in late August and September to escape the northern winter. Some 140 million insects travel to small forests in southern California (west of the Rocky Mountains) and Mexico (east of the Rockies, via central and coastal Texas) from as far as Minnesota and New England. In late spring, they will journey north again. Given that their lifespan is four to six weeks, the butterflies making the annual return migration are the grandchildren of the grandchildren of the butterflies that over-wintered ten months previously.

A butterfly garden to attract these beautiful insects and others can be an inspiring class project. Often PTO funds can be made available for flower or seed purchases and mulch or soil fertilizers, if needed. Some teachers have had success in writing science grants to develop a garden. Students will learn which plants larvae feed on and which plants adult butterflies turn to for nectar. Once the garden has been planted, keep track of caterpillars and butterflies with *The First Guide to Caterpillars*, by Amy Wright (Houghton, 0-395-91194-2, ages eight to twelve), and *The First Guide to Butterflies and Moths*, by Paul Opler (Houghton, 0-395-90665-2, ages eight to twelve). Both are in the Peterson's guide series mentioned above.

Several other books have information about butterflies and the kinds of gardens that attract them. Lois Ehlert's *Waiting for Wings* (Harcourt, 0-15-202608-8, ages three to seven) will delight young readers. The initial point of view is that of a caterpillar growing into a butterfly and its reliance on flowers for food and shelter. The second part of the book is told from the flowers' point of view and their dependence on butterflies. Back matter contains information on the flowers that are particularly attractive to butterflies. Joanne Ryder's *Where Butterflies Grow* (Penguin, 0-14-055858-6, ages four to seven) is a lush introduction to the life cycle of butterflies and contains back matter on gardens. Deborah Heiligman's *From Caterpillar to Butterfly* (HarperCollins, 0-06-445129-1, ages four to eight) and *The Butterfly House*, by Eve Bunting (Scholastic, 0-590-84884-4, ages five to ten), have good information, too. The first book is nonfiction, the second is a story about a girl and her grandfather building a butterfly house. For an exquisite journey with a monarch butterfly, read Laurence Pringle's *Extraordinary Life: the Story of a Monarch Butterfly* (Orchard, 0-531-30002-1, all ages).

(24)

Autumn Equinox

September 22 or 23

September 22 or 23 is the first day of autumn in the northern hemisphere. *Equinox* is derived from two Latin words that mean "equal night." On this day, the daylight hours are nearly equal to the number of hours of nighttime all over the earth. That's because the sun is positioned directly above the equator. In the northern hemisphere, this heralds the arrival of autumn and signals that winter is approaching. In the southern hemisphere, it's the arrival of spring.

In science class, focus on prediction. Scientists make predictions based on their observations and experiences. Ask students to think about what occurrences they have observed in the past as autumn approached. Now zero in on the area in your community. If there are trees on the school grounds, let students predict what colors the leaves on each tree will turn and the dates they think certain trees will lose their leaves. Predict when the first frost will occur. Have students make a chart that lists their predictions and see which ones prove most accurate. Draw conclusions about tree species, color, and leaf loss.

Ask them to notice any signs of animal behavior that signals autumn is approaching. Two common signs are V-shaped formations of bird flocks and squirrels burying nuts, and the appearance of certain kinds of insects, like caterpillars.

Younger children will enjoy leaf-related science activities found in *Red Leaf, Yellow Leaf*, by Lois Ehlert (0-15-266197-2, Harcourt, ages four to eight), and the art projects in Morteza Sohi's *Look What I Did with a Leaf* (Walker, 0-08027-7440-7, ages four to eight). *Fall Leaves Fall!*, by Zoe Hall (0-590-10079-3, Scholastic, ages three to six), is a good book for preschoolers and primary students. *Autumn Leaves*, by Ken Robbins (0-590-29879-8, Scholastic, ages seven and up), is a beautiful photo book of leaves.

In health class you might want to note how clear, cloudless autumn skies and a tingle in the air seem to promote higher energy levels. See if students have noticed that stuffy, overly warm classrooms are conducive to sleepiness. Some college campuses have overheated libraries where you can find more students napping than studying on any given day. What effects do they think this could have on learning? If your students are rural they may have noticed that farm animals get frisky and run around more as the weather cools.

In the old days autumn was a time of much hard physical labor to prepare for the hard winter months. People harvested and prepared food for storage, butchered and smoked or canned meats and cut, hauled, split, and stacked piles of wood. You may want to read a chapter from any of Laura Ingalls Wilder's books where she outlines these preparations.

The autumn equinox is also an opportunity to focus on the harvest season. *The Autumn Equinox: Celebrating the Harvest*, by Ellen Jackson (0-7613-1442-3, Millbrook, ages eight and up), provides a wealth of information about the equinox and the many ways that cultures celebrate the harvest season. A collection of art and culinary activities is included at the end of the book. One of them, in keeping with the thanksgiving theme often associated with harvest, is a lovely variation on the fortune cookie. It uses crescent rolls and penciled notes of thanksgiving.

(25)

Rediscovering Lewis and Clark

Lewis and Clark Expedition Returns, September 23, 1806

When Thomas Jefferson became president in 1801, the western boundary of the United States was the Mississippi River, and about two-thirds of the population lived within fifty miles of the Atlantic. President Jefferson commissioned his private secretary, Captain Meriwether Lewis, and his friend, Lieutenant William Clark, to lead an expedition to explore routes to the west that would lead to the Pacific Ocean.

The Jefferson-dubbed "Corps of Discovery" began their trek in May 1804 by traveling up the Missouri River. They spent the winter of 1804–1805 in what is now North Dakota. The following spring and summer their party crossed the Rocky Mountains. They canoed across several river systems, finally paddling down the Columbia River and reaching the Pacific Coast in November 1805. Native Americans helped the explorers survive the harsh winter that followed. They arrived back in St. Louis in September 1806, after traveling more than eight thousand miles.

Lewis served as the expedition's naturalist. His detailed daily journal recorded descriptions and drawings of the many rock formations, plants, and animals he saw.

Have students read excerpts from Lewis's journal (look for copies in the public library or on the website noted here) that described the natural surroundings. *Spider* magazine had a serial story on Lewis and Clark in the fall months of 2002. Your library will likely have these on file. The story is amazing and the illustrations will draw every elementary student into the drama.

Go on an expedition outside the school building. Ask students to pretend they are naturalists from another planet. Have them describe the plants, animals, and other things they see as reports that will be transmitted back to their home planet.

Also for science, have students compare and contrast the kinds of rock, flora, and fauna that Lewis encountered in two ways. First, how did they change as Lewis and Clark made their way across the territory? Second, how did what Lewis saw differ from the flora and fauna in the area where you live?

For geography, chart the course of Lewis and Clark's trip, labeling the major rivers, mountains, and other physical boundaries they encountered, including weather phenomena. Ask, How many states came from the territory Lewis and Clark traveled in?

Literature connections include: *How We Crossed the West: The Adventures of Lewis and Clark*, by Rosalyn Schanzer (National Geographic, 0-79-223738-2, grades 3 to 7). *My Name Is York*, by Elizabeth Van Steenwyk (Northland, 0-87358-650-6, grades 2 to 4), is an account of the expedition told through the eyes of York, a slave who accompanied them. *Seaman: The Dog Who Explored the West with Lewis and Clark*, by Gail Karwoski (Peachtree, 1-56145-190-8, grades 4 to 8), is a novel that dramatizes the story of Seaman, the Newfoundland dog that joined the expedition.

The website for the PBS television program "Lewis and Clark: The Corps of Discovery" has classroom resources at pbs.org/lewis andclark.

26

Dogs with Jobs

Dogs have long been touted as "man's best friend," but throughout the years they've been one of humankind's best helpers, too. The partnership between people and dogs has been solidly established for thousands of years. In prehistoric times, wild dogs probably were slowly domesticated to serve as companions and watchdogs. Later, shepherds realized their value for herding and protecting livestock. Hunters used dogs to flush out and retrieve game. Dogs have been used to pull carts loaded with packed goods or harnessed to sleds for transporting goods across snow-covered areas.

Why not focus a classroom lesson on working dogs? Today, dogs are helpful in many ways. Many police departments maintain a K-9 corps, which is used for sniffing out illegal drugs and explosives. Police dogs are trained to track and hold criminals. Bloodhounds, with their ultrasensitive and discriminating noses, track missing persons. And after an earthquake or a disaster like the one at the World Trade Center, tracking dogs are brought to the sites of fallen buildings to help search the rubble for survivors.

Because dogs are intelligent, reliable, and highly trainable, they have carved out a niche as helpers to people who are blind or hearing impaired. Those who use a wheelchair sometimes have a dog for assistance as well.

For a classroom section on dogs contact the local police department to see if they have a K-9 presentation that they could bring to your school. The same option could be explored with a guide dog for a blind or hearing-impaired person. If you are fortunate enough to have a working canine visitor come to your school, be sure to emphasize to the children that the dog will be behaving appropriately and they must behave appropriately to it. (Remember, September is also Children's Good Manners Month!) Ask the dog's owner or handler questions beforehand to determine what behavior is appropriate for the children while the dog is near them.

Books about working dogs are readily available. There are plenty of general books about the jobs that working dogs do, including *Working Dogs: Tales from Animal Planet's K-9 to 5 World*, by Colleen Needles (Discovery Books, 1-5633-1843-1, ages twelve and up); *Dogs with Jobs: Working Dogs Around the World*, by Merrily Weisbord (Pocket, 0-671-04735-3, ages twelve and up); *A Dog's Gotta Do What a Dog's Gotta Do*, by Marilyn Singer (Holt, 0-8050-6074-X, ages seven to ten); and *Dogs with a Job*, by John Patten Jr. (Rourke, 0-8659-3456-8, ages six to nine).

Dogs that help with police work or as guide/aide dogs are also featured in several titles, including *Aero and Officer Mike: Police Partners*, by Joan Plummer (Boyds Mills, 1-56397-931-4, ages five to eight); *Jake: A Labrador Puppy at Work and Play*, by Robert Jones (Farrar, 0-374-43713-0, ages five to ten); *Buddy: The First Seeing Eye Dog*, by Eva Moore (Scholastic, 0-590-26585-7, ages seven to nine); and *My Buddy*, by Audrey Osofsky (Holt, 0-8050-3546-X, ages six to eight).

Another way to celebrate dogs is to invite someone from a canine club to visit your classroom and discuss how dog owners can be good neighbors. Too often, we forget to emphasize with children that it is the dog owner's responsibility to train his or her dog to behave in public. Just as good manners are appreciated in people, dogs with good manners are a pleasure to be around.

For a great read-aloud for younger students try this fun title: *Maxi, the Hero*, by Debra and Sal Barracca (Puffin Pied Piper, 0-14-055497-1, ages five to eight). Older students will enjoy *James Herriot's Treasury for Children* (St. Martin's Press, 0-312-08512-5, all ages interest, reading level upper elementary), by the famous British veterinarian, which has several excellent stories about dogs.

(27)

Local History Day

It might be fun to begin the school year with special acknowledgment of the city where your school is located. So create your own Local History Day. Announce that at some point during the year, it will be your city's birthday. Ask if anyone knows when it might be. See what stories, if any, students know about the town. Are there any particular highlights that come to their mind? Estimate exactly how old the town is. Everyone should hazard a guess. Cities on the East and West Coasts, because of historical settlement patterns, are likely to be older than some in the middle regions of the country.

After making estimates of the age, brainstorm about how and where students can go to find out the city's founding date. Students could work in pairs or threes, with each group reporting its findings to the class. Talk about the possibility of holding an informal birthday party for the city, perhaps with cookies and juice for the class during recess or snack time. Younger children will even enjoy singing "Happy Birthday."

In addition to discovering the "birthday" of your city, let students discover the roots of the city's name. Was it named after a person, a place in Europe, or might the name have Native American roots? With a little planning, students can easily generate enough information for a classroom book on the historical facts of the city's founding. This book could be shared with other classes in the school.

Giving students a sense of place and pride in their community's past is like nurturing a tiny seedling's root. Once the root begins growing, it often yields a greater commitment to community involvement in the present and future. Students come to realize that many other people have built homes, lived, worked, raised children, and died in the area they now call home and that they are part of a continuum.

As part of a local history project, students could also seek out local historical landmarks. These could be a statue, a building, an old tree, a historic park, an old cemetery, the site of an old athletic stadium, even an old mine or abandoned train track. Have students choose a landmark that interests them and write a short story about it, telling the story from the perspective of the historical landmark. Describe what the area and political climate was like when the landmark was erected, planted, or built and what changes it has seen over the years.

George Gershwin

Birth, September 26, 1898

George Gershwin is one of America's most famous composers. He wrote many songs and concert pieces that are still very popular today. The son of Russian immigrant parents, Gershwin began writing popular songs at age fifteen—the age when many of today's teens who play in local bands are first trying out their composing skills. His brother, Ira Gershwin, wrote the lyrics for many of George's show tunes. Biographies of Gershwin for children include *Introducing Gershwin*, by Roland Vernon (Silver Burdett, 0-382-39161-6, grades 3 to 6), and *George Gershwin*, by Mike Venezia (Children's Press, 0-516-04536-9, grades 3 to 6).

There are many ways Gershwin's music can be incorporated into the curriculum. From a language arts perspective, "I Got Rhythm" is a wonderful lead-in to poetry units where students will be exploring rhythmic patterns. Gershwin's last symphonic piece was a piano and orchestral version of "I Got Rhythm" played with variations of the main musical theme. Discuss with your class how musicians play with notes and poets play with language. Rap is all about rhythm, and is a fun way for students to make a contemporary connection.

Rhapsody in Blue and *An American in Paris* are exciting musical pieces and introductions to quintessential American jazz and rhythmic compositions. Students can be encouraged to look for the movie *An American in Paris*, a musical with a plot constructed around Gershwin's piece. It's available on videocassette—free in public libraries. Also, don't miss *Porgy and Bess*, Gershwin's black folk opera, probably the best known of all American operas.

Recordings of Gershwin's music are widely available. If you don't have any in your personal music archives, public libraries offer cassettes, CDs, and LPs. Celebrating Gershwin's birthday rounds out September as National Piano Month. See Idea 15, "Tickling the Ivories," for more information.

(29)

An Apple a Day

Johnny Appleseed, Birth, September 26, 1774

John Chapman, better known as Johnny Appleseed, was born September 26, 1774, in Leominster, Massachusetts. When he was in his twenties, Chapman began a lifelong apple-planting mission along the American frontier (Ohio and Indiana), that later catapulted him into folk-legend fame. He earned the name "Johnny Appleseed" as a result of his widespread orchard plantings. Chapman died in 1845.

September is the perfect time to celebrate an apple grower's life. One activity might be to hold a classroom apple tasting. This could be patterned on a blind taste-tasting style event. Buy several varieties of apples from your local supermarket and make a list of them. Keep the varieties separated from one another. Set up apple "orchards" in numbered stations around the room. Leave one apple of each variety whole. Cut the rest into small pieces—enough to let each student have a taste.

Before students visit each "orchard," have them make a comparison grid, listing taste, crunchiness, color, size, etc. across the top. List orchard numbers down the side of the paper. At each station, students can evaluate the apple they see and taste. Young students might want to draw a picture on the back of their grid.

After everyone has sampled and observed, graph student findings as a whole, and see if their observations can help them correctly name each apple variety. (You will need to have a list of characteristics of each variety on hand.)

Later, the whole apples from each station can be cut in half and used to make apple print gift wrapping. Students can plant the seeds in containers and monitor their growth. Plant them at the end of the year.

Books to complement these activities include: *Johnny Appleseed*, by Patricia Demuth (Putnam, 0-448-41130-X, ages four to six); *Johnny Appleseed*, by Reeve Lindbergh (Little, Brown, 0-316-52634-7, ages four to eight); *The Real Johnny Appleseed*, by Laurie Lawlor (Albert Whitman, 0-8075-6909-7, ages nine to twelve); *The Life and Times of the Apple*, by Charles Micucci (Orchard, 0-531-07067-0, ages seven to ten); and *Apples*, by Gail Gibbons (Holiday House, 0-8234-1497-3, ages eight to eleven).

October

---

(30)

Digging for Dinosaurs

International Dinosaur Month, October

Whether fearsome or placid, dinosaurs intrigue adults and enthrall elementary school children. Bring dinosaurs into your classroom and take advantage of this high-interest topic. Dinosaurs first appeared on the Earth about 230 million years ago. Different dinosaur species lived at different times. You can use dinosaurs to introduce students to the concept of geologic time periods. For example, stegosaurus lived during the early Jurassic period, allosaurus during the late Jurassic, plateosaurs during the late Triassic, iguanodons during the early Cretaceous, and velociraptors during the late Cretaceous.

Try making a timeline across one wall of your room. If you construct it proportionately, (perhaps with an inch for each million years or so), starting with the Mesozoic era and working up to the Cenozoic era (the present), children gain a better understanding of how long dinosaurs lived on the Earth in comparison to the relatively short time people have. This is a key concept for children to grasp, so be sure to help them "see" it even if you only draw a simple line on a chalk or white board. To assist you in this project, here are the years of each era, period, and epoch.

The Mesozoic era is made up of the three periods listed below with their beginning dates (estimated millions of years ago, or *m.y.a.*).

Cretaceous period	135 m.y.a.
Jurassic period	200 m.y.a.
Triassic period	250 m.y.a.

The current era is called the Cenozoic, and is made up of two periods divided into epochs, which are listed below, most recent first, with the estimated beginning date for each.

Quaternary Period

Holocene epoch	10,000 years ago
Pleistocene epoch	1.9 m.y.a.

Tertiary Period

Pliocene epoch	6 m.y.a.
Miocene epoch	25 m.y.a.
Oligocene epoch	38 m.y.a.
Eocene epoch	55 m.y.a.
Paleocene epoch	65 m.y.a.

Primary students can begin learning the principles of scientific classification by sorting dinosaurs. First ask them to divide dinosaurs into two-legged and four-legged species. Then sort meat-eaters and plant-eaters. Other criteria could include horned, big and little, water and land creatures, and so on. Students should understand why each dinosaur is a member of its group. Have them label each category with a topic sentence such as: "[Dinosaur name] belongs in this group because it [characteristic]." Here is an opportunity to introduce terms such as *like* and *unlike* and *similar* and *different*.

As a science project, middle school students can compare the anatomy of the two major divisions of dinosaurs: the ornithischians (bird-hipped) and saurischians (lizard-hipped). New research indicates that some birds and dinosaurs may be related. Students can compare and contrast the structure and physiology of modern birds, transitional birds, and possible dinosaur ancestors.

Studying fossils and how they are made is an offshoot of dinosaur units. Create your own fossil "dig" with a large box, plaster of Paris, a few bones from the supermarket, some leaves, and some soil. You can make dinosaur footprints or leaf prints in the same way molds of student handprints are often made as classroom art projects. For a more layered "rock" approach, have students mix the plaster of Paris and, while it's still soft, put several bones on the surface. Position some of the bones upright. When the mixture dries, cover the bones with a second layer of plaster of Paris and top with a layer of soil. Using small chisels or dental instruments, conduct a classroom dig. If students follow proper scientific techniques, they should remove the plaster in layered increments, diagram the location of bones, and measure the bone positions in relation to the whole plaster unit.

Dinosaur poetry is always fun. *Dinosaur Rap* (Rock n' Learn, 1-878489-59-3, audiocassette and book) has catchy rhythms, and *Bone Poems*, by Jeffrey Moss (Workman, 0-7611-0884-X, grades 2 to 6), has several funny dinosaur poems that will stimulate creative thought.

Literature connections include: *Dinosaur Babies*, by Kathleen Weidner Zoehfeld (Harper, 0-06-445162-3, grades K to 3); *A Dinosaur Named Sue*, by Fay Robinson (Scholastic, 0-439-09983-8, grades 2 to 4); and *Did Dinosaurs Live in Your Backyard?*, by Melvin and Gilda Berger (Scholastic, 0-439-08568-3, grades 1 to 4).

(31)

What Did Dinosaurs Look Like?

International Dinosaur Month, October

The world of paleontology changes with each new discovery. In the past, dinosaur artists have always depicted the "terrible lizards" with the nostrils placed high on the head and back away from the tip of the dinosaur's snout. Laurence Witmer, a scientist at Ohio University, believes the nostrils belong much nearer to the front of the snout and closer to the mouth. Witmer studies animal noses and even has a project underway called DinoNose. There is a fascinating article by Witmer in the August 3, 2001, issue of the journal *Science* ("Nostril Position in Dinosaurs and Other Vertebrates and Its Significance for Nasal Function," pages 850–853), and a shorter, less technical column by Erik Stokstad ("Dinosaurs Nostrils Get a Hole New Look") on page 779 of the same issue. The news was also reported in many national newspapers in summer 2001. Paleontologists are excited by Witmer's theory and feel the evidence he presents is very strong.

The subject of dinosaur metabolism and whether they were cold-blooded or warm-blooded has raged for more than a decade. New scanning equipment used for medical diagnoses, plus some startling fossil finds, are opening up a whole new area of dinosaur study. *Outside and Inside Dinosaurs*, by Sandra Markle (Simon and Schuster, 0-689-82300-2, ages seven to ten), is a good general introduction to the internal physiology of dinosaurs. *Dinosaur Eggs*, by Jennifer Dussling (Grosset, 0-448-42093-7, ages six to nine), is good for younger readers who want to learn more about what paleontologists have learned about juvenile dinosaurs from studies done on fossilized dinosaur eggs.

One of the ways students can enjoy this new theory is by comparing it with how dinosaurs have been depicted throughout the years. An exciting new book, *The Dinosaurs of Waterhouse Hawkins*, by Barbara Kerley (Scholastic, 0-439-11494-2, ages eight and up), recounts the story of Benjamin Waterhouse Hawkins, the first person to build life-size dinosaur models.

Hawkins built the models in London for Queen Victoria and Prince Albert's new art and science showplace, the Crystal Palace, in 1854. The story of how he reconstructed the dinosaurs from fossil evidence gathered at the time and made clay and iron models is absolutely delightful. And his dinner party to convince paleontologists to go along with his idea is a hoot—too good to give away the surprise. When the exhibit opened, it was the first time members of the public had any concrete presentations of dinosaurs.

The comparison of Hawkins's models with those found in present-day museums is startling. Children will immediately notice the iguanodon, built with a horn on its head. Later scientific fossil finds showed the "horn" was actually the large "thumb."

Digging for Bird Dinosaurs, by Nic Bishop (Houghton Mifflin, 0-395-96056-8, ages eight to twelve), is an engrossing nonfiction book that discusses the work of paleontologist Cathy Forster and her quest for fossils of a primitive reptilian bird, *Rahonavis*. Readers accompany Forster on her fossil dig in Madagascar and become "virtual paleontologists" involved in all aspects of excavation, preservation, and the laboratory reconstruction of the bones she finds. This is a great inside peek for students who are interested in becoming paleontologists.

Feathered Dinosaurs, by Christopher Sloan (National Geographic Society, 0-7922-7219-6, ages ten and up), examines, in depth, the most recent information about the connection between birds and dinosaurs. Skeletal comparisons, scale and feather developments, interesting photographs of feathered fossils, and imaginative paintings of feathered dinosaurs make this a helpful tool for history of life units. Examining a feather visually and then comparing the naked-eye observations with those found while examining the same feather with a microscope will amaze students.

The skeleton of Sue, the largest and most complete *Tyrannosaurus rex* ever discovered, is now on display at Chicago's Field Museum. Perhaps this would be a good time for a field trip to a natural history museum if you are fortunate to have one within a reasonable drive. If you have older books that depict dinosaurs in ways that are likely to be quite different from today's museum displays, you may want to bring them on the trip so students can compare and contrast how new discoveries have changed our ideas about these creatures.

(32)

Charlotte's Web

First Published, October 1952

In a review for *The New York Times Book Review*, famed author Eudora Welty pronounced the just-published *Charlotte's Web* "just about perfect." And this book by E. B. White became one of the best loved of all children's books. Even with the tremendous recent sales of the Harry Potter books, *Charlotte's Web* is the bestselling children's book of all time.

Although *Charlotte's Web* is often used as wonderful read-aloud in primary classrooms, we seldom use it with older students. However, a revisit with *Charlotte's Web* at the upper middle school or junior high level is one way to familiarize students with the elements of literature. *Charlotte's Web* has easily identifiable foreshadowing, character types and development, irony, setting, and a linear plot that make a literature group discussion of these elements interesting and fun. Students love seeing the story in a new, more mature light.

Extend Charlotte into the science curriculum with a unit on spiders. Books and articles about spiders will help students overcome their fears and learn to appreciate the spider's role in the ecosystem. Do your students know that Arabella and Anita, two common cross spiders, were sent into space in 1973 to study the effects of gravity? Arabella spun the first web in space.

E. B. White's *Stuart Little*, like *Charlotte's Web*, explores the theme of friendship. Students will appreciate these novels by drawing comparisons between Stuart and Wilbur, who lend themselves well to character development study.

Children who want to read other books with animal protagonists can look for Miss Spider books by David Kirk (preschool to grade 2); Beverly Cleary's Ralph Mouse novels (grades 2 to 5); *The School Mouse*, by Dick King-Smith (Little, Brown, 0-786-81156-0, grades 2 to 5); Ian Falconer's Olivia books (grades K to 2); and Cynthia Rylant's Poppleton Pig series (grades K to 2).

33

Hooray for Home Runs!

Barry Bonds Hits Seventy-Three Home Runs, October 7, 2001

On October 5, 2001, Barry Bonds broke Mark McGwire's 1998 home run record when he hit his seventy-first home run in a season. Bonds finished the season with seventy-three home runs—the record that still stands today. Previously, McGwire's seventy slammers broke the record of sixty-one home runs in a season, a record held by Roger Maris, an outfielder for the New York Yankees. And the legendary Babe Ruth set the pace with sixty home runs long before.

October is World Series month, and students can have math fun with baseball accomplishments in many ways. If you plan ahead and are doing a unit on estimation and prediction, have students predict how many home runs they think specific players will hit by the end of the season. Choose professional baseball players whose club plays near your community or solicit names of favorites from your students. Ask them to estimate how many total home runs are hit by a team during a typical season. Post the student estimations. Let several students research how many were actually hit by that team each year for the past three or four years. Many interesting sites for students of baseball math are available online—one that includes historical averages, among other things, is the "teachersfirst" site listed at the end of this entry. Ask the students to present their findings to the class. Revise and record new predictions based on the students' research.

Older students who are learning percent and ratios may have fun figuring out what percent of all Bonds's hits were home runs. What percent of his "at bats" were home runs? How does the number of home runs compare with the number of singles, doubles, etc?

Students learning graphing skills can graph the gradual monthly rise in Bonds's or a favorite player's season. They also can create a bar graph that compares the total number of home runs hit by each professional team. This type of exercise can be modified to fit seasonal sports records from other (perhaps local) athletic games.

Teachers will find a host of great baseball math Internet sites with activities free for the downloading by simply using the phrase "baseball math" in a search. A teacher site that features all the distance measurements and so forth that you might need in designing custom baseball math problems is colonial.net/schoolweb/willard/web/stuff/beattie/ideas/resources/html. One-stop shopping with excellent links to baseball physics sites and some truly inspired math problems is teachersfirst.com/baseball.html.

(34)

Kids Love a Mystery

Kids Love a Mystery Month, October

It doesn't take a world-class detective like Sherlock Holmes to deduce that kids (of all ages) love a good mystery. Fortunately, there are plenty of good mysteries written for young readers.

Begin a unit on the mystery genre with a reading of Jane Yolen's *Piggins* (Harcourt, 0-15-261686-1, preschool to grade 3). The puzzle is clearly presented and not overly difficult. Piggins, the trusty butler, is an engaging character (he reappears in sequels) who pokes sly fun at the stereotypical image of "the butler did it." Other picture book mysteries include *The Mary Celeste: An Unsolved Mystery from History*, also by Jane Yolen (Simon and Schuster, 0-689-81079-2, grades 2 to 6), which features the mysterious disappearance of a ship in 1872, and nicely complements social studies units. Middle school and junior high language arts classes could create solutions for the various peculiar circumstances found in *The Mysteries of Harris Burdick*, by Chris Van Allsburg (Houghton Mifflin, 0-395-353-3-9, all ages). For a lighthearted look at finding out secret information about why grown-ups make rules, try *The Secret Knowledge of Grown-Ups*, by David Wisniewski (Lothrop, 0-688-15339-9, ages seven and up), and its sequel.

For early readers, the Nate the Great series by Phyllis Sharmat provides a satisfying introduction to the genre. Moving a level or two higher, Ron Roy is working his way through the alphabet with the A to Z Mysteries series. The three young detectives featured in this series experience a wide variety of adventures from missing mummies to absent authors.

Middle school students will enjoy the National Park mystery series written by Gloria Skurzynski and Alane Ferguson. The first book in the series is *Wolf Stalker* (National Geographic Society, 0-7922-7034-7, ages eight to twelve). It and others in the series are also available in paperback. The sleuths are two middle school students, brother and sister. All the mysteries/adventures take place in U.S. National Parks. Environmental themes provide the focus for most of the mysteries, which makes them complement many science units. The various geographical settings provide relevance for social studies units as well.

For a stand-alone book (not part of a series) at an early reader level, try *Someone Is Following Pip Ramsey*, by Ron Roy (Random House, 0-679-987498-4, ages seven to ten). If laughs are up your alley, the secrets—hidden and divulged—in *The Secrets of Ms. Snickle's Class*, by Laurie Hornik (Houghton Mifflin, 0-618-03435-8, ages eight to twelve), will have students rolling in the aisles.

Junior high readers love the Sammy Keyes mystery series, written by Wendelin Van Draanen. Sammy is a gutsy junior high–age sleuth, whose determination and spunk enable her to save the day. Two good stand-alone mysteries for junior high readers are *Dovey Coe*, by Frances O'Roark Dowell (Simon and Schuster, 0-689-83174-9), and *Silent to the Bone*, by E. L. Konigsberg (Simon and Schuster, 0-689-83601-5).

Middle school and junior high students have fun trying their luck at decoding secret messages. For an interesting artistic slant on language and the abstract nature of language and art, see *The Abstract Alphabet*, by Paul Cox (Chronicle, 0-8118-2940-5, ages eight and up). Students could be encouraged to invent their own secret alphabets.

More mystery writers popular with children include: David Adler, Gertrude Chandler Warner, Joan Lowery Nixon, Barbara Wallace, Willo Davis Roberts, Dorothy and Thomas Hoobler, Peg Kehret, Mary Downing Hahn, and for junior high and high school readers, Nancy Werlin and William E. Coles.

If your class is inclined to be creative, why not write your own mystery? One funny way to encourage writing is to start a mystery and then give it to individual students or groups to continue. Decide on the length of each additional piece ahead of time. It could be as little as a few sentences for younger students (or reluctant writers) or as much as a whole chapter. Each addition should end with a hanging sentence or plot twist so the next installment will have to build on the one that precedes it. The resulting story can be edited by the class and rewritten until it makes sense and is easy to follow but still mysterious.

(35)

Pasta Appreciation

National Pasta Month, October

October is National Pasta Month. The wide variety of pasta shapes and the many cultures that eat it make pasta a fun and informative classroom topic. The word *pasta* comes from an Italian word that means "dough." As pasta has become trendy, its shapes have gotten fancier, including shells, wagon wheels, and letters. The addition of all kinds of vegetables has given us a rainbow assortment to choose from.

The song "On Top of Spaghetti," an old camp favorite, taught us that meatballs grow on trees. Well, pasta grows in fields. See *From Wheat to Pasta*, by Robert Evans (Children's Press, 0-516-26069-3, ages seven to ten), for the details on its "growth." *Pasta Factory*, by Hana Machotka (Houghton Mifflin, 0-395-60197-5, grades 1 to 4), shows how pasta is made. Teacher Created Materials has published *Pasta and Pizza: Thematic Units*, by Larry Bauer (1-5769-0374-5), for use with primary students.

The obvious first choice for a pasta activity is to incorporate it into the art curriculum. Students have been creating pasta art for decades. Instead of the traditional pictures children usually make, why not use pasta to teach texture and line? The flat, smooth sides of linguine and lasagna noodles contrast nicely with the ridged sides of rigatoni. Lasagna noodles have lovely wavy edges that direct the viewer's eye in a different way than spaghetti or elbow noodles do.

Another project is creating pasta mosaics. Let students find mosaic patterns and geometric designs from several cultures. Turkish and Italian tile murals, Native American or Australian Aboriginal geometric designs, or Tibetan sand mandalas provide good examples. Use tiny pasta, or even couscous, to create the pictures.

Many cultures flavor pasta in a number of different ways. Three books, *Everybody Cooks Rice, Everybody Bakes Bread*, and *Everybody Serves Soup*, by Norah Dooley (Lerner, 0-8761-4591-8, 0-8761-4895-X, and 1-5750-5422-1, grades K to 3), would serve as good models for your own classroom book about pasta. Each child can bring in a favorite pasta recipe from home. Encourage them to use traditional recipes that may have been handed down from grandparents or relatives from countries other than the United States. If your student population lacks cultural diversity, let students choose a culture and seek recipes from books. Libraries usually have cookbook sections that feature ethnic cuisines.

In science, you might want to call attention to the nutritional information found on the side of pasta boxes. Enriched pasta is a source of B vitamins and is high in carbohydrates, a good source for quick energy. (Many school athletic teams hold a pasta supper the night before a game.) You might wish to discuss the food pyramid and where pasta belongs on it. Many students will not have had the opportunity to sample pastas made from whole grains. Whole wheat pasta contains more fiber, vitamins, and minerals and can be very tasty and more filling. Pastas made from other grains such as corn, quinoa, and rice are available in health food or specialty stores. Regular grocery stores should at least carry rice noodles in their Asian section. Perhaps your class could have a sample party and taste some of these. Be careful not to overcook, which ruins the texture of pasta— the Italian phrase *al dente* means that the pasta should be cooked "to the tooth," or so that you can bite through the pasta easily but it is not mushy and overly soft.

Don't forget how silly pasta can be. Most children like to suck in spaghetti. Some cultures even encourage pasta slurping! For a silly story about pasta, read Tomie de Paola's *Strega Nona* (Simon and Schuster, 0-671-66606-1, preschool to grade 3) and other books in the series. Children love Big Anthony's overflowing pasta pot.

(36)

Popcorn Poppin' Projects

National Popcorn Popping Month, October

While we're on the subject of food, October is also National Popcorn Popping Month. Since we are a nation of popcorn eaters, why not have some food fun with a favorite snack?

Europeans first encountered corn and popcorn when they reached the New World. Native North and Central Americans, who had known about popcorn for more than a thousand years, introduced them to it. Indians ate popcorn and also used it for decoration and in ritual ceremonies.

Popcorn kernels are usually smaller than seed corn kernels. A popcorn kernel's soft, moist interior is protected by a hard outer covering. But it's the moisture inside that drives the "pop." When a kernel is heated, the moisture inside expands as a gas. When it does, the kernel explodes and becomes a piece of fluffy, white popcorn.

Children can have lots of fun with popcorn. Art projects may include unpopped kernel mosaics. Use different colored corn seed (or other dried seeds) for contrast. Mention how many Christmas trees in the past were hung with strings of popped corn, perhaps with cranberries for contrast. It's a great family activity that can be done easily while sitting around talking or watching TV. With care, the strands will last for years. The strands can also be hung outside for birds and other backyard wildlife.

In language arts, students can have fun writing poems about popcorn. Focus on their experiences with it and their eating habits. Mention alliteration. The explosive "p" is satisfying and appropriate to the subject.

In math, unpopped kernels can be used for simple counting tasks and for estimation purposes. Fill different sized containers and let students estimate what the quantity might be. Encourage them to first measure a certain number of kernels. Add the measurements and then divide to find the average kernel size. Or, fill a known area (one cubic inch, for example) with kernels and count the number of kernels inside. Estimate from that number how many kernels are in a much larger container. They will have to calculate the volume of the larger container.

Play with popcorn volume, too. Again, measure out small amounts of kernels—perhaps a teaspoon, a tablespoon, and a quarter cup. Have students predict how much space the same kernels will fill after they have been popped. Use a hot air popper to avoid oily spills, and caution students about proper, safe use of the popper.

Popcorn also can be used to play a game of place value. Make up sheets with columns (ones, tens, hundreds, thousands, and so forth) appropriate to the mathematical level of your students. Give each student a handful of popped corn. The teacher says a number (or have students take turns drawing a number from a hat) and the class tries to put the appropriate number of popcorn pieces in each column. This can be done in teams or individually. The teacher or a student can check results. So if you call out "four hundred eighty seven," the students should move four pieces into the column marked "hundreds," eight pieces into the column marked "tens," and seven pieces into the column marked "ones."

In science, several experiments can be carried out in a short span of time. Corn germinates in about a week. Plan ahead and have available a few different kinds of corn seed. Have each student plant one kernel on moist paper and five others in moist dirt. Mark the location of each seed with a toothpick. At three-day intervals, uncover and observe how the seeds have changed. Replant if the students want to keep the seeds growing. To make the study more complicated, have students keep their plantings in different parts of the room, especially in darker or colder areas. Chart resulting growth and compare results.

In social studies, students can research how Native Americans (North and Central) used *maize*. Their planting techniques were varied and interesting. For geography, students might shade areas on a U.S. map to reflect the states that are major corn producers.

Related literature includes: *Popcorn at the Palace*, by Emily McCully (Harcourt, 0-15-277699-0, grades K to 3); *Popcorn: Poems*, by James Stevenson (Morrow, 0-688-15261-9, grades 3 and up); *Four Seasons of Corn: A Winnebago Tradition*, by Sally Hunter (Lerner, 0-8225-9741-1, grades 3 to 6); *Popcorn Plants*, by Kathleen V. Kudlinski (Lerner, 0-8225-3014-7, grades 2 to 3).

(37)

Diversity Awareness Month

Our nation is quite diverse, but some classrooms are not. Now is the time to get your students thinking about what makes us the same and what makes us different. The possibilities for celebrating this month in the classroom are endless. Here are a few that will get your creative thought processes flowing.

For the youngest primary students begin on a smaller scale, one that is concrete to very young children. Take a classroom poll on favorite colors. List students' names under each one. Make up other favorite categories: food, TV shows, books, animals. Talk about how some students share favorites, others don't. Art projects focusing around the "likes" that students share provide a visual and concrete expression of similarities. Talk about our similarities: we are all people, everyone breathes, thinks, and feels emotions. Other similarities include two eyes, ears, legs, and arms. Then, discuss differences like hair, eye, and skin color. Include discussion of differences caused by physical disabilities.

Emphasize the way student differences make the classroom a more interesting and exciting place. Explore the old saying that "You can't judge a book by its cover."

Older students may wish to explore differences by writing about family traditions that celebrate ethnic backgrounds. A bulletin board with pictures (student generated!) of the many cuisines we eat is a good idea. Do students celebrate birthdays, religious initiations, seasonal changes, certain holidays? Ask students to think of ways they celebrate special days in their household and then illustrate these to share with the class.

Literature and music provide myriad opportunities for students of all ages to explore cultural differences. Ask students to share family favorites with their classmates. Teachers who need books that treat specific ethnic groups and/or promote discussion of diversity can consult the following: *Against Borders: Promoting Books for a Multicultural World*, by Hazel Rochman (American Library Association, 0-8389-0601-X), which lists books for students in grades 6 to 12; *Our Family, Our Friends, Our World: An Annotated Guide to Significant Multicultural Books for Children and Teenagers*, by Lyn Miller-Lachmann (Bowker, 0-8352-3025-2); and *This Land Is Our Land: A Guide to Multicultural Literature for Children and Young Adults*, by Althea K. Helbig and Agnes Regan Perkins (Greenwood, 0-313-28742-2).

Older students can talk about stereotypes and misconceptions people hold about people who are a different gender, have a different physical ability, race, or ethnic background. A teacher can provide prompts and moderate if the discussion gets too intense. Class discussions of somewhat taboo topics like race can be awkward, but are important because they allow students to get things out in the open and provide an opportunity for the teacher to set a tone of respect.

Older students can be encouraged to begin a pen pal exchange via E-mail or postal mail with someone very different from themselves. Many teachers have found that colleagues at different schools can be helpful sources to match students. *Scholastic* magazine often offers a "pen pal service" that teachers can use to connect their students with a pal from someplace very different. If you decide to make this a classroom project be sure to put up a map with pins or Post-it Notes showing each person's pal and his or her general location.

Encourage writing by setting aside some classroom time for writing letters or "prewriting" E-mails. Students may wish to have help with correcting spelling or grammar, or you can just let them write privately and freely. Prompt students to ask their pen pals about how they celebrate holidays, or other questions that can help the class understand the diverse ways humans live.

Writing may prove easier at first if students are given some optional opening sentences and a list of possible questions to pose in the first few letters. Some of your students may never have had a letter exchange at all, so you may have to help by putting the addressing and stamping protocol up on the board. Keep a few extra stamps on hand for those students who may not have access to stamps at home. Encourage students to reply to their pal within a few days of receiving a letter, so that the letters can stay current and reply time is brief. After a few weeks ask students what they have learned about their new friends and make a chart of the type of diverse information students have gained (perhaps geography, new understanding of customs, and so forth).

38

World Space Highlights

United Nations World Space Week, October 4-10

The United Nations has set aside one week every October to celebrate the contributions of space science and technology to the betterment of the human condition. October 4, 1957, marks the anniversary of the first satellite, *Sputnik*, and October 10, 1967, marks the anniversary of the Treaty on Principles Governing the Activities of States in the Exploration and Use of Outer Space. Students should thrill to a section on world space highlights. Celebrate by researching many firsts.

Since students were not yet born when our astronauts first made their way into space you will find there is much to cover when you focus on space exploration. You may wish to begin with a commemoration of the first moon landing on July 20, 1969. Millions of people, glued to their television sets, watched as Neil Armstrong stepped down from the lunar landing module and said, "That's one small step for a man, one giant leap for mankind."

For language arts, bring in several pictures of Earth taken from space. Ask students to imagine they are astronauts leaving Earth for the first time. Have them write a poem about the sounds heard during a blastoff or write a letter to their families describing how they feel about the trip.

In science, look at the changes in technology regarding the shape and size of rockets, space shuttles, and landing capsules. There have been many modifications over the years. Also, chart the path taken by rockets to the moon, including any earth orbits prior to heading for the moon. Students can research what life is like on a space station. The International Space Station is being funded jointly by sixteen nations. The first astronauts moved in in November 2000. For more information, visit the ISS website at spaceflight.nasa.gov/station/index.html.

Try to get videos of the moon landing. See your learning center director for help in locating them. There are also videos about space exploration.

Discuss the risks of space exploration, such as the tragic launch pad fire of the *Apollo 1* mission on January 27, 1967, the *Challenger* space shuttle explosion on January 28, 1986, and the *Columbia* tragedy of February 1, 2003. Many people were moved to write poems describing the *Challenger* disaster. The death of high school teacher Christa McAuliffe, a member of the crew, was particularly felt in the education community. Many classrooms had TV hookups that day to watch and celebrate the much-anticipated liftoff.

Looking toward the future, compare the kinds of information probes we send out now to those of the past. Have students hypothesize about manned expeditions to Mars. How long would the trip take? What would they need to take along? Also, using newspapers and magazines, students could research the new investigations into possible life forms that may have existed on Mars.

Did your students hear about the failed landing a few years ago of an unmanned research vehicle on Mars? The very expensive crash was caused in part because the scientists working on the radio-controlled landing had not agreed upon whether distances were to be cited using the metric system or the American system of inches/feet/yards and so forth. This might be a good time to discuss the importance of good communication in space efforts. Think of the difficulties in communication aboard the International Space Center, which is occupied by scientists who speak many different languages and may measure using different systems. This may help explain why a standard measurement system and language can be helpful, thus answering one of the common whines about studying the metric system: "Why do we have to learn this?"

There are many excellent books about space exploration. *First on the Moon*, by Barbara Henner (Hyperion, 0-7868-0489-0, grades 3 to 7); *Spacebusters: The Race to the Moon*, by Philip Wilkinson (Dorling Kindersley, 0-7894-2961-6, grades K to 3); and *One Giant Leap: The Story of Neil Armstrong*, by Don Brown (Houghton Mifflin, 0-395-88401-2, grades K to 4), are all about moon exploration. *Close Encounters*, by Elaine Scott (Hyperion, 0-7868-0147-6), is a good teacher resource space overview. *Space Exploration*, by Carole Stott (Knopf, 0-679-88563-3, grades 3 to 7), contains interesting photos concerning all aspects of space exploration.

The History News: Space, by Michael Johnstone (Candlewick, 0-7636-0490-9, grades 3 to 7), offers a newspaper-style overview of space exploration. *Discover Mars*, by Gloria Skurzynski (National Geographic, 0-7922-7099-1, grades 5 to 10); *Is There Life in Outer Space?*, by Franklyn Branley (Harper, 0-06-445192-5, grades 2 to 4); and *Floating in Space*, by Franklyn Branley (Harper, 0-06-445142-9, grades 2 to 4), all contain helpful material regarding the exploration of the universe and other planets. Also visit the NASA for Kids website at nasa.gov/kids.html.

(39)

Fire Safety

Fire Prevention Week, First Week in October

Each year, fires in homes are responsible for the loss of life and property. Many of these fires and the accompanying heartbreak could have been prevented.

All children should be educated in fire prevention and what to do in case of fire. Panic during a fire can lead to tragic results. That's why school fire drills are so important. An orderly evacuation plan saves lives. Unfortunately, many homeowners never take the time to plan ahead. That's where you can help.

Fire departments across the nation observe Fire Prevention Week in early October. Call your local unit and request a fire prevention assembly. Visits to the fire station may be possible. If not, your local unit may be able to bring an engine to the school. One of the things to point out to children is the importance of leaving fire hydrants clear. In today's crowded cities, people seem to ignore parking laws and forget to park well away from hydrants.

During science, it's important to discuss the mechanics of fire. A fire cannot burn unless oxygen is present. A simple experiment can illustrate this. Bring in a small birthday cake candle. Light it and let it drip onto a saucer. Blow out the candle and fix it upright in the wax drop on the saucer. Light the candle again. Explain how the candle's flame burns as long as oxygen can reach it. Cover the candle with a drinking glass. After a few seconds, as the flame uses up the oxygen available under the glass, the flame will dim and then go out. That's why children are taught to "Stop, Drop, and Roll" if their clothing should catch fire: the rolling "suffocates" the flames. It is also an important illustration to explain why many stove-top fires can be put out using a tight lid or by smothering flames with baking soda. Explain to your students that they should never dump water on a grease fire as the resulting spatters can set clothes, hair, or the rest of the kitchen on fire.

When you speak with firefighters about a visit, ask if they have a video (or experiment) that shows the danger of smoke. It's easy to tell kids smoke rises and to stay low, but if you can visually demonstrate it for them, they will remember better. Many departments have access to a model "house" that can illustrate to students how smoke fills a room and why crawling along the floor can save lives. Younger students may enjoy practicing by crawling or slithering under a waving blanket held only six to eight inches or so from the floor.

Talk with students about safety measures the school building has: smoke alarms, sprinklers, etc. Ask each student to talk with his or her parents about fire safety in their home. List and graph the kinds of preventive devices the class as a whole has in their homes. Create a "My Home Is Safe—We Have a Fire Plan" classroom goal. At the very least, every child should be able to articulate an escape plan. Encourage them to draw a map of ways they could escape from their home if a fire started. Discuss why children should *never* reenter a burning building to save a toy or pet or even a sibling.

Discuss 911 and how it operates. Children can work in pairs and act out 911 call scenarios. Stress the serious nature of using 911 and that it is never acceptable to call it for fun. See if you can get a 911 call receiver to visit your classroom. He or she will help reinforce the message. Even children as young as two have saved people's lives by calling 911. Be sure kids understand that they need to stay on the line and talk with the operator, so that the call can be traced and emergency vehicles dispatched to the scene.

Fire prevention in parklands is also important. Younger students can become acquainted with Smokey the Bear. While the symbol was created in 1944 by the National Forest Service, in 1950, a real Smokey Bear was found in New Mexico's Lincoln National Forest. For more information, go to smokeybear.com.

Have a poster campaign to illustrate the danger of fire and its prevention. Display all the posters in the school hallways and find out if the municipal building or the public library would be willing to display them as well. If you have a shopping area, merchants might be willing to participate and hang the posters in their store windows. It's worth a try, and makes for good public relations. The National Fire Protection Association website has lesson plans for elementary and middle grades at nfpa.org. Their "Sparky the Fire Dog" site (sparky.org) has information for kids.

(40)

Camille Saint-Saëns

Birth, October 9, 1835

Born in Paris, France, on October 9, 1835, Camille Saint-Saëns quickly captured the attention of the music community. He was a child prodigy and an accomplished pianist. By the age of ten he could play all of Beethoven's piano sonatas. Saint-Saëns was a marvelous organist. In fact, Franz Liszt called him the world's greatest organist. Saint-Saëns is perhaps best remembered for the melodic tunes and phrases in two compositions that have great child appeal: *Danse Macabre* and *The Carnival of the Animals*. Fortunately, both are readily available and easily brought into the classroom.

Carnival of the Animals, by Camille Saint-Saëns (Henry Holt, 0-8050-6180-0, all ages), is a picture-book retelling of the music, with explanations of which instruments represent each animal and why. It comes packaged with a compact disc recording of the piece.

Since Halloween is just around the corner, let Saint-Saëns bring a holiday atmosphere to your classroom. *Danse Macabre* is a wild piece that gets all of the graveyard residents up and dancing about. Its wonderful orchestration really shows off skeletons and ghosts at their best. The xylophone perfectly captures the frenetic pace of the skeleton and its rattling bones. Older elementary, middle school, and junior high students will enjoy this piece. Turn the lights down low and let students' imaginations wander. The Orlando Pops Orchestra has a recording entitled *Fright Night* that includes *Danse Macabre* and other Halloween-like classical pieces. You can also find it on other recordings. Check your public library.

Several books perfectly extend the concept of dancing bones and lend some fun to language arts and science units as well. *Shake dem Halloween Bones*, by W. Nikola-Lisa (Houghton Mifflin, 0-395-73095-3, ages 4 to 8), offers lots of moving and shaking fun. *The Dancing Skeleton*, by Cynthia Defelice (available in libraries), is a great read-aloud for elementary students ages seven and up. *The Big Book of Bones: An Introduction to Skeletons*, by Claire Llewellyn (Peter Bedrick, 0-8722-6546-3, ages seven and up), provides a look at bones and the skeletal system. *Dem Bones*, by Bob Barner (Chronicle, 0-8118-0827-0, ages three to eight), is a first look at the human skeleton for younger readers, based on the old "knee bone connected to the thigh bone" song.

Mayan Heritage

Día de la Raza, October 12

In Mexico, this day (October 12) observes not only the discovery of the Americas by European explorers, but also the cultural heritage of the Native American peoples who lived in the region before the arrival of Europeans. For more than four thousand years, the Maya have lived in the area now called the Yucatán, in Mexico and in nearby Central American countries such as Guatemala and Honduras. The Mayan civilization was one of the greatest civilizations of the New World and it flourished from 250 to 900 A.D.

The Maya built bustling city centers that often traded goods among themselves. Tikal, Chichen Itza, Palenque, and Copan are some of the major cities in Mayan history. Farmers who lived in the surrounding areas provided food items needed to sustain the city populations. In the cities, stone craftsmen and architects constructed stone pyramids crowned with a temple. Priests held important religious ceremonies in the temples, including sacrifices to the gods, and important rulers were buried inside the pyramids.

Large stone stelae were used to record the important events that occurred in Mayan communities and the lives of their rulers. The Maya wrote their records in hieroglyphics that conveyed information by using pictures that represented a word, a phrase, an idea, or a phonetic syllable.

For many years, there was a dearth of information geared toward children about this fascinating culture. Social studies teachers will be happy to know that a number of books for young readers are now available. Before delving into the past, take a look at *Mayeros: A Yucatec Maya Family*, by George Ancona (Lothrop, 0-688-13465-3, ages seven to ten). This account of a modern Mayan family shows students that the descendants of the ancient Maya are still living in the region. *Mayan Weaving: A Living Tradition*, by Ann Stalcup (Rosen, 0-8239-5331-9, ages five to nine), depicts, in colorful photographs, the production of traditional weaving. In *Mario's Mayan Journey*, by Michelle McCunney (Mondo, 1-5725-5203-4, ages seven to ten), a modern-day boy goes on a dream voyage to discover his Mayan roots.

Examine Mayan culture with *A Maya*, by Frederico Linares (Runestone Press, 0-8225-1922-4, ages ten to thirteen), and *Your Travel Guide to the Ancient Mayan Civilization*, by Nancy Day (Runestone Press, 0-8225-3077-5, ages ten to fourteen). Both are full of photographs, maps, and diagrams. Day's book is written with a light, travel-guide tone that quickly grabs a young reader's interest with descriptions and discussions of the everyday life that he or she would experience if a time-travel visit were possible. *Popol Vuh: A Sacred Book of the Maya*, by Victor Montejo (Groundwood, 0-88899-334-X, ages ten and up), contains the mythical and historical tales of the Mayan people in Guatemala.

Peter Lourie's *The Mystery of the Maya: Uncovering the Lost City of Palenque* (Boyds Mills, 1-56397-839-3, ages eight and up) takes the reader on a visit to the heart of the Mexican jungle. Lourie describes the work of archaeologists as they explore one of the recently unearthed thrones of an ancient Mayan king. A first-page account of a run-in with a deadly fer-de-lance viper grabs the reader's attention immediately.

Secrets in Stone: All About Maya Hieroglyphics, by Laurie Coulter (Little, Brown, 0-316-15883-6, ages eight to twelve), presents Mayan hieroglyphics to young readers. Many children are familiar with Egyptian hieroglyphics, but most don't know about Mayan hiero-glyphs. Readers will be fascinated by the story of how hieroglyphs and the tales they tell were deciphered. Raised glyph templates enable children to create their own secret code messages.

Two novels for middle grade readers are *Secrets in the Mayan Ruins*, by P. J. Stray (Silver Burdett, 0-3822-4704-3, ages twelve and up); and *The Well of Sacrifice* by Chris Eboch (Clarion, 0-395-90374-2, ages eight and up). The first is a modern-day mystery set against the backdrop of a Mayan ruin; the latter is the story of Eveningstar Macaw, a young Mayan girl of the ninth century, and is full of drama and suspense.

For current articles (and videos) on Mayan archeological expedi-tions, try *National Geographic* magazine and the National Geographic Society. They have funded many expeditions, including some at Copan.

42

Dictionary Doings

Noah Webster, Birth, October 16, 1758

Noah Webster compiled the first dictionary of American English, which contained seventy thousand entries and took Webster more than twenty years to research. He must have been a person who loved words. Enjoying words—their look, sound, and definitions—makes reading and writing pleasurable. Sometime during the birth month of

Noah Webster, ask your students to think about dictionaries. When did the first one for English speakers appear? While dictionaries were used in ancient Chinese, Greek, and Islamic cultures, the modern dictionary really only got its start in the eighteenth century.

To encourage vocabulary building you can start a "word jar" or box and a designated dictionary (it can be an inexpensive paperback) in which words placed in the word jar will be highlighted with a yellow marker. Begin the collection with several words you think your students will find interesting. Your contributions might include *onomatopoeia*, really long words, silly words, or useful words.

Write each word on a slip of paper about the size of an index card. Include on the card the correct spelling of the word, its definition, an example of how it is used in a sentence, and your name. Share your words with your students. Then hand out slips of paper to the class. Ask them to write down a word they like, along with the information suggested above. Emphasize that all words must have a student's name on them and that no profanity will be permitted. (If any finds its way in, throw it away without public acknowledgment.) Words deposited can be shared with the class in a daily or weekly word study period, on a blackboard list, in a spelling lesson, or as a prompt for a writing assignment.

On a weekly basis, students' slips are given to an official highlighter (rotate to a different student weekly), who highlights the words in the designated classroom dictionary. This dictionary is always available. Students checking out the page with their contribution will see what other words are on the page. Before they know it, they've read another word and definition—perhaps one to add to the jar.

If you add at least one word per week, it will continue stimulating student interest. By using words that occur during instructional periods or read-aloud sessions, you can model the behavior you hope your students will use.

The index card slips can be stapled into weekly word booklets (with covers) that students can sign out, take home overnight, or read at their desks. It's also fun to share them with other classes. Children love to watch the yellow highlights increase in the dictionary, and it gives them a sense of accomplishment.

A book that provides a great model for a classroom book of word definitions is *Serendipity*, by Tobi Tobias (Simon and Schuster, 0-689-83373-3, all ages). Tobias defines the word *serendipity* by creating fun examples and illustrations to define the essence of the word. These help students remember what the word means and understand how to use it. They also highlight the pleasure of saying a lovely word that flows off one's tongue. Two examples from the book include: "Serendipity is when the big boys need another player on their team, and you happen to be carrying your mitt," and "Serendipity is a hole in the sweater you've always hated." Let students write and illustrate definitions for interesting words they find: *delicious* or *problematical*, for example.

(43)

Franz Liszt and Hungarian Rhapsody No. 2

Birth, October 22, 1811

Franz Liszt was one of the most popular pianists of the nineteenth century. He was born on October 22,1811, in the town of Raiding, Hungary, which is now part of Austria. Liszt was a child prodigy, and by the time he was twelve years old, he had performed piano recitals in Hungary, Germany, and Austria. His father, an amateur musician, taught young Franz how to play the piano, but it soon became apparent that Liszt's talent and affinity for music needed more scope than his father could provide. Liszt began his formal music education in 1823, when he traveled to Paris to attend music school to learn composition and music theory.

Everywhere he played, Liszt astounded people with his keyboard virtuosity. His skill at improvising, plus his engaging personality, made him a crowd favorite. He began his career as a composer in 1848.

A wide variety of music composed by Liszt is readily available in library collections and music stores. He composed many solo pieces for the piano, as well as ballads and waltzes. One of his compositions, Hungarian Rhapsody no. 2, is a musical classic that every child should learn to appreciate and recognize. (If you hear a recording of this piece, you will immediately recognize the music even if the name is unfamiliar!) The first half of Rhapsody no. 2 opens with a slow introductory section dominated by the stringed instruments. It represents the anguish and hardships suffered by Hungary's gypsies as they wandered throughout the countryside. Short clarinet solos periodically reflect this somber theme during the piece. A whimsical, lighthearted, and capricious tone takes over the second half of the piece. Students will immediately feel like dancing and many may say, "This sounds like a circus," or "I've heard this before!" (And they're right: Hungarian Rhapsody no. 2 was used as background music for loads of cartoons.)

Say "Happy Birthday, Franz!" by playing the Hungarian Rhapsody no. 2. Children can respond to it by drawing pictures that reflect their own mood and how it changes as the music and tempo build. Older students can write prose or poetry to reflect their moods. Perhaps they could discuss what the music tells the listener about a gypsy's life.

Or you could just listen and appreciate the music. Your students will love it and probably ask for an encore.

The Erie Canal

Opened, October 26, 1825

After eight long years of construction, the first barge, the *Seneca Chief*, floated the length of the Erie Canal on October 26, 1825. For many years people dreamed of a waterway connecting the Great Lakes to the Atlantic Ocean. The first important waterway built in the United States, the Erie Canal had a length of 363 miles. Travel time from Troy and Albany, in eastern New York on the Hudson River, to Buffalo, on Lake Erie, was reduced from several weeks to less than ten days.

Learning about the Erie Canal is especially important for units on settling the American West. The opening of the canal paved the way for a flood of settlers and manufactured goods into the country's interior. Also, agricultural products and timber from the western areas could be carried swiftly to the East Coast.

Students can plot and trace the route of the canal on a map of New York. Discuss why that particular route was chosen and how difficulties were solved. The construction of locks was crucial. A group of students could draw diagrams or build a model of a lock.

Older students could enact DeWitt Clinton's petition to the New York state legislature for funds to build the canal. (The federal government had denied Clinton's request for building funds.) They could also compare and contrast the building of the Erie Canal with that of the Panama Canal, discussing the impact each had on its respective time period. Finally, they could research early railroads in America and the impact they had on canals.

Because October 26 is also Mule Day (yes, really!), students should know that mules supplied the power needed to pull the barges along the canal. *The Amazing, Impossible Erie Canal*, by Cheryl Harness (Simon and Schuster, 0-02-742641-6, grades 3 to 8), is an entertaining introduction to the building of the canal. Visit the New York State Canal System's website at canals.state.nys.us/canals/erie_canal.htm for additional information on the canal's history and recreational use today.

45

Theodore Roosevelt

Birth, October 27, 1858

Theodore "Teddy" Roosevelt, born on October 27, 1858, was one of the four children of Theodore and Martha Roosevelt. As a child Roosevelt was somewhat frail, very nearsighted, and suffered from asthma. He was an avid reader and liked learning about nature and being outdoors. Indoors, he maintained a large collection of dead animals that he had brought to his room for nature study. By the time he reached his teen years, Roosevelt had become a fitness devotee and frequently exercised in the family's home gym. His workouts helped him to overcome his asthma and enabled him to pursue boxing, hiking, and hunting.

After graduating from Harvard University, Roosevelt served in the New York State Assembly for several years. He left politics after his wife and his mother died in 1884 and "retired" to the Dakota Territory, where he ran two cattle ranches. Two years later, he was back in New York and had remarried.

During the Spanish-American War, Roosevelt organized and commanded the cavalry unit known as the Rough Riders. The regiment's success during the war made him a national hero. He was elected governor of New York. In 1900, he was elected vice president of the United States. He became president in 1901 when President McKinley was assassinated.

Roosevelt was an avid hunter, but he was also concerned about preserving natural areas. He established the first federal wildlife refuge in 1903 and added more than one hundred million acres to the nation's forest reserve areas.

Students will enjoy meeting Teddy Roosevelt. One way to celebrate his birthday is with a Teddy Bear School Visit Day. The toy bears were named after Roosevelt. Students might have fun researching that story and the political cartoon that gave rise to the name. Roosevelt was also well known for "Bully!"—his energetic shout of approval. Language arts fun could involve writing stories to explain how the phrase came about.

Roosevelt approved a treaty with Panama that granted the United States control over a narrow strip of land in that country. That led to the construction of the Panama Canal, which Teddy considered one of his greatest achievements. Take a moment to look at an atlas or globe to show how this canal shortened a ship's route from one continent to another. Older students can investigate and discuss the importance of the canal to shipping and trade and the handover of its control to Panama at the end of 1999.

The Roosevelt children were a rowdy bunch. A bit of research will turn up amusing stories about their many White House adventures, which often revolved around their menagerie of animals. *So You Want to Be President*, by Judith St. George and David Small (Scholastic, 0-439-31756-8, grades 3 to 6), contains some of these amusing tales.

Teddy Roosevelt was the first U.S. president to have much of his life chronicled on film. Recently, more than one hundred films in the Library of Congress's film collection were made available on the Web. Students can get a firsthand glimpse of this energetic man at memory.loc.gov/ammem/trfhtml.

Literature connections include: *Young Teddy Roosevelt*, by Cheryl Harness (National Geographic, 0-7922-7094-0, grades 2 to 5); and *Bully for You, Teddy Roosevelt*, by Jean Fritz (Paperstar, 0-698-11609-7, grades 5 to 8).

(46)

The Internet in the Classroom

Internet "Born," October 1969

Initial hookups that would in later years become the Internet began during the month of October in 1969. Today, the Internet has become a widespread information source and plays a role in many aspects of our lives, from pleasure to work. E-mail has established instantaneous connections between peoples who live far from each other. Chat rooms have become popular, especially with students in middle school through college. In many cases, chat rooms have become the new telephone for young people.

The Internet has taken its place as a resource and learning tool in many schools, and politicians have often been heard pledging their support for an Internet hookup in every school as a desirable goal. Internet usage in schools does require supervision. Because of the diverse nature of information available on the Internet, it's important that student use of the Internet during the school day be focused on information that pertains to the curriculum. There are many websites that complement and extend the school curriculum. Each teacher, before recommending a website, should explore its content.

One source to use to locate interesting websites is the Webby Awards. These awards, presented by the International Academy of Digital Arts and Sciences, began in 1997. The award categories range from humor to volunteering and social activism. Some are wacky and definitely for adults or for out-of-school hours. Others pertain to kids and are very helpful. For more information, see: webbyawards.com /main/webby_awards/winner_list.html.

Past Webby Award winners in the children and education categories include nationalgeographic.com and factmonster.com. The former is wonderful for exploring many aspects of the natural world, science, and world cultures. The latter provides links that help children with homework, while also providing fun for those who love browsing trivia. Both sites are kid-friendly.

The Internet is also a source for newspapers. Many of them maintain websites, some of which are free. The *New York Times* and the *Chicago Tribune* are just two of the major U.S. newspapers available on the Internet. Both are great school resources.

Many books are available that introduce children to the Internet and its use as a research tool. Scholastic Professional Books has published several activity books that guide and direct student use. See *Getting Started with the Internet*, by Peter Levy (0-439-14114-1, ages nine to fourteen), and *10 Quick and Fun Internet Field Trips*, by Deirdre Kelly (0-439-27165-7, ages eight to eleven). All of the Scholastic books specifically target social studies and science curricula. New books are coming out all the time. Ask your learning center director what he or she has seen recently.

One quick tip: if children are using the Internet for a school report on animals or plants, suggest they first find out the scientific name for their Internet search. It helps make the search more accurate. Use a dictionary or encyclopedia. For example: searching for information on the white rhinoceros under its scientific name *Ceratotherium simum* excludes the extraneous sites, such as those on rhinoceros beetles, that would also be found by searching under the keyword "rhinoceros."

A final note of caution: Stress that information found on the Internet should be confirmed by another (print) source. The Internet is not infallible. There are plenty of errors. The children in your classroom today will become Internet users in college and later in their careers, so be sure they understand that no one is really "in charge" of the Internet and that not all that is there is worthy of time or consideration. The ability to sift through the heaps of information so readily available is a skill that will be needed in the future.

47

Fabulous, Frightening Fangs

"I vant to suck your blood" is the classic vampire line. Of course, there aren't any human vampires, but the real truth about vampire animals is, they don't suck out blood. (They also don't kill their victims.) The vampire bat uses its fangs to nip a small piece of flesh from its victim. Then it uses its tongue. The vampire bat has an unusual tongue, with grooves along its sides and on the bottom. When the bat sticks its tongue into the victim's wound, blood runs into the grooves. Capillary action pulls it upward into the bat's mouth. By this point, you may be saying, "Yuck, that's disgusting!" So will children—but they'll be paying really close attention and wanting to hear more. As Halloween approaches, introduce "Fabulous, Frightening Fangs" as a theme.

Many animals have sharp fangs, which are great for grabbing and stabbing prey. Fangs may be defensive weapons to use against predators. Animals have different types of fangs. Divide students into pairs or small groups. In their groups, students can brainstorm reasons why fangs may have evolved. If they go to the learning center, ask them to see what information they can find about fangs in general. For example, some fangs are used to inject venom. Others are used for ripping or shredding flesh. This is a good time to introduce specific tooth names such as incisors and canines.

Create four larger student groups named Fish, Mammals, Reptiles, and the Ancient Ones. Before researching, children should list animals with frightening fangs that belong in their group. Suggestions include:

Fish: sharks, viperfish and other deep-sea fishes, barracudas, and piranhas.

Mammals: lions, tigers, bears, and shrews (they have venom glands).

Reptiles: mambas, rattlesnakes, alligators, crocodiles, and Gila monsters (venom, again).

Ancient ones: carnivorous dinosaurs, saber-toothed tigers, and other fossil finds.

Prior to any research, ask the students to list what information they know about each animal. Then, let the groups go on a "Fun Fang Fact-Finding Foray." After they collect information, ask each group to create a "myth versus reality" fact sheet about one or more of their animals. Students who enjoy art projects can supply drawings, paintings, and/or collages of their group's animals. Close-ups featuring what the fangs look like will give the room an appropriately scary atmosphere. Perhaps they would want to make masks featuring certain animals. If you speak with the learning center director in advance, perhaps you can arrange for all the books located in one research period to be checked out as a group loan to your classroom. That way they could be used as classroom decoration and free-time browsing stops during the length of the focus on fangs.

Some books that will interest students are: *Bats*, by Gail Gibbons (Holiday House, 0-8234-1457-4, ages five to eight); *Bats! Strange and Wonderful!*, by Laurence Pringle (Boyds Mills, 1-56397-327-8, grades 1 to 3); *All About Rattlesnakes*, by Jim Arnosky (Scholastic, 0-590-46794-8, ages seven to eleven); *Shark Attack!*, by Cathy East Dubowski (Dorling Kindersley, 0-7894-3440-7, ages six to eight); *Outside and Inside Alligators*, by Sandra Markle (Atheneum, 0-689-81457-7, ages eight and up); *Vampire Bats*, by Laurence Pringle (out of print, but available in libraries, ages ten and up); *Ferocious Fangs*, by Sally Fleming (NorthWord Press, 1-55971-587-1, ages seven and up).

IDEAS FOR
November

---

(48)

Q and A Day:
Learning How to Get
Questions Answered

All parents have been hit at an utterly odd moment with an amazingly profound question from their child, only to realize they have no answer ready. Teachers get this too. Today can be a day of eliciting questions from your students without demanding they be "on topic." This exercise can prove a way to get nagging questions answered, but much more important, it provides a perfect excuse to teach something really important: research skills!

We live in world of baffling complexity, and as adults we tend to screen out those little niggling voices that occasionally ask, "Gee I wonder how this cell phone actually works?" It is understandable that there are not enough hours in the day to really allow us to fully comprehend the items in our lives, much less the bigger philosophical questions of being a human being at this time in our history. However, answering some of these questions, even if not perfectly, will make our lives richer and more filled with meaning. Understanding how to find answers is a skill that is more important than any set of facts you could ever hope to make kids memorize. It is a skill used by just about every career person in the world, and it makes a person much more valuable as a worker and more effective as a member of a community.

So, for today's focus on Q and A, start by asking your students if they ever had what they felt was a really good or important question that either they never asked, or they asked but no one could really answer. Have them write down those questions. Be prepared to be amazed. You are likely to get some fantastic questions. Don't try to answer any of them, but remain encouraging: "that's a good question," or "interesting!" should be your stock response. Once children have written down their one or two most important or interesting (to them, not you or other kids) questions you are ready to begin.

Explain that most important discoveries in science, archaeology, medicine, or even religion began with a question. Then tell the students that their job now is to figure out how to find the information they need to get their questions answered. Talk about ways of finding information: fact books, experts, reference sites online, and so forth. Have some books to place at stations around the room or in your reading nook. You may also need to have phone books handy as students with really specific questions may need to call a local expert to learn more. Students can make their call after school from home on their own if old enough, or send a note home asking for parental assistance for younger students.

After spending some time pursuing this project, some students will hit dead ends. A dead end is a perfectly normal result in a quest for information. Be sure to reassure students that they can find another way to get their question answered and provide some guiding questions if they need a little shove in the right direction. Try to make this as child-led as possible for best results. Students who get an answer early on can try to answer a second question or can be asked to assist students who are having a harder time.

Visible Ink puts out a series of excellent reference books that are arranged by topic. A few are listed here: *The Handy History Answer Book*, edited by Rebecca Nelson (1-57859-068-X, upper elementary to adult); *The Handy Science Answer Book*, compiled by the Science and Technology Department of the Carnegie Library of Pittsburgh (1-57859-099-X, upper elementary to adult). The series includes a geography and weather book as well.

Another fine reference book is *The New Way Things Work*, by David Macauley (Houghton Mifflin, 0305038473, all ages), which is the bright and funny new version of an old favorite that was called simply *The*

Way Things Work and is likely available at your school media center. *The New Way Things Work* also comes as a CD-ROM.

Beside the books and CDs, the *Way Things Work* folks have an outstanding, and I do mean outstanding, website that teachers, students, and parents all swear by. Visit them today and register for the free E-mail newsletter and you can keep "Q and A Day" happening all through the year: howstuffworks.com. Take the virtual tour to learn more about the site. Children will find it very easy to use, just fill in a blank, "how _____ works," and the computer does the rest. As they say, you can put in almost anything from sunglasses, to engines, to nuclear reactors, to Christmas!

49

Exploring Native American Heritage

National American Indian Heritage Month, November

By presidential proclamation, November has been declared National American Indian Heritage Month. Each day this month feature a Native American who has figured prominently in history. Or, you might want to choose a specific aspect of Native American culture. One way to grab children's attention and create a sense of anticipation is by making a "Fact of the Day" box.

Use a cardboard box the size of those used to package reams of copier paper. Tape the lid securely to the box. Cut a hole about five inches by five inches in the top. Paint the outside of the box and decorate it with art motifs found in Native American cultures: for example, patterns used to decorate Pueblo Indian pottery (see *Children of Clay*, by Rina Swentzell, 0-8225-9627-X, Lerner, ages eight to twelve).

On twenty to thirty blank index cards (or comparable size poster board) write several sentences that tell about a Native American fact. You might describe famous leaders such as Sitting Bull, Cochise, Geronimo, and Wilma Mankiller. One card could feature the anniversary of the Battle of the Little Bighorn, which is on June 25. Some cards could include information about writers whose heritage is Native American. Joseph Bruchac, Michael Dorris, Gayle Ross, and Louise Erdrich have written many books for young readers. Do a book talk on a title for each author. Don't forget sport figures such as Jim Thorpe. There are several famous monuments dedicated to Native Americans as well. The monument to Crazy Horse is one of them.

Glue or tape a heavy metal washer or several large paper clips to the back of each card. Put all the cards into the decorated box. Get a stick about twelve inches long—dowel rods come in many diameters and are cheap. Tie a string about eighteen inches long to the tip of the stick and a magnet to the other end to create a "fact-finding fishing rod."

Set aside a few minutes at the beginning of each day as a time for thinking about the heritage of Native Americans and their contributions to the history of the United States. Let each student have a turn to "fish" through the hole for an index card. After the student reads the card aloud, post it on the board for the day and let students reread it as the opportunity presents itself. The fun of fishing makes everyone look forward to his or her turn. (You may have to do two facts on certain days in order for everyone to have a turn.) The mystery of what interesting fact will come next heightens student interest and anticipation.

Because tribes are so diverse, small student study groups are more effective if they focus on one geographical region. Information can be presented to the class for comparing and contrasting with regional cultures studied by other groups.

Historical treatment of Native Americans is integral to a well-balanced social studies curriculum. Chief Joseph's attempt to lead his people, the Nez Percé, to freedom could be contrasted with the Cherokee people's forced march, called the Trail of Tears, from the southeastern states to Oklahoma.

Teachers should be cautioned against studying only historic Native American cultures. It's important to include information about the lives of modern Native Americans. The thirteen volumes in Carolrhoda Books' series *We Are Still Here: Native Americans Today* contain a wealth of information on the lives of contemporary Native American children.

Literature to connect with this month's theme includes: *Crazy Horse's Vision*, by Joseph Bruchac (Publisher's Group West, 1-88-000094-6, ages six to nine); *Indian School*, by Michael Cooper (Clarion, 0-395-92084-1, ages ten and up); *The Long March*, by Mary Louise Fitzpatrick (1-8836-7291-0, ages seven to ten); *Sitting Bull and His World*, by Albert Marrin (Knopf, 0-525-45944-8, ages twelve and up); *An Algonquian Year*, by Michael McCurdy (0-618-00705-9, ages seven to nine); *A Braid of Lives*, edited by Neil Philip (Clarion, 0-395-64528-X, ages eleven and up); *Home to Medicine Mountain*, by Chiori Santiago (Children's Book Press, 0-892-39155-3, grades 1 to 3). Russell Freedman's *Indian Chiefs* (Holiday House, 0-823-40625-3, grades 3 to 8) is a fine collection of biographical sketches and photographs of famous chiefs.

For a bibliography of additional materials, see *American Indian Reference and Resource Books for Children and Young Adults*, by Barbara J. Kuipers (2nd ed., Libraries Unlimited, 1-56308-258-6).

(50)

International Beats

International Drum Month, November

Most people respond to the beat of drums. Their rhythmic patterns seem to reach deep inside listeners and connect in an elemental way. It's almost impossible to avoid tapping a finger or toes or nodding one's head in response to a drum. There are many different forms of drums in the world. During International Drum Month, you might wish to focus on different regions and the styles and drums found there.

Steel drum bands flourish in Trinidad. In fact, steel pans were invented in Trinidad in the years after World War II. The pans, which range from short-sided, higher-pitched lead pans to deep bass pans, are made from empty oil drums left behind in Trinidad at the war's end. People created notes by hammering indentations in the flat end of the can. Traditional songs reflect the Caribbean heritage, but a growing number of bands are exploring the diversity and new sound that steel pans bring to classical pieces and modern compositions. Liam Teague is an outstanding pan player. A soft-spoken, highly talented young musician from Trinidad, Teague has taken the concert stage by storm and is bringing worldwide attention to the versatility and fun of this unique drum. You can visit his website at liam teague.homestead.com. His CDs *Hands Like Lightning* and *Emotions of Steel* are truly inspired.

Japanese taiko drums are huge, deeply resonant drums. They require enormous energy to play, and it's very exciting to watch a group of musicians perform taiko compositions. Two excellent websites are: Tqjunior.thinkquest.org/5997 and Taikodojo.org/play -taiko.html. The first site is geared specifically to children and has a lot of information about the drums' history and playing. Photos feature young players. The second site is sponsored by San Francisco Taiko Dojo, the only United States–born taiko company. The videos and sound samples of each type of taiko drum will captivate students. CDs of San Francisco Taiko Dojo music are available. A fun literature connection is the picture book *The Drums of Noto Hanto*, by J. Alison James (Dorling Kindersley, 0-7894-2574-2, all ages).

Hand drums are found in many cultures. Latin American music often features bongos and congas. *Tabla* are pot-shaped Indian hand drums, played while sitting cross-legged on the floor. Ireland's *bodhran*, often accompanied by a fiddle, is played with the hands or with a short beater stick. Drums are important in African culture. Babatunde Olatunji's CD, *Drums of Passion*, is a good example of African drumming.

Timpani, the deep kettledrums used in orchestras, are tunable drums that are capable of low murmurs or thunderous rumblings.

If possible, try to arrange for high school or college drummers in your district to visit the school for a short assembly. Many high schools own snare drums, a drum set, and timpani. Well-equipped music departments may have several international drums as well. They could play pieces that feature different rhythmic patterns such as jazz, rock, marching beats, and salsa. Remember that moving drums can be awkward and time-consuming. Contact band directors several weeks in advance to arrange for a date. If cost is involved, approach your school's parent-teacher organization for funds. Drum assemblies really "rock" with kids.

You can also connect Drum Month with poetry. Both require an underlying rhythmic pattern, so they complement each other well.

Older students might try writing short poems that reflect specific drum rhythms.

If you have a percussion student in your class, she or he might be willing to conduct a short drum lesson. If you live in a large community you may even have a formal drum club or an informal rhythm group that gets together to play drums and other rhythm instruments. If you see a poster for such a club, perhaps you could get some of the members to come play for your class. Many such clubs are amazingly diverse, attracting female, male, young, and elderly folks from many cultural backgrounds. Drumming pulls people together.

You can see if you have any budding drummers in your class by handing out an assortment of "instruments" either from your music department or homemade from oatmeal canisters and so forth. You will beat a rhythm on your desk and see if they can answer it on their instruments. Wooden chopsticks or unsharpened pencils make adequate substitute drumsticks for whole-class participation in drumming rudiments and rolls. This form of call and response is a very traditional and time-honored method of teaching, so go for it and have fun!

Also, students might enjoy discovering the joys of tap dancing, which is actually foot drumming of a sort. Savion Glover is a hot young performer who is dazzling kids with his footwork and his focus and commitment to excellence. *Savion! My Life in Tap*, by Savion Glover and Bruce Weber (Morrow, 0-688-15329-0, ages ten and up), is perfect for all those pencil tappers in your room. The rhythms in this book, spelled out in large, colorful letters, are fun to chant aloud.

Play any CD by internationally acclaimed drummer Mickey Hart, *Drumming on the Edge of Madness* or *Planet Drum*, for instance, and you will have every student's attention. Mickey Hart is an award-winning drummer from the band The Grateful Dead. He has his own web page where all his recordings are listed. Or ask your librarian if your library has the World Series of drum recordings—*Planet Drum* is just one of a whole list, each with a focus like rainforest or Native American drumming.

Put on a CD, move the desks back, and let children move to the beat. If students are having trouble with memorization of facts, try having them vocalize to a beat. This simple change may be enough to cause a breakthrough for those suffering from inability to recall math facts or spelling lists. Rhythm can be a powerful force in learning. Drumming can also be a force in healing, and in fact Mickey Hart has testified to Congress about the important role drumming can play in healing the elderly. Many cultures use drums for healing in century-old ceremonies all over the world.

(51)

Fantastic Flying Machines

Aviation History Month, November

Today we board an airplane and minutes or hours later arrive at a destination that a century ago would have been impossible to reach in such a short time. It has been only one hundred years since Wilbur and Orville Wright's first powered flight took place on December 17, 1903. However, people have been fascinated by the idea of flight for many hundreds of years. Indeed, most people have dreamed at least once of being able to fly. A classroom observance of November's Aviation History Month can be a rich and rewarding experience.

In ancient Greek mythology, Daedalus fashioned wings made of feathers and wax so he and his son Icarus could escape from Crete. There are many published versions of this myth and also that of Pegasus, the flying horse. Students can illustrate their own versions of these myths.

Leonardo da Vinci drew a prototype for a flying machine with flapping wings in about 1500. A picture of this machine can be found in *Leonardo da Vinci*, by Diane Stanley (Morrow, 0-688-10437-1, grades 2 and up). Many people experimented with variations of da Vinci's machine in the eighteen hundreds. Students might research and compare them with da Vinci's. A fun and interesting historical fiction video that features one of da Vinci's early flying machines may be a fun way to spend a November afternoon: *Leonardo: A Dream of Flight* (Steeplechase Entertainment, 1894449002, rated G).

The hot-air balloon, first flown in France in 1783, was used for spy missions during the American Civil War. Hot-air balloonists have circled the globe. Students can compare modern-day balloons with older models. Perhaps a balloon enthusiast could pay a visit to your school. There are many children's books featuring hot-air balloons, including: *Full of Hot Air: Launching, Floating High, and Landing*, by Gary

Paulsen (Delacorte, 0-385-30887-6, grades 4 and up); and *Spy in the Sky*, by Kathleen Karr (Hyperion, 0-7868-1165-X, grades 2 to 5).

There are many ways to bring the history of engine-powered flight into the classroom. Videos about Charles Lindbergh, Amelia Earhart, and other early aviators, and film clips of early flying machines are available. Check your local library and the Internet for sources. An antique airplane enthusiast might be available in your area. Call small local airports to ask about clubs. Many children build and fly model airplanes. See if students in your school can organize a schoolwide exhibition.

Children's literature abounds with books on aviation firsts. To get started, look at: *Fly, Bessie, Fly!*, by Lynn Joseph (Simon and Schuster, 0-689-81339-2, grades 1 to 4); *One Giant Leap: The Story of Neil Armstrong*, by Don Brown (Houghton, 0-395-88401-2, grades 1 to 4); *The Glorious Flight: Across the Channel with Louis Bleriot*, by Alice and Martin Provensen (Puffin, 0-14-050729-9, grades 3 to 6); and *First on the Moon*, by Barbara Henner (Hyperion, 0-7868-0489-0, grades 3 to 7). For easy readers and novels try: *First Flight*, by George Shea (Harper, 0-06-444215-2, grades K to 3); and *Airfield*, by Jeanette Ingold (Harcourt, 0-15-202053-5, grades 6 to 10).

52

Like Author, Like Daughter (or Son, or Sister ...)

National Author's Day, November 1

One of the questions children ask authors who visit their schools is, "Doesn't it get lonely, just writing alone?" But authors belonging to certain writing families know they aren't alone in their career because another member of the family is also an author. If you're celebrating National Author's Day on November 1, introduce some famous authors and illustrators who have chosen to follow in their parents' footsteps.

Brian Pinkney is well known for the lovely scratchboard artwork he creates for the many books he has illustrated. *Cendrillon*, a Caribbean Cinderella variant, and *Bill Pickett: Rodeo-Ridin' Cowboy* are two of his recent books. Myles Pinkney, Brian's brother, is a photographer. *Shades of Black*, written by Myles's wife Sandra, features his stunning photos of African American children. Brian and Myles are the sons of illustrator Jerry Pinkney, winner of many prestigious awards. Pinkney recently adapted and illustrated such classics as *Aesop's Fables*, *Rikki-Tikki-Tavi* by Rudyard Kipling, and *The Ugly Duckling* by Hans Christian Andersen.

Crescent Dragonwagon has written several children's books, including *Home Place* (which is illustrated by Jerry Pinkney). Dragonwagon's mother, Charlotte Zolotow, is the author of the sensitive story *William's Doll* and dozens of other wonderful books for young readers.

The Crews family makes quite a splash in children's literature. Nina Crews's collage illustrations, which often incorporate computer-generated images, are lots of fun. *You Are Here* is the picture-book story of two girls who have an imaginary adventure in their home. Nina's father, Donald Crews, is well known for his graphic design illustrations in books such as *Freight Train*. And Nina's mother, artist Ann Jonas, is the author/illustrator of *Round Trip*, a creative book that really involves the reader and his or her imagination.

After her father Robert C. O'Brien died, Jane Leslie Conly wrote two sequels to his much-beloved *Mrs. Frisby and the Rats of NIMH*. Her books, *Racso and the Rats of NIMH* and *R.T., Margaret and the Rats of NIMH* have matched the popularity of his Newbery Award–winning title.

Christopher Myers, the award-winning illustrator of *Fly!*, *Harlem*, and *Black Cat*, is the talented son of Walter Dean Myers, author of the middle-grade reader *Me, Mop and the Moondance Kid*, and young adult award winners that include *Fallen Angels* and *Monster*.

Authors' Day could include a research "mystery trip" to the learning center. Let students go to the library with some of the above names in hand. Have them check out books they find that are written or illustrated by these authors and artists. Let the students figure out what the familial relationships are. This may involve a consultation with the librarian regarding biographical source materials. In the case of the Pinkney family, it's especially fun to compare and contrast the media and different illustration styles each one uses. Challenge students to seek out other authors/illustrators who have family members who work in the field of books.

(53)

The International Space Station

First Inhabited, November 2, 2000

The grand opening of the international space station (ISS) occurred in November of 2000. This installation, orbiting 230 miles above the Earth, is a permanent one that will be occupied by crew members from many different nations. In November of 2002, records for longest time spacewalking were broken when astronauts spent many hours working on the outside of the structure. The station is being built in stages, with the cooperation of over a dozen nations, and should be completed by 2006. William Shephard was the first commander with a crew of Russian astronauts, Yuri Gidzenko and Sergei Krikalev. Their two-day flight took them to the space station for a three-month-long stay (November 2000 through February 2001). Each team of astronauts is replaced by a new set after its mission is completed.

The space station is expected to serve as a study center for the next fifteen years. Orbiting the Earth at about 17,500 miles per hour, the space station is quickly becoming one of the most brightly visible objects in the night sky as more and more sections are added.

Students can learn more by searching the Internet for updates on the station's construction and current crew. The NASA site at space flight.nasa.gov/station should be the first stop. If possible organize a star-watching night and see if you can spot the station. The Real Time

Station Data section of NASA's website has information on when the station can be best seen from your location. *Sky and Telescope*, the astronomy magazine, also has up-to-date information at skypub.com. Look at the "Sights/Satellite Observing" section. Newspapers and local planetariums will also have this information.

As a writing project, students could write what they think life on a space station would be like. Ask them to think about daily necessities like air, water, food, exercise, sleep, toilets, showers, etc. You might wish to send letters to NASA, asking for information. You can gain insight by watching a "NOVA" TV special, which is available on the Web at pbs.org/spacestation. The Discovery Channel also has information on its site at school.discovery.com/schooladventures/space station/index.html.

In art, ask students to design their idea of a perfect space station. Compare them with the real thing. How are they the same and different? Two books elementary students will find interesting are: *Floating in Space*, by Franklyn Branley (HarperCollins, 0-06-445142-9, grades K to 3), and *The International Space Station*, by Franklyn Branley (HarperCollins, 0-06-445209-3, grades K to 4). For danger and drama see *Space Station: Accident on Mir*, by Angela Royston (Dorling Kindersley, 0-7894-6686-4, grades 2 to 4).

Students can put their ideas to the test by participating in NASA's Ames Research Center's Space Settlement Contest for students in grades 6 to 12. Students are asked to submit designs for an orbital space settlement (deadline is always March 31 each year). All participants receive a certificate, and winners present their submissions at California's NASA Ames Research Center in June. For contest information go to belmont.k12.ca.us/ralston/programs/itech/Space.

The International Space Station heralds an exciting era in space exploration. The important lessons learned from the building of and living in the ISS will provide the framework for future missions to places much farther away then the skies of Earth.

54

The Discovery of King Tut's Tomb

November 4, 1922

The beautiful gold mask that covered King Tutankhamen's mummy is one of the most famous of all Egyptian antiquities. But the mask was only one of the amazing treasures found in the boy-king's tomb. Children will especially relate to the everyday objects, such as ship models, games, and a trumpet that can still be blown. Children also relate to King Tut because he was only about nine years old when he became pharaoh, in 1347 B.C. He died at the age of eighteen or nineteen.

Tutankhamen's short reign was undistinguished in Egypt's history. His more famous relatives include Akhenaton, the heretic pharaoh, who may have been his brother or father (scholars are not in agreement), and Akhenaton's queen Nefertiti. Young readers will love *Tut's Mummy*, by Judy Donnelly (Random House, 0-394-89189-9, ages five to eight). Middle school students will enjoy the photos in *DK Discoveries: Tutankhamon: Life and Death of a Pharaoh*, by David Murdoch (Dorling Kindersley, 0-7894-3420-2, ages eight to twelve). For young adults see *Tutankhamen: Life and Death of a Boy-King*, by Christine El Mahdy (St. Martins, 0-312-26241-8). There are many books for adults about Tutankhamen that have pictures children will enjoy. The 1923 edition of *National Geographic* that reported the find is on the Web at nationalgeographic.com/egypt.

Many people, including children, are fascinated by the exotic allure of ancient Egypt. A marvelous idea for an art perspective would be to compare and contrast the difference in the style of art found in traditional wall and tomb reliefs with the freer, more natural style found in art of the Amarna Period (Akhenaton's reign).

Children love experimenting with hieroglyphics—ancient Egyptian writing. The pictures represent sounds. A bit of research into sound/picture equivalents may allow students to transcribe their names into hieroglyphics. Older students could compare and contrast the nature of hieroglyphics with the writing systems of other civilizations. Good books for younger readers include: *Seeker of Knowledge: The Man Who Deciphered Egyptian Hieroglyphics,* by James Rumford (Houghton Mifflin, 0-395-97934-X, ages seven to eleven); *The Shipwrecked Sailor,* by Tamara Bower (Atheneum, 0-689-83046-7, ages seven and up), is a translation of a story from an ancient papyrus scroll that includes phrases in hieroglyphics.

The science of mummification has tremendous classroom appeal. There are many books about mummies. You might want to let students research mummies from different cultures. Here are a few books to get your students started: *Secrets of the Mummies,* by Shelley Tanaka (Hyperion, 0-7868-0473-4, ages eight to twelve); *Mummies, Bones, and Body Parts,* by Charlotte Wilcox (Carolrhoda, 1-57505-428-0, grades 4 to 7); *Mummies and Their Mysteries,* by Charlotte Wilcox (Lerner, 0-8761-4643-4, ages eight to twelve); *Cat Mummies,* by Kelly Trumble (Houghton Mifflin, 0-395-96891-7, ages eight to eleven); *Bodies from the Bog,* by James M. Deem (Houghton Mifflin, 0-395-85784-8, ages eight to twelve); *Ice Mummy: Discovery of a 5,000 Year Old Man,* by M. and C. Dubowski (Random House, 0-679-85647-1, ages eight and up); *Discovering the Inca Ice Maiden,* by Johan Reinhard (National Geographic, 0-7922-7142-4, ages nine and up).

National Geographic magazine features information on Egyptian antiquities on a regular basis. Ask your media center if you can borrow some back issues for students to look at during your free reading time or any other period that would be appropriate. You may wish to gather books on this topic to have available as well.

55

Benjamin Banneker

Birth, November 9, 1731

Considered to be the "first black man of science," Benjamin Banneker was born November 9, 1731, at Ellicott's Mills, Maryland. He was the grandson of Bannaky, an African slave, and Molly Walsh, an indentured servant from England. Benjamin's family lived on a tobacco farm. Benjamin taught himself astronomy and higher mathematics. He wrote an almanac, first published in 1802, which provided information that helped farmers and travelers. He was a member of the surveying team that designed and planned Washington, D.C. Banneker also carved wooden clockworks and built the first clock that was completely made in America.

One way you might celebrate Benjamin Banneker's contribution to history is by looking at the building and design of our nation's capital. Prior to the city's completion, the land was swampy and often mosquito infested. Named after George Washington, it was the most elaborately planned American city of its time. Washington, D.C. celebrated its bicentennial in 2000.

You might also have students research Banneker's almanac and compare the kinds of information it contained with that of modern almanacs.

For biographies about Banneker and his family see: *Molly Bannaky*, by Alice McGill (Houghton Mifflin, 0-395-72287-X, all ages); *Dear Benjamin Banneker*, by Andrea Davis Pinkney (Gulliver, 0-15-200417-3, grades K to 3); and *What Are You Figuring Now?*, by Jeri Ferris (Lerner, 0-87614-521-7, grades 3 to 6). Several websites feature Benjamin Banneker: for example, web.mit.edu/invent/www/inventors A-H/Banneker.html.

56

Armistice Day

Anniversary, November 11, 1918

Veterans Day, or Armistice Day, as it is called in many countries outside the United States, has been a legal federal holiday since 1938. However, many children today do not know its significance or why people wear red poppies. This day commemorates the end of World War I in 1918. In 1919, President Woodrow Wilson proclaimed it as Armistice Day, to remind all Americans of the tragedies of war. In 1954, Congress changed the name to Veterans Day, to honor and recognize veterans of all wars.

This is a day for reflection on the sacrifices made during wars. Compromise and nonviolent conflict resolution are alternative topics. There are many books available on war and its effects. *In Flanders Fields: The Story of the Poem by John McCrae*, by Linda Granfield (Doubleday, 0-385-32228-3, grades 3 and up), intersperses double-page spreads of the poem with information about World War I, including the significance of red poppies. *Casey Over There*, by Staton Rabin (Harcourt Brace, 0-15-253186-6, grades K to 3), is a picture book about one family's experience during WWI. *After the Dancing Days*, by Margaret Rostkowski (HarperCollins, 0-06-440248-7, grades 6 and up), is about a young girl's relationship with a WWI veteran who is recovering in a veteran's hospital. *War and the Pity of War*, edited by Neil Philip (Clarion, 0-395-84982-9, grades 6 and up), is an anthology of poems inspired by war. The poems reflect a range of experiences, including heroism, sardonic humor, and horror.

Teacher's wishing to add more geography or history can do a large time line showing wars from the last hundred years. A series of maps highlighting which countries were involved in which wars may help students understand more about the world wars and why they are called that. Use large red cutout arrows to show major offenses and label them with which countries were involved. Ask students to team up to research some of the major battles of the wars you are featuring. How many died on each side? What mistakes were made? Did weather or geography play a major role? How did this battle influence the outcome of the war?

(57)

Celebrate Aaron Copland's Birthday

Birth, November 14, 1900

Aaron Copland was one of the greatest American composers. His music—filled with interesting rhythms, syncopation, and many musical themes that are great for humming—celebrates American life and music. He incorporated elements of jazz and folk songs.

Copland was born in Brooklyn, New York, November 14, 1900, to parents who had immigrated from Lithuania. Copland's father ran a dry goods (department) store and the family's living quarters were above it.

Many of his compositions are music that young listeners will enjoy. *Billy the Kid* (1938), *Rodeo* (1942), and *Appalachian Spring* (1944) are three ballets that are particularly appealing. The first two epitomize the spirit of the American West. Use selections from them to add musical depth to units on westward expansion. *Appalachian Spring* celebrates the building of a new farmhouse in a rural Pennsylvania farming community during the early eighteen hundreds. The repeated theme from the Shaker hymn "Simple Gifts" is very stirring and develops into an emotional fullness that echoes the richness found in the lives of the people and in the soil that supports their farms. Every child should be introduced to this piece, for which Copland won the 1945 Pulitzer Prize for Music.

All of this music is easy to find. If you are willing to dig deeper, try to locate *Lincoln Portrait*, which features a narrator reading aloud writings by Abraham Lincoln. There are several different recordings—Carl Sandburg and Melvyn Douglas are two of the narrators. *El Salón México* is another piece worth hunting for. This features some light Mexican folk music themes.

Before sharing these pieces with children, you might want to summarize the story of the ballets. Prior to playing a dance selection, it may help to include a comment to start student imaginations rolling. For example: "Can you imagine horse-drawn wagons rolling down a dirt-covered Main Street," before playing "Street in a Frontier Town," from *Billy the Kid*. Or "Imagine the fun these dancers are having. How would you move around if you were one of them?" before playing "Hoe-Down" from *Rodeo*. When playing *Appalachian Spring*, identify the musical theme of "Simple Gifts" and ask children to notice how it changes as the piece continues.

The best way to celebrate Copland is by playing his music. However, some children may want additional information about the composer. Steer younger readers toward Mike Venezia's *Aaron Copland* (Grolier, 0-516-44538-3, ages nine to twelve). High school students may enjoy browsing the in-depth adult biography *Aaron Copland: The Life and Work of an Uncommon Man*, by Howard Pollack (University of Illinois Press, 0-252-06900-5).

Georgia O'Keeffe

Birth, November 15, 1887

Georgia O'Keeffe is one of America's best-known artists. Born in 1887 in Sun Prairie, Wisconsin, she later moved to New York and had her first showing in a gallery owned by Alfred Steiglitz, whom she later married. Her paintings of flowers and desert landscapes, particularly those including wildlife skulls, command instant recognition. Of her work, O'Keeffe said "When I was still a little girl, I used to think that since I couldn't do what I wanted to . . . at least I could paint as I wanted to and say what I wanted to when I painted." Students will enjoy looking at her artwork, which can be found reprinted in books, calendars, and postcards. Discuss the way O'Keeffe explored shape and varying light conditions. Talk about her use of bright, vibrant colors.

O'Keeffe's work was closely tied to nature. This provides a tie-in to the science curriculum. Units on plants, animals, and rocks and minerals are full of materials well-suited to an O'Keeffe celebration and exhibit. Ask students to find a rock, leaf, or twig with an interesting shape. If outside observation is possible, students can look at cloud shapes and tree bark patterns, the shapes found on an animal's paw or the texture of its fur. An assignment would be to draw or paint the object they have seen, paying special attention to shape, texture, and color. Encourage students to highlight the part of their object that intrigues them most by drawing it larger than life-size.

An additional activity could include a list of descriptive and sensory words for the object the student has drawn or painted. The list will provide a starting point for the student to write a poem or short essay. Artwork and written pieces should be displayed in the classroom or hall.

There are a number of juvenile and adult biographies about O'Keeffe: for example, *My Name Is Georgia: A Portrait*, by Jeanette Winter (Harcourt Brace, 0-15-201649-X, grades 2 to 4). Check your library for video interviews and documentaries about her life and work.

(59)

Bold, Beautiful Books

Do you have read-aloud sessions in your class? If not this would be a great habit to start. Let students script a short picture book, early reader, or a section of a novel (depending upon skill level and age). Use the script and student readers to stage a reader's theater presentation. If different students present each day, everyone can have a turn by week's end. If students work in teams reluctant readers can contribute shorter lines of dialogue or narration, and the hams of the class will have a chance to strut their stuff.

Get parents involved in your celebration of beautiful and bold books. Ask if any parents are willing to come in for just a few minutes to give a quick (less than five minutes) book talk on their favorite book from childhood. If parents can't visit, ask kids to interview them and fill out a "virtual book talk" form. These can be read aloud or posted on a bulletin board.

For a middle school change of pace, bring picture books into the language arts class and read them aloud. Try *Click, Clack, Moo: Cows That Type*, by Doreen Cronin (Simon and Schuster, 0-689-83213-3); *Tommy at the Grocery Store*, by Bill Grossman (available at libraries); *And the Dish Ran Away with the Spoon*, by Janet Stevens and Susan Stevens Crummel (Harcourt, 0-15-202298-8); *Book! Book! Book!*, by Deborah Bruss (Scholastic, 0-439-13525-7); and *Humpty Dumpty Eggsplodes*, by Kevin O'Malley (Walker, 0-8027-8756-8). All of them are quick reads and very funny—perfect for witty sixth, seventh, and eighth graders!

Students can also celebrate books by engaging in other book-related activities. Each student could design a bookmark for his or her favorite book. Post recommended titles on the bulletin board. Nominate and vote for favorite book of the week (an activity that could carry on throughout the school year). You can expand this activity and perhaps expand reading interests by specifying different genres each time: nonfiction, science fiction, mystery, and so on.

Think about holding a cover critique session. Choose books from the school learning center and canvas students' desks for books. Ask students to compare cover illustrations with the actual story inside. Does the cover illuminate or support the story? Is the cover inviting or a turnoff? Encourage students to give their own ideas on what makes a good cover and how they would change an existing cover, if they feel one doesn't work. Students can develop a list of things that they feel make a good cover. This can be a small-group project or done on a student's own. Checklists for covers can become a class resource when looking at books as they are presented throughout the year.

Older students could extend this activity by summing up their conclusions regarding specific book covers. If they are able to edit their first draft they can develop a letter suitable for sending to the Children's Book Marketing Department of the book's publisher. Addresses and names are often available on the Internet, or ask your librarian for assistance in locating them. Being able to write and send an appropriate letter to a business is an important life skill, and so is being able to appreciate *and* critique books.

Pirate Tales for Gray Days

Edward "Blackbeard" Teach,
Death, November 22, 1718

In the gray fall days of November, it can be fun to liven things up with pirate tales. Blackbeard the Pirate is a name many children might have heard from legend.

This English pirate of the Caribbean and American Atlantic met his end at Ocracoke Island, North Carolina, in hand-to-hand combat with British naval forces defending coastal cities of the colonies. Born around 1680 at Bristol, England, Teach (sometimes known as Drummond) had a notorious reputation in a pirate career that lasted from about 1716 to 1718 aboard his ship *Queen Anne's Revenge*. Teach went to great pains to make himself legendary and feared across the seas: he grew his hair and beard to long lengths and plaited them. He also put lighted cording in his hair and beard to create evil-looking smoke around him!

Pirates weren't all as colorful as Blackbeard or the fictional peglegged Long John Silver from Robert Louis Stevenson's *Treasure Island* (1883). In fact, although Stevenson based *Treasure Island* on pirate legends of the time, a lot of what he wrote was for dramatic effect: the pirate talk and treasure map were unique to the book and not to real pirates. Pirates did, however, use distinguishing flags (many featuring skulls and skeletons) to frighten the ships they sought to plunder.

It's hard to go wrong with reading from *Treasure Island* to thrill a class, but you can also use nonfiction books to give the true history of these notorious criminals. One good start is *Eyewitness: Pirate*, by Richard Platt (DK Publishing, 0-789-46608-2, ages nine to twelve), which is filled with photos of pirate flags, weaponry, plunder, dress, and more.

And perhaps an educational treasure hunt can liven the day? Instead of following a map for gold and pearls, students might solve math problems to lead to a treat!

61

Thanksgiving

George Washington Declares Thanksgiving, November 26, 1789

Giving thanks at harvest time is a tradition shared by many cultures. Some celebrations have their roots in ancient times; others, such as Thanksgiving Day as observed in the United States, are more recent. Although we often think of the Pilgrims as holding the first Thanksgiving in America, the very first one was celebrated in 1619 on a plantation in Virginia. Settlers gathered together for a time of thanksgiving that was observed with prayer and not feasting.

The first Thanksgiving in New England was celebrated in the autumn of 1621. The three-day festival was attended by colonists and Native Americans. Feasting was an important part of this celebration, as were prayer and some outdoor activities. Our traditional turkey dinner is a reminder of the four wild turkeys shared that day.

George Washington declared November 26, 1789, as Thanksgiving Day. But after that, many states celebrated Thanksgiving on different days. Thanksgiving was not actually designated as a nationwide holiday until 1863, when Abraham Lincoln proclaimed the last Thursday in November as Thanksgiving Day. Each year after that, the president proclaimed the holiday anew. Congress ruled that after 1941, Thanksgiving Day would be celebrated on the fourth Thursday in November. Because being thankful for what you have is not just a feature of our culture you will find that other countries, like Canada, have their own celebrations of Thanksgiving. Make finding more celebrations of thankfulness a class treasure hunt and see how many are out there. How do these differ from one another?

There are a number of recently published children's books that will extend and complement the activities you have planned for the holiday. *The Autumn Equinox: Celebrating the Harvest*, by Ellen Jackson (Millbrook Press, 0-7613-1442-3, ages seven to eleven), begins by looking at harvest festivals as they have been celebrated in different worldwide cultures during the past hundreds of years. She discusses the holiday in the United States. The last few pages of the book contain a number of multicultural activities with giving thanks as their theme. Students could share the different traditions their families observe each year.

This First Thanksgiving Day, by Laura Krauss Melmed (Morrow, 0-688-14554-X, ages three to six), is a simple counting book that depicts Native American and colonist children as they gather items and prepare for the coming festival. *Giving Thanks: The 1621 Harvest Feast,* by Kate Waters (Scholastic, 0-439-24395-5, ages seven to ten), is a photographic re-creation of the first Thanksgiving. Models in costume portray the participants and carry out activities that were likely to have occurred during the days preceding the celebration. The viewpoint switches back and forth between a Wampanoag boy and a Pilgrim boy.

The Story of Thanksgiving, by Robert Merrill Bartlett (Harper, 0-06-028778-0, ages seven to twelve), describes early harvest times and celebrations and then recounts the history of Thanksgiving in the United States. He describes the foods that were eaten and the socialization between the Pilgrims and Native Americans that occurred after the meal was finished. The contributions George Washington and Abraham Lincoln made toward making Thanksgiving a national holiday are included at the end.

62

Turkey Day!

While we're on the subject of Thanksgiving, introduce your students to an unfamiliar historical fact about turkeys.

In a January 26, 1784, letter to his daughter Sarah, Benjamin Franklin expressed his unhappiness over the choice of the eagle as the symbol of America—he preferred the turkey. "I wish the bald eagle had not been chosen as the representative of our country; he is a bird of bad moral character," wrote Franklin, "like those among men who live by sharping and robbing; he is generally poor, and often very lousy. The turkey is a much more respectable bird, and withal a true original native of America."

Ask your students to share what they know about turkeys, making a list on the board. Next, tell them that Franklin preferred the turkey. When your students finish laughing, ask why they think he liked this bird and list their reasons.

Have students gather information from the learning center about turkeys and eagles. First, they should discover that there are domesticated turkeys, like those raised as a food crop, and wild turkeys, which were what Franklin had in mind. They should find enough similarities and differences to compare and contrast both kinds of turkeys and eagles.

Jim Arnosky's book *All About Turkeys* (Scholastic, 0-590-48147-9, grades 1 to 5) contains a wealth of information about turkeys. *Soaring with the Wind: The Bald Eagle*, by Gail Gibbons (Morrow, 0-688-13730-X, grades 2 to 4), gives a good overview of bald eagles.

After students have done some research, read aloud the section of the letter Franklin wrote to his daughter on the subject (quoted earlier in this section).

As a persuasive writing extension, ask students to write letters to the country's founding fathers in support of Franklin's candidate. Another extension would be to ask students to choose another animal they feel best represents this country and write a statement telling why the animal should be chosen.

63

Discovering Canada: The Canadian History Time Line Project

Here's a quick treasure-hunt style project for the end-of-November doldrums. Since Canada and the United States share so much history it is also a way to see our connectedness as nations and neighbors. Start by visiting the websites listed below during a prep time. Be sure they are still at these addresses, as you will be sending students there during the treasure hunt to find answers. "100 Great Events in Canadian History" can be found on the Web at tceplus.com/Time line/100Events_frame.html. "Important Moments in Canadian History" can be found at arts.okanagan.bc.ca/finearts/his_home.html. These two sites alone should be able to provide the information your students will need to put together the big events in Canada's history. Students may wish to fill in with book research on their own, and you may wish to assign more reading and writing if time allows.

If computer access is tight, assign groups of students to work together or divide the project into different parts of the day so students all have time at a computer station to do their work. The first group should come up with at least twelve things to place on a time line of Canadian history that occurred before 1800. The next group can work on the dates between 1800 and 1867. Assign these dates to other groups: 1868 to 1918, 1919 to 1945, 1946 to 1967, and 1968 to present.

Each group should be able to put a date on the time line and add a paragraph describing what happened and why it is important. After each group has added their information and the time line is complete take some time to draw comparisons to the dates that are important in the history of the United States. Do we share some of the same ones? Can students see how different the Canadian government is on account of Canada's association with Britain? Is Britain still in charge of Canada? In what ways is this still true or less true than in the past? Here are some extra credit questions for the treasure hunt:

- What is lacrosse? What is its origin? (Lacrosse is Canada's national sport, invented by native people, witnessed by Europeans in 1608.)
- How many native people were living on the continent of North America around the year 1600? (The native population was estimated at 250,000.)
- What is the meaning of the phrase "First Nations"? (It refers to the native population of Canada.)
- What is Bill 101? (Bill 101 is a controversial Quebec language law, which among other things banned most English-only signs in Quebec.)
- What is a "Loonie?" (In 1989 the dollar bill was replaced by a coin with a loon on it, now referred to popularly as a "loonie.")
- When did Prince Edward Island get connected to the mainland of Canada by bridge? (The very controversial almost nine-mile Confederation Bridge was completed in 1997.)

December

---

(64)

Bingo's Birthday Month

Bingo Invented, December 1929

In December 1929, Edwin Lowe invented a game called "Lowe's Bingo." Since then, bingo has become one of the most frequently featured fund-raising games in the United States. As the holiday season approaches, students begin to get antsy. Take a short break for a classroom game of bingo. If you know you are going to be absent, suggest it to the substitute.

You can buy your own bingo set, or students can make their own. Play the standard bingo game just for fun, or create your own version of it. The standard version is a fun way to get primary students to recognize numbers.

For math, instead of a single number in the columns beneath the letters B-I-N-G-O, put simple math problems. With planning, you could design boards with equations. For example, under the "B" column one board might contain 1 + 1; 1 + 2; 1 + 3; etc. The caller would pick and read out the sum, for example, "B3." Players would have to recognize that 1 + 2 equaled the sum of 3. This is a very complex version; a simpler version would be to place single numbers in each column. They could represent sums or products, etc. The caller would pick and read out the equations. Kids would do the math in their heads and search for the correct answer in the designated column.

An alphabet bingo could be structured for students who are learning the alphabet, or for emergent readers, using simple words such as *dog, and, cat, the, we, she,* etc.

For those who enjoy a wacky extension of the bingo theme, suggest students read Betsy Byars's humorous Bingo Brown books. *The Burning Questions of Bingo Brown* is the first volume. There are three sequels, and all are available in libraries and as paperback novels for readers ages nine to twelve.

(65)

Winter Is Coming: Understanding Snowflakes, Glaciers, and Icebergs

During the frigid days of December, feature snow, ice, and glaciers in your classroom.

Create a snowy atmosphere in your room. As an art project, let students cut out paper snowflakes and hang them from the ceiling and on the walls. Point out that in real life no two snowflakes are the same. On January 15, 1885, Wilson Bentley, a nineteen-year-old man, took the first photograph of a single snowflake. He took thousands more after that. His original photographs have been published, and Caldecott Medal–winner *Snowflake Bentley*, by Jacqueline B. Martin (Clarion, 0-395-86162-4, grades 1 to 5), is a lovely picture-book biography about Bentley's work.

In science, investigate crystals and how snowflakes form. Discuss snow accumulation and how snowflake crystals change as they are subjected to pressure. In climates where the snow cannot melt each spring and summer, it continues to accumulate and eventually forms a glacier. *Icebergs and Glaciers*, by Seymour Simon (Morrow, 0-688-06186-9, preschool to grade 3), and *Glaciers: Ice on the Move*, by Sally M. Walker (Carolrhoda, 0-87614-373-7, grades 3 to 6), both describe the process and contain photographs and diagrams.

After learning about how glaciers form and move, it's easy to turn the focus to icebergs. When a glacier flows into a body of water, large chunks of ice calve, or break, from the main body of ice and float away. They are called icebergs. Large icebergs pose threats to ships that travel through frigid waters (and one caused the *Titanic* to sink). Students can make mini-icebergs for a concrete understanding of the hidden danger an iceberg poses. All they need to do is plop a piece of ice in a glass of water. Ask them to observe the ice and draw how it appears above and below the water. Measure the ice and determine what percent sticks out of the water.

In geography, students can track the course of a gigantic present-day iceberg called B-10A. This iceberg broke off from Antarctica in 1985 and began moving away from the continent in 1992. It broke in half in 1995. B-10A is the piece now drifting toward the southern Atlantic Ocean. Have your students look in newspapers and news magazines for articles about B-10A. The National Oceanic and Atmospheric Administration's National Ice Center maintains a website with photos and the latest news about the iceberg at natice.noaa.gov.

(66)

Georges Seurat

Birth, December 2, 1859

Celebrate the birth of Georges Seurat (pronounced "suh-RAH") and familiarize students with an interesting style of painting. Born in Paris, France, December 2, 1859, Seurat was one of the inventors of pointillism, a painting style that experiments with pure color and dots rather than brush strokes. In pointillist paintings, facial expression and detailed textures are not as important as capturing the intensity of color and the play of light. Seurat's most famous pointillist painting is *Sunday Afternoon on the Island of La Grande Jatte*, painted in 1886, which depicts a crowd of people enjoying a Sunday afternoon on an island in the Seine River. Shown strolling, fishing, or relaxing on blankets, the people and the surrounding landscape are an exploration and celebration of color.

Pointillists did not mix colors. Instead, they used dots of pure color positioned side by side. Different shades were obtained by varying the intensity, or number of dots, of a particular color in certain areas. When seen from a distance, the viewer's eyes blend the colors.

Bring in examples of Seurat and pointillist-influenced paintings done by Paul Gauguin, Vincent van Gogh, Claude Monet, and Jan Vermeer. Many art books contain color reproductions of their work. Encourage students to draw or paint their own pointillist art. In addition to pen and paint, markers work well for pointillist pictures. Before beginning the actual art piece, have students experiment with dot intensity. For example, investigate how adding yellow dots in varying numbers changes a blue or a red dotted area. How much yellow must be added before the viewer's eye blends the blue and yellow into green? Display student work in a classroom exhibit.

A research project could include an investigation of pointillism in modern technology. The pictures on color television are made with dots of color. The number of pixels, or dots, on a computer's monitor screen control the clarity and intensity of the images we see. Use a magnifying glass or microscope to look closer at advertisements in magazines or newspapers. Up close most reveal discrete dots of color. Do any of your students have the older kind of computer printer known as "dot matrix"? Before laser and jet ink printers, dot matrix printers printed letters by laying down a series of dots.

(67)

Ferdinand's Friends

Munro Leaf, Birth, December 4, 1905

The Story of Ferdinand, by Munro Leaf (Penguin, 0-448-42190-9, ages four to eight), first published in 1936, is a classic that has won the hearts of generations of children. Mr. Leaf was born December 4, 1905. His gentle story, with black-and-white illustrations, tells the tale of Ferdinand, a bull bred for the bullfighting ring. Strong, fierce-looking, and huge, it appears that he will be a formidable fighter. Ferdinand, however, prefers smelling flowers. He's a gentle bull who is sensitive and friendly.

Every child should read (or listen) to this charming book that not only encourages peace over aggression, but gently underscores that it is OK to be different. *The Story of Ferdinand* is a good discussion opener for topics such as bullies and fighting. Students could start by listing the characteristics the bull breeders attribute to and expect from Ferdinand. Then, list the personality traits that the reader actually sees in Ferdinand. Ask if they have ever assumed something about a person based on his or her appearance.

Odd Velvet, by Mary Whitcomb (Chronicle, 0-8118-20004-1, ages four to eight), complements *The Story of Ferdinand* very nicely. Young Velvet is different from her classmates. She collects milkweed pods and finds eight crayons more than enough to draw rich pictures.

Although laughed at to begin with, Velvet's gentle, creative, and caring personality, which always remains true to itself, persuades her classmates to understand that being different is nothing to be feared.

Patricia Polacco's new book, *Mr. Lincoln's Way* (Penguin, 0-399-23754-2, ages five and up), also complements the theme of Leaf's book. Mr. Lincoln is a cool principal. Everyone likes him, except Mean Gene, the bully who picks on kids from minority groups. When Mr. Lincoln discovers that Gene loves all species of birds, it gives him the key for helping Gene free himself from his prejudices. A surprise ending deals with a family of ducks that nest in the school's atrium.

Turning an enemy into a friend is explored in *Enemy Pie*, by Derek Munson (Chronicle, 0-8118-2778-X, ages four to eight), an engaging story about a boy who has decided the new kid in town is his enemy. He carefully follows his father's suggestions and recipe for making an enemy pie. During the process, the boy is surprised to find he makes an unexpected friend. *Marianthe's Story: Painted Words, Spoken Memories*, by Aliki (Morrow, 0-688-15661-4, ages five to ten), is the story of a girl as she struggles to make friends in a new country.

Bill Pickett and the Cowboy Life

Birth, December 5, 1870

Born in Texas on December 5, 1870, Bill Pickett grew up to become one of the most famous African American cowboys. Almost every child dreams of becoming a famous cowboy or cowgirl at one time in his or her life. There's something so exotic and alluring about life on the trail—not to mention the derring-do of steer wrestling, roping, and horseback riding.

Bill Pickett was the second of thirteen children born to Thomas Jefferson Pickett and his wife, Mary. By the time he was eleven, Bill was hired out as a ranch hand. Over the next several years, he perfected skills in riding, roping, and "bulldogging." By the time Bill was sixteen, he was known nationally. Later, he performed in international rodeos.

Pickett died on April 2, 1932, of a fractured skull, the result of being kicked by a horse. In 1971, Bill Pickett was the first African American cowboy to be admitted to the National Rodeo Hall of Fame.

Take some time to create an attribute list of the skills or personality traits young Bill had to have to become such a successful cowboy. Can students think of modern-day jobs that require a similar skill set? Older students might be assigned a "chapter" in Pickett's life to write up as historical fiction.

Biographies about Pickett include *Bill Pickett: Rodeo-Ridin' Cowboy*, by Andrea Pinkney (Harcourt, 0-15-202103-5, ages four to eight), and *Guts: Legendary Black Rodeo Cowboy Bill Pickett*, by Cecil Johnson (Summit, 1-5653-0162-5, ages young adult and up).

Because cowboys are so popular with elementary students, you might want to consider developing a cowboy unit. Three books that may help are *Black Cowboys*, by Gina De Angelis (Chelsea House, 1-7910-2590-X, ages ten and up); *Cowboys*, by Martin Sandler (0-06-446745-7, ages ten and up); and *Cowgirls*, by Ubet Tomb (Bellerophan Books, 0-88388-188-7), which tells students about a whole host of wild, brave, and athletic women.

Social studies projects could include identifying other famous cowboys. Bob Lemmons and George Mcjunkin are two well-known African American cowboys. Students can research and describe life on a working ranch in the late eighteen hundreds. They could also map specific routes that cowboys frequently used while driving herds. Discuss how the advent of railroads altered the cowboys' way of life. Try *Black Frontiers*, by Lillian Schlissel (Simon and Schuster, 0-689-80285-4, ages eight to twelve), for a look at African Americans in the West. Girls may want to research the role of women cowpersons and present their findings to the class.

Have fun in language arts with *The Cowboy ABC*, by Chris Demarest (DK Ink, 0-7894-2509-2, ages three to six), and *Home on the Range: Cowboy Poetry*, by Paul Janeczko (Dial, 0-8037-1910-8, ages five to nine). Young adult audiences may enjoy Baxter Black's poetry, including *Coyote Cowboy Poetry* (Coyote Cowboy Co., 0-939-34300-2). Tony Johnston's fairy tale *The Cowboy and the Black-Eyed Pea* (Putnam, 0-698-11356-X) will delight students of all ages.

In math, students can have fun creating their own cowboy word problems. Enterprising older students may be interested in creating cost analysis "spreadsheets" on the money needed to outfit and run a cattle drive, including items like feed and stock purchases and saddles and branding equipment. The popular computer game "The Oregon Trail" gets students to think about the costs of items and their ultimate utility in a cross-country trip by wagon. Chances are good that your school owns this game, or that many of your students do. If you have access to computers in the classroom, why not offer this learning game to back up what students are learning about the life of a cowboy.

Regardless of whether you incorporate cowboys as a unit or as individual studies of people such as Bill Pickett, at this time of year students' minds are starting to go into holiday shutdown. Dusty trails, chuck wagons, and some roughriders may be just what's needed to hold their attention.

69

United Nations International Volunteer Day

December 5

In our busy lives we often forget the importance of volunteering our time to organizations and people who need a helping hand. Out of a growing concern that some children do not understand the value of being a volunteer, some school districts are making community service hours a graduation requirement. Familiarizing primary and middle school children with volunteer service helps them discover the rewards—on personal and community levels—of helping others. Parent-teacher groups within the school system are an example of how volunteers make a difference in students' lives. Many towns have service organizations, such as Kiwanis, Knights of Columbus, food pantries, and homeless shelters.

Students can volunteer in school: sorting the Lost and Found items, reading aloud to younger students, setting up a tutoring program, and helping with playground trash pickup are a few volunteer projects that don't involve transportation. With access to transportation, usually with parent volunteers, students can donate time at local nursing homes or soup kitchens with age-appropriate activities and supervision. Many old folks are lonely at this time of year, and young people singing holiday songs or making crafts at the elbow of residents is a welcome event. Call any local nursing home and you will probably be invited to "tea and cookies" or activity time.

Encourage students to find stories of people engaging in volunteer work. Collecting newspaper stories and photographs showing people involved in disaster relief after floods, tornadoes, earthquakes, or hurricanes is one way to illustrate volunteerism. A "We Make a Difference" bulletin board of volunteers schoolwide keeps students aware of areas that can use help. The key to success is making students aware of needs in the community.

Community-based groups may be willing to provide a school speaker. A speaker from a homeless shelter, teen help hot line, or women's shelter may be able to provide age-appropriate real life stories of serious needs met by volunteers. Be sure to tell the speaker what your students' ages are and what you would like the speaker to discuss. Students can create a thank-you card for each speaker.

(70)

The Borrowers

Mary Norton, Birth, December 10, 1903

Mary Norton, author of the children's literature classic *The Borrowers*, was born on December 10, 1903, in London, England. Not much is known about her life, but her books are world famous. Encourage your students to read and discuss them. There is a biography about her works and life written for adults. It is entitled *Mary Norton*, written by Jon Stott (Macmillan, 0-8057-7054-2, adult).

The Borrowers (Harcourt, 0-15-209990-5, ages eight to twelve), published in 1953, is the first of Norton's five books that chronicle the adventures of Pod, Homily, and Arriety Clock, a family of tiny people who live under the floorboards in an English home. This fantasy family must use discarded and "borrowed" materials from the large house to create their own comfortable home. Their ingenuity is totally charming and often laugh-out-loud funny. The other four books in the series are: *The Borrowers Afield*, *The Borrowers Afloat*, *The Borrowers Aloft*, and *The Borrowers Avenged*. All are readily available in school and public libraries and in paperback in bookstores.

As is usually the case with fantasy involving tiny people, normal-sized humans pose the greatest threat to the continued existence of the little people. This issue is one children relate to, perhaps because they themselves are trying to make their own way through a world inhabited by larger people.

A fun way to enjoy and explore the themes and situations found in the Borrowers series is to have children read them (as part of a fantasy genre unit, perhaps) and also the excellent Mennym series by Sylvia Waugh. The Mennyms are a family of life-size, living rag dolls who live in a house in England. *The Mennyms* (Morrow, 0-380-72528-2, ages nine to thirteen) is the first book of the series and is followed by four more. Set in modern times, the Mennyms have many exciting adventures as they foray out into the world of humans. There are sufficient similarities and plenty of differences to make them a good example of how literature can be compared and contrasted.

As a writing project, children might enjoy writing about where the Borrowers would live in their house, if they were to move in. What kinds of things would pose a threat (pets?), and what items would they be likely to "borrow"? Some mothers have been known to blame "borrowers" for the lack of one sock in a pair. What if they were to inhabit your school?

(71)

Discussing Human Rights

Human Rights Week, December 10-16; Human Rights Day, December 10; and Bill of Rights Day, December 15

Often, when we feel vexed at the outcome of a disagreement, we say in a frustrated tone, "But I have the right . . ." There is sometimes confusion about the difference between a "right" and a "privilege." A right is a protection that our government (or individuals) must grant to its citizens (or other human beings). A privilege is a benefit that is given but is not mandatory, like a driver's license.

All students can list what they feel are their rights. As a class, discuss the items listed and work at sorting out the "rights" from the "privileges." (This is almost an adjunct list to a description of "needs" and "wants," which you might want to discuss first. It helps clarify the topic for younger students.)

Begin the discussion with basic human rights: dignity, respect, love, etc. Guide students to talk about ways that people infringe upon those rights on a national scale. Gradually turn the discussion to ways that human rights are infringed upon around them. Focus on a classroom and peer level. Many students do not perceive that their actions and comments can actually infringe upon others' rights. Ask students for their suggestions on small things each of them can do to protect the rights of others, which in turn protects their own rights. Perhaps these suggestions could be announced over the PA system during the week.

Students can research and write about groups that seek to demean, harm, or take away the rights of others. Media attention has been focused on what actions constitute hate crimes. Students can discuss the motivating emotions (fear and low self-esteem are two) behind these harmful behaviors.

Children also can talk about what rights they have as students. The American Civil Liberties Union has a website at aclu.org. Talk about the rights we are entitled to under our form of government and why those rights were included as part of our Constitution. Have students make Bill of Rights signs. Each one might feature a specific amendment and an example of what it guarantees as it relates to us today.

Also, students can be encouraged to research the way children are treated in various countries, including the United States. All children are not given education, nor are they protected from abuses in the workplace. Many consumer goods and sports products we use regularly are produced by child labor.

Literature connections include: *A Kid's Guide to America's Bill of Rights*, by Kathleen Krull (Avon, 0-380-97497-5, grades 5 and up); *Living the Bill of Rights*, by Nat Hentoff (Harper, 0-06-019010-8, grades 8 and up); *Human Rights*, edited by Mary Williams (Greenhaven, 1-56510-796-9, grades 5 to 12); and the five titles in the What Do We Mean by Human Rights? series (Franklin Watts, grades 4 to 8).

Antarctic Exploration

South Pole Reached, December 14, 1911

Roald Amundsen (born in 1872) was a Norwegian explorer who sailed the first single ship through the Northwest Passage in 1906. He turned his sights south when he found out that Robert Peary had reached the North Pole (1909). At about the same time, Robert Scott put together a British Antarctic expedition.

Students could compare and contrast the routes and transportation methods of the two groups. (Scott's ill-fated mission relied on ponies rather than sled dogs.) How do present-day expeditions differ from early Antarctic explorations? How have new equipment and technology like satellite positioning changed the life of the explorer? Will Steeger's polar expeditions in the late 1990s featured daily reports typed into a laptop computer in his tent and beamed up to a satellite for teachers and others to read.

It was big news when Amundsen's expedition reached the South Pole on December 14, 1911. Have your students write and publish an Antarctic newspaper reporting the momentous occasion. Columns might include a cooking section (what they ate), weather reports, transportation (the latest in sleds), a column featuring the Amundsen/Scott race, Letters to the Editor, and feature articles.

Amundsen made history again in 1926 when he flew in an airship over the North Pole seeking to make the first transatlantic Arctic flight (Richard Byrd flew the same path three days earlier, but there is dispute over who actually crossed the pole). Two years later, Amundsen and his crew vanished while on an Arctic rescue mission. Students interested in researching what may have happened to them can also explore other famous disappearances, like Amelia Earhart's.

There are many ways to expand the Antarctic exploration theme. A creative writing focus is *Black Whiteness*, by Robert Burleigh (Atheneum, 0-689-81299-X, grades 4 and up), a lyrical journal-like account of Richard Byrd's six-month period alone in the Antarctic. *Shipwreck at the Bottom of the World,* by Jennifer Armstrong (Crown, 0-517-80013-6, grades 5 and up), is a don't-miss, riveting survival story about Ernest Shackleton's expedition to cross Antarctica in 1914. This intense story will stimulate a number of classroom discussions and raise some interesting moral issues.

An additional exploration theme might be modern-day explorers and the places they go. The ocean floor and space are two examples.

Sitting Bull

Death, December 15, 1890

Sitting Bull, also known by his native name, Tatanka Iyotaka, was a famous and highly revered Hunkpapa Lakota warrior and leader. He was a *wichasha wakan,* the Lakota words for a holy man or seer. One of his prophetic visions was of "soldiers falling into camp," which many believed foretold the results of the Battle of the Little Bighorn.

He was born around 1831, the son of Her Holy Door and Sitting Bull (his father's name). At the baby's naming ceremony, his father named him Jumping Badger, but the young boy soon received the nickname "Slow." Slow was known as a keen observer and a quick learner. He spent a lot of time with horses and was an excellent horseman. When he was about fourteen years old, Slow went on his first war party, against Crow warriors. That was when he scored his first coup—he whacked a Crow warrior with his coup stick. (Many Plains Indian "wars" were not so much about killing warriors from an "enemy" tribe, but often involved gaining honor by touching or unhorsing an opponent.) That blow caused the Crow warrior to miss his shot and earned great honor for Slow. Later, when the war party recounted their victory, Slow received his adult name. His father

acknowledged his son's bravery by giving his most valuable posses-
sion—his own name—to his son. From then on, Slow was known as
Sitting Bull. Sitting Bull drew many pictures that depicted his deeds.
He represented his presence in a scene with a drawing of a sitting
buffalo bull. A brave warrior, Sitting Bull had a reputation for uphold-
ing strict moral principals and obeying the tribe's rules.

Sitting Bull was one of the Native American leaders at the Battle
of the Little Bighorn, on June 25, 1876. The Native American warriors
defeated the U.S. Army's Seventh Cavalry, commanded by George
Armstrong Custer.

Inflamed by the defeat, the army became determined to conquer
and capture Sitting Bull. Sitting Bull's belief and request, often
repeated, that Native Americans be free to choose their own way of
life, was ignored. A series of wars broke out. Finally, Sitting Bull and
a small band of followers fled to Canada, where they remained until
1881. Then, faced with starvation after two brutal winters, Sitting Bull
and his people were forced to return to the United States.

In the summer of 1885, Sitting Bull accompanied Buffalo Bill Cody
and his Wild West Show and appeared in New York, Philadelphia, and
Washington, D.C. He led the parades and greeted visitors to the show
in his lodge. After one season, Sitting Bull returned to live on the
Standing Rock Reservation in South Dakota. While there, he supported the Ghost Dance, which many believed would bring ancestors
back to aid their people in a time of terror and hopelessness. Whites
saw this as a threat and attempt to renew the Indian wars. Sitting Bull
was shot and killed on December 15, 1890, when Native American
police officers attempted to arrest him.

Two books for young readers include: *A Boy Called Slow*, by Joseph
Bruchac (Putnam, 0-698-11616-X, ages five to eight), and *Sitting Bull
and His World*, by Albert Marrin (Dutton, 0-525-45944-8, ages eleven
and up). Marrin's book is a comprehensive biography that includes
information about the Lakota and how changes brought by the
expansion of white society affected them. He presents all issues with
perspectives from both sides, making this an excellent choice for class
discussion. Some moments in this book will bring tears to your eyes.
Most of all, your students will understand and respect Sitting Bull, a
unique and charismatic leader.

74

The Three Cs: Cross-Cultural Communication

Sitting Bull and his life may open the door to discussions of what anthropologists call "cross-cultural miscommunication." Sitting Bull tried very hard to be a good leader of his people and often ran afoul of the United States government and its people because there was very little understanding across cultures.

A fine example of cross-cultural miscommunication is the fact that many cultures do not encourage eye contact. In fact, many Native American cultures see direct eye contact as a sign of disrespect. Ask students to consider how they would view a person who does not make eye contact. Chances are you will hear "untrustworthy," "suspicious," or even "evil." Now ask them what happens when one person's cultural rules say not to meet a person's eyes and the other culture tells one to always make eye contact.

There are many examples of physical and communication rules. Some cultures encourage people to speak in quiet, almost monotone voices. What does this kind of speech mean in your community's mainstream culture? Some cultures encourage men to hold hands when they walk and talk on the street, and to kiss when greeting or leaving one another. Other cultures do not encourage any touching in public at all. In some places if you compliment a person by saying, "That is a lovely vase," the person will have to give the vase to you and would be insulted if you did not take it. Have students list rules in our culture such as shaking hands, what is said when answering the phone, and so forth. Pretend you are writing a guidebook for a person from a very different land. The list of rules we take for granted every day, because we are insiders in this culture, is sobering.

If your students have seen the very funny film *My Big Fat Greek Wedding*, they may recall the scene where the Greek Americans in the church are sort of spitting at the bride. This practice is seen as warding off the "evil eye," or keeping the gods from being jealous! Some cultures believe that a little spit should follow any compliment to protect the person who was complimented. That could be quite uncomfortable to someone who did not know about this practice! These sometimes subtle and sometimes out-front differences can make for trouble not just in the classroom but in business and politics as well.

Students may want to ask parents or friends for examples of times when their expectations ran afoul of another person's cultural rules. Stories of travelers' errors abound and many are very funny. Have students research cultural differences and write a fictional story about a misunderstanding. These can be acted out, given as speeches, or just read as a report.

The Boston Tea Party

Anniversary, December 16, 1773

On December 16, 1773, colonists angered at the East India Company's monopoly of the tea market tossed 342 chests of tea into Boston Harbor. They feared the monopoly could put American merchants out of business. They also resented the imposition of British laws on American people.

Students can research a number of details about this event. How many people participated in the protest? Did they represent the way most people in the community felt? Had they presented their grievances to the authorities in any other way first? Middle school students can write letters to King George III protesting the British policies. They can also use American ingenuity to come up with advertising campaigns for a new drink alternative to tea. Support the new drink with posters that advocate turning away from British-supplied tea. Have them write flyers that urge a boycott against the East India Tea Company.

Other historical questions to research include a focus on tea itself. Why was tea so important to the colonists? Where did the tea come from? When did tea drinking become such a widespread habit in Europe? Science connections can include understanding the stimulant nature of black teas, the climate needed for the growing of tea, and the medicinal uses for herbal teas.

Another research project might include investigating the York Tea Party, which occurred in York, Maine, in 1774, when a group of Maine patriots burned tea in a warehouse. Compare and contrast it with Boston's Tea Party.

Today, an action like the Boston Tea Party might be regarded as vandalism. Britain's response was to impose more taxes, some of which the colonists regarded as harsher than the original ones. Middle school and junior high students can research how our government would be likely to respond to these actions now. Have them write a letter to an elected official and ask for his or her perspective on how the government would respond. They can also research other protests involving the destruction of property and see how frequently violent acts invoke violent responses. Have them look into possible nonviolent alternatives to the Tea Party. They might want to have more modern figures (like Gandhi, or Martin Luther King Jr.) agree to "meet" with the Tea Party members and present their cases for other means of protest. Ask them to script some of the alternatives and present them for the class.

Among the many books about this historical event are *The Boston Tea Party*, by Laurie O'Neill (Millbrook, 0-761-30006-6, grades 3 to 6), and *The Boston Tea Party*, by Steven Kroll (Holiday, 0-823-41316-0, grades 3 to 6).

76

Holiday Memory Chain

December includes several holidays—Hanukkah, Christmas, and Kwanzaa—that are often celebrated by families gathering together to share prayer, gifts, meals, and memories. As we grow older, we realize that gifts from the heart are the ones we cherish most. Why not encourage your students to make a family gift that will become a cherished gift and a chronicle of their family's life?

Each student will be making a five- to ten-link paper chain. (Some students will really get into this and can be encouraged to create more.) Offer several colors of construction paper. Students will need permanent markers or crayons.

Cut paper into strips that measure six and a half inches long by one to one and a half inches wide. Students can scallop or nick edges if they want.

On each strip the students can write a short phrase (or draw a picture) that recalls a particular moment of their life, or that of a family member. (Students should write their names in small letters, too.) For example, family milestones like, "We got our puppy _____ this year." "Grandma taught me to how to _____." "My sister was born on _____." "Our family moved to _____." Encourage students to remember some of the times when the family laughed together over something silly: "The dog jumped on the kitchen table and ate John's birthday cake."

Each phrase should include just enough description to jar comments of "Oh, yeah—and remember what else happened . . ." or "And after that we . . ." or "Let's let Susie tell all of us the whole story."

After the individual links have been written, paste or staple them together. This short chain becomes the nucleus for a chain that family members will add links to each year. The chain can be stored away with holiday decorations and rehung (and lengthened) the following year.

This is a fun way to get families to share memories with each other. Suggest children ask grandparents to add links right away. It's also a great way to reinforce the importance of oral tradition. Many cultures, like the Hmong of Southeast Asia, have managed to pass thousands of years of history on to the next generation without the benefit of a single written word! Oral history is so important because as old-timers die they can take important unwritten memories with them. The chain and your students can be the catalyst for the jarring of memories and the telling of family tales. What could be a better gift this holiday season?

(77)

Understanding World Religions

December is a month that often encompasses a number of religious holidays. These holidays can provide a peek into a foreign world for us. Our nation is known for its tolerance of religious differences, while some nations have a state-approved religion. While public schools are encouraged to keep religion separate from school, that doesn't mean we are not to educate our young people about religions. Learning that the world religions have a lot in common with each other is eye-opening, and it is a way to promote peace and under-standing—two things our world certainly needs. Be sure to reassure students that this unit will not ask them to question their personal beliefs or to share them with others unless they wish to do so.

A good place to start is to ask kids to list the religions in the world (there are four major ones: Islam, Christianity, Judaism, and Bud-dhism). Let them brainstorm and write all answers on the board no matter how odd they may appear. Then perhaps get out the diction-ary and define *religion*. From here you can whittle away at the list until it has four religions that the class would like to explore. At this point you can assign research to four (or more) teams. Ask them to look for these key pieces of information using any research tool available in your class or media center: (1) In what way(s) do people in this religion state their faith? (2) What are the key duties and responsibilities of a person of good faith? (3) What are the special or most holy times of year? (4) Which places are considered holy? (5) Where do people of this faith practice their religion? (6) What are the names of the holy books that contain the wisdom or laws of this faith? Have the questions on a work sheet or up on the board for reference.

A site by the Peace Corps (where a variant of the questions above can be found) is a great starting place for the children who are researching Islam: peacecorps.gov/wws/guides/kgrgyzstan/islam.html. Using Kgrygyzstan as a launching point, the site includes much information (and lessons) for teachers and students. The Different Drummer site teachingaboutreligion.com also offers lesson plans that include information about free thinking and religious liberty. The exercise recommended in the next few paragraphs comes from this excellent Teacher's Choice site aimed at middle school and up: ama rilloart.org/lp_6_.6_ss_identifyreligion.html. There you will find lesson ideas broken down by topic (like art or history) and by grade level from grade 6 up.

Once your students have answered the questions on their work sheet it is time to come back together and share what the teams have learned. Start by drawing a Venn diagram on the board. A simple Venn diagram is just two circles that overlap in the middle. If your class chose to research Judaism and Christianity, ask those two research teams to fill in the circles. Circle A contains characteristics of one religion, Circle B contains characteristics of the other. The place where they overlap should contain those items that are shared characteristics of both religions. For example in the case of Judaism and Christianity both share the words and laws of the Old Testament.

Next you can make the class work harder by drawing bigger circles, once for each religion, and have them overlap in the middle so that each circle has a space for characteristics that are unique to that faith. The overlapped areas now can be filled in with characteristics shared by two, three, or even all four religions. This effort will be repaid with a graphic reminder that these faiths, while wrapped in different symbols and practices, share at their core very important fundamental pillars. It also helps students understand the differences.

Now you can launch into questions and answers. Many students have probably had questions about other faiths they were never allowed to ask. If you feel overwhelmed by your class and cannot in good faith provide answers you should feel free to use the best phrase in a teacher's lexicon: "That is a good question. I don't know the answer, but I will find out and get back to you." This gives you time to look up an answer or even line up a speaker or speakers (A professor of world religions? A lineup of religious leaders of various faiths?) who can address the questions. Better understanding usually leads to tolerance. In a world with biological and nuclear weapons in the hands of all sorts of fanatics, it behooves us to help our students become better world citizens, and by understanding other faiths we can get a clearer picture of motivations and beliefs.

(78)

Crossword Puzzle Fun

First Published, December 21, 1913

Chances are likely that students are getting excited about the approaching school vacation. Attention spans are shortening and their minds (yours, too?) may not be totally focused on academic matters. Why not have some crossword fun and celebrate the anniversary of the first publication of crossword puzzles on December 21, 1913? If you plan ahead, you can ask the school secretary to save paper targeted for recycling and use the backs of those sheets for copying.

During first period, divide the students into groups of four or five. Arrange groups so that each one includes a couple of students who can be relied upon to keep the process moving along. Assign each group a subject: science, math, reading, gym, etc. The group should brainstorm a list of words they are currently using in that part of the curriculum. Limit the list to ten so they don't get bogged down trying to think of terms. Unrelated words can be used to fill other squares.

Give the students a blank grid with ten boxes across and ten down. (For copying purposes, make them small enough to fit two grids per sheet.) They can lightly pencil in their words, blended together crossword style. While one student is doing this, the others should be writing clues for each word across and down. Blacken the boxes where no letters appear. Number the boxes after unused boxes are colored in, so students can number the clues consecutively. Students should number the clues according to the box where the word begins. Erase the lightly penciled letters from the grid. Hopefully, the creation of the puzzles will not exceed two class periods.

When the crossword puzzles are finished, copy them and give them to students to fill out that afternoon or to take home for fun during vacation.

(79)

An Amazing Find

Coelacanth Discovered, December 22, 1938

On December 22, 1938, Marjorie Courtenay-Latimer, the young curator of South Africa's New London Museum, sorted through a pile of fishes on the deck of a fishing trawler. Not expecting to find anything out of the ordinary, the sight of a beautiful blue fin surprised her. She was even more surprised when she uncovered the rest of the fish. It was almost five feet long and had scales that resembled armored plates. But it was the strange, lobed fins on the fish's underside—which looked like legs with fins instead of feet—that really caught her attention. Courtenay-Latimer had seen many different fish, but never any that resembled this one.

When ichthyologist Dr. James L. B. Smith identified Courtenay-Latimer's find as a coelacanth, shock waves rippled throughout the scientific community and newspaper headlines round the world exclaimed the news. The reason everyone was so excited was that coelacanths had previously only been found as fossils. Scientists had believed coelacanths were extinct. Courtenay-Latimer's discovery was like finding a live dinosaur.

The search for a second specimen of a coelacanth lasted fourteen years, and it wasn't until 1987 that researchers in a manned submersible managed to find coelacanths in their natural habitat. Subsequent discoveries in Indonesia and, more recently, in South Africa, continue to make headline news as scientists seek to unravel the many mysteries concerning this highly unusual fish.

Unexpected scientific discoveries often lead to scientific quests that have fascinating stories. Unfortunately, many students never learn of these exciting adventures and continue to subscribe to the myth that "science is boring." Why not tempt students with real-life scientific mysteries and quests that will change their minds and encourage them to look beyond their own horizons? A number of books are available.

Pertaining to the discovery of coelacanths, see *Fossil Fish Found Alive: Discovering the Coelacanth*, by Sally M. Walker (Lerner, 1-57505-536-8, ages ten and up), and for high school students, Samantha Weinberg's *A Fish Caught in Time: The Search for the Coelacanth* (HarperCollins, 0-06-019495-2).

A good collected source for many scientific mysteries and discoveries is *The Case of the Mummified Pigs and Other Mysteries in Nature*, by Susan Quinlan (Boyds Mills, 1-563977-83-4, ages ten and up). Learn how forensic scientists track down a poacher in *The Wildlife Detectives*, by Donna M. Jackson (Houghton Mifflin, 0-395-86976-5, ages nine to twelve). *Asteroid Impact*, by Douglas Henderson (Dial Books, 0-8037-2500-0, ages nine and up), explores what might have occurred when the comet or asteroid possibly responsible for the extinction of the dinosaurs hit Earth. *The Search for the Giant Squid*, by Richard Ellis (Penguin, 0-14-028676-4, ages fourteen and up), is an in-depth account of finding this huge ocean creature, as well as an overview of how the animal has been regarded through history.

Younger readers will enjoy *Ice Mummy: Discovery of a 5,000 Year Old Man*, by M. and C. Dubowski (Random House, 0-6798-5647-1, ages six to nine), and *Giant Squid: Mystery of the Deep*, by Jennifer Dussling (Grosset and Dunlap, 0-448-41995-5, ages six to nine). *The Mystery of the Hieroglyphs: The Story of the Rosetta Stone*, by Carol Donoughue (Oxford University Press, 0-19-521554-0, ages ten to fourteen), is a good choice for budding Egyptologists.

80

Endangered Animals: Our Changing Landscape

Endangered Species Act of 1973,
Approved by Congress December 28, 1973

Encourage students to realize the causes that have led to the very real possibility that certain animals are in danger of extinction. Have them make a list of well-known endangered mammals. Then, make the idea of threatened species immediately relevant to your students by extending the theme to include animals, fish, insects, and plants threatened in your own community or state.

Housing subdivisions and industrial complexes are being built at an astounding rate. In many cases, their construction encroaches on undeveloped lands that often include forests, fields, and wetlands. Environmentalists and conservationists are concerned about the threat to many species of animals and plants. Loss of habitat has led to a number of species' inclusion on lists of threatened or endangered species. What's happening in your state? Exploring this question should lead to many project ideas.

Supplement the geography curriculum by dividing the state into its natural geographical regions. Point out the importance of including population densities within each geographical province. State geological surveys can supply information, and often maps. Have groups of students research the animal and plant life that are typically found in those areas today. The thrust of this project is to make children aware of how to access valuable primary source materials that concern their state. Find out if your state has a plan to protect and/or encourage the maintenance of open space as part of construction plans. An example is "Illinois Tomorrow," a program that encourages municipalities to work together and plan ways to preserve open space and rebuild urban areas. Your state governor's office or the U.S. Fish and Wildlife Service can steer students toward appropriate sources and agencies that will have information for your state.

A social studies project would focus on past usages of the state's lands. Depending on where you live, choose an increment of years appropriate to your area. Again, students should focus on human population density and its influence on the land and animal and plant life in the area. If you live on the plains or in the West this discussion might include the impact of fencing.

Math projects have many possibilities. For example: several pie charts showing the percentages of animals, people, and undeveloped lands for different time periods. A line graph that reflects human population increases could be plotted on the same graph with animal population densities. See *Tiger Math: Learning to Graph from a Baby Tiger*, by Ann Whitehead Hagda and Cindy Bickel (Henry Holt, 0-8050-6248-3, grades 2 to 5).

Discover if any animals and plants have been listed as endangered or protected species in your state. Examples include: Gila monsters, snowy owls, certain species of stickleback fish, and lady slippers. In some regions, protecting endangered species has caused major conflicts between environmentalists and industry, particularly when restrictions involve loss of jobs. For a state-by-state list of endangered animals, go to the U.S. Fish and Wildlife Service's website at endangered.fws.gov.

One book you may find useful is *The Environmental Movement*, by Laurence Pringle (HarperCollins, 0-688-1562-22, ages ten and up). Students will gain insight into many of the environmental issues suggested here. The end of the book includes a number of addresses for environmental and government agencies, plus a suggested reading list. For younger readers, see *There's Still Time*, by Mark Galan (National Geographic Society, 0-7922-7092-4, ages nine to twelve).

81

Revisit Fall Goals This Week

This last week before the holiday break may be a good time to look back at any classroom goals you may have set as a teacher or as a class (see Idea 1 in August), and for any students who set their own individual goals to see how they did. This can also be an opportunity to get parents involved in their children's education.

Prior to vacation, make a simple handout that can be given to parents during the break. Use a heading such as "Go for the Goal." The text of the handout might read, "[Student's name] has already achieved one goal this year. He/she has worked hard and can [accomplishment]. [Student's name] and I have talked. We think a worthwhile new goal is [goal], and you can help [student's name] achieve it. As a class we are committed to achieving our goals. Please give [student's name] the gift of your time and work with him/her to achieve the goal he/she has set for the coming new year."

Talk about setting personal goals with your students. Mention goals you have set for yourself. Ask them to discuss goal setting with their parents. What have been some of the goals their parents have set? Stress that even small goals can be stepping-stones to a successful day. Brainstorm with students and create a blackboard list of goals they might want to choose. Suggest addition and subtraction, handwriting, reading, spelling, or sitting quietly while attendance is being taken. Guide students who may have difficulty attaining certain goals into choosing appropriate goals that will challenge but not frustrate them. Successful achievement is important for encouraging goal-setting habits. Plan to revisit goal setting and achievement in the spring (see Idea 141, "Go for the Goal," in the month of April for ideas).

82

Money, Money, Money

Euro Currency Adopted, January 1, 2002

On January 1, 2002, euro bills and coins were adopted in twelve nations of the European Union. Currency such as drachmas, francs, marks, lire, and pesetas, which had been used for hundreds of years in such countries as Greece, France, Germany, Italy, and Spain, are no longer in circulation. Do your students really understand what money is? You may need to review the facts: money is anything accepted in exchange for goods or services. What is a good? Anything that can be seen and sold, like a house, a car, or food. A service, on the other hand is something a person does for you. Have students list services we all pay for (teaching, medical care, acting, dog-walking, and so forth). Currency is the form money takes in exchanges; in our country it is made up of paper bills and metal coins.

A fun lesson in money comes from explaining that in most of humankind's history currency has been made up of whatever people in a region regarded as valuable. See the *Kid's Almanac* book listed later in this section for more ideas, but here are some common and not-so-common currencies: furs, whales' teeth, feathers, animals, stones, shells, tea, nuts, snails, beeswax, fishhooks, and salt. This last item was used by many cultures including the Romans, who built many roads just to transport salt and paid workers "salaries" from the Latin word for salt. Thus the saying we still use, "not worth his salt," for a worker who doesn't earn his pay. We also still say people are "salting it away" when they are saving their pay.

In the United States, the big news on the currency front has been the introduction (beginning back in 1999) of state quarters. The U.S. Mint is introducing five distinct quarters each year honoring individual states. They are being released in the order in which the states joined the Union. The first coin honored Delaware, the first state, and Hawaii, the newest state, will be on the fiftieth quarter, to be released in 2008. Can your students figure out what rank your state has in the order of admissions to the union, and thus when your state quarter was or will be released?

Each state legislature has been able to select the design for one side of their state's quarter. Do your students know what the design will be on your state's quarter and what its significance is? Perhaps someone in the class had been collecting these quarters and can bring in a set for examination. Give your students the assignment of researching the meaning of each quarter currently available. For example, Caesar Rodney, who is on the Delaware quarter, was one of the signers of the Declaration of Independence: he rode eighty miles from Delaware to Philadelphia in July 1776 to cast the historic tie-breaking vote that assured unanimity between the colonies in declaring independence from Britain.

For more information on the state quarters, visit the U.S. Mint's website at usmint.gov where there are lesson plans for teachers. The Mint also has a site for children at usmint.gov/kids. Using these sites and some books on coin collecting from your media center you will be able to create a number of days' worth of activities on coins and money. A great reference to have in an upper elementary classroom is *The Kid's World Almanac of Amazing Facts about Numbers, Math and Money*, by Margery Facklam and Margaret Thomas (Pharos Books, 0-88687-634-6), which contains lots of astounding facts about money and many fun activities that are sure to astound your class.

83

Ellis Island

Opening Anniversary, January 1, 1892

Some 40 percent of all Americans can trace their family tree back to an immigrant who passed through the halls of Ellis Island. In operation from 1892 until 1954, Ellis Island was host to millions of immigrants and deportees, as well as being used for over a decade as a Coast Guard station.

Meticulously restored, it has now become a very important museum of immigration. If you are close enough to visit, organize a field trip that will stay with children forever. If you are too far away, take a virtual tour thanks to the website of Queensbury Middle School (capital.net/~alta/index.html), which had the interesting idea of doing a simulation of Ellis Island with children and parents in costume. Follow four students as they leave home, arrive at Ellis Island, and then jump bureaucratic hurdles set up by the immigration authorities.

You can also visit the Ellis Island official site (ellisisland records.org) to locate any ancestors who came through the island. To get started, all your students need is a last name, but it helps to have more information like the first name, year of entry, and possible alternate spellings of the last name. This site, long wished for by genealogists, became a reality when the Church of Jesus Christ of Latter-day Saints entered all the information from ships' passenger lists. It is a nicely laid-out site and would be appropriate for older children to use on their own. There are also interesting photos of ships themselves.

You may wish to assign some research on immigrant history to your students. Children can learn about their own family history to share with the class. Another option is to ask teams to research a certain area of the world that sent us many immigrants. Find out why so many people from Ireland, Greece, Italy, Sweden, Norway, and other countries came here in waves. Which sets of years had the greatest waves of migration? How did the groups fare once they got here?

Were they treated fairly? How did the laws passed by Congress affect immigrants' chances of becoming American citizens?

It might also be interesting to research the current immigration situation. What groups are immigrating to our country now? Where do they come from, and why did they leave their homes to come here? Recent stories of Cuban and Haitian refugees can be particularly compelling.

Books about Ellis Island for younger children, ages four to eight, include *The Memory Coat,* by Elvira Woodruff (Scholastic, 0-590-67717-9), which offers an upbeat look at immigration without downplaying how scary the process of getting through Ellis Island actually was. *Dreaming of America,* by Eve Bunting (Troll Association, 0-8167-6520-0), received the International Reading Association's Teacher Choice Award, and it tells the true story of Annie Moore, a young Irish immigrant who was the first person to be processed at Ellis Island on its opening day. A picture book by the same author offers a contemporary view of Ellis Island and the Statue of Liberty: in *A Picnic in October* (Harcourt, 0-15-201656-2, ages four to eight), a boy thinks everything is corny until he meets a new immigrant and is struck by the deeper meaning hidden in these special places. A book with an older protagonist (thirteen), but written at an easier reading level, is *When Jessie Came Across the Sea,* by Amy Hest (Candlewick Press, 0-7636-0094-6, ages four to eight). Ages nine to twelve might enjoy *Journey to Ellis Island,* by Carol Bierman (Hyperion, 0-7868-0377-0), or *Letters from Rifka,* by Karen Hesse (Puffin, 0-14-036391-2), which is a moving and true account of a brave girl's trials in getting through Ellis Island.

(84)

Jacob Ludwig Grimm

Birth, January 4, 1785

Jacob Grimm and his brother Wilhelm collected and published many of our most beloved fairy tales, including *Sleeping Beauty*, *Rumpelstiltskin*, *Hansel and Gretel*, *Rapunzel*, and *Cinderella*. Traditional literature (fairy tales) introduces children to a wide variety of cultural groups and has universal appeal. Familiarity with traditional literature characters and situations is part of being culturally literate. Think of all the times these tales are referred to in other literature, and even in conversation. All children need to be introduced to the fairy tales we hold in common in this country and should also have some familiarity with tales from other cultures.

The rich, descriptive language found in original versions of the Grimms' tales exposes children to an enriching experience. Moral issues are very clear in Grimms' fairy tales. Good and evil are very distinct. Good triumphs in the end, often with harsh consequences for the wrongdoers.

Grimms' fairy tales are wonderful read-alouds for students in grades K to 8. Many picture-book versions are suitable for adapting into plays or as reader's theater scripts.

A scholarly, but fun, treatment is to compare and contrast one of the Grimms' tales with its variants found in other cultures. Make a literary criticism chart with the headings Title, Hero or Heroine, Setting, Magic, Wrongdoers, Punishment, Story's End. As a group, read the original Grimms' version of the tale. Then choose two or more cultural variants of the same tale. Divide the class into groups and assign one tale to each group. After reading and discussing them, regroup as a class. Each group reports to the class and fills in their information on the classroom literary criticism chart. Discuss ways the different cultures have adapted the tale.

Cinderella is a good first choice. Its many variants include: *The Golden Sandal: A Middle Eastern Cinderella Story*, by Rebecca Hickox (Holiday House, 0-8234-1331-4, grades K to 3); *Mufaro's Beautiful Daughters*, by John Steptoe (Morrow, 0-688-04045-4, grades K to 3); *The Way Meat Loves Salt: A Cinderella Tale from the Jewish Tradition*, by Nina Jaffe (Holt, 0-8050-4384-5, grades K to 3); *Kongi and Potgi: A Cinderella Story from Korea*, by Oki Han (Dial, 0-8037-1571-4, grades K to 3); *Sootface: An Ojibwa Cinderella Story*, by Robert San Souci (Doubleday, 0-385-31202-4, grades 1 to 4); *Cendrillon: A Caribbean Cinderella*, by Robert San Souci (Simon and Schuster, 0-689-80668-X, grades K to 3); and *Yeh-Shen: A Cinderella Story from China*, by Ai-Ling Louie (Paperstar, 0-698-11388-8, grades 1 to 4).

Why not have some fun with this story during language arts? Instead of a fairy-tale locale, set the story in a traditional folk style found in your geographical area. Incorporate old-time language or words from the cultures found in the region. Students can give the story their own title. If written as a classroom story, where each student adds his or her own bit, you can provide an opportunity for the classroom artists to go wild.

(85)

Sir Isaac Newton

Birth, January 4, 1643

Newton got a rough start. He was born prematurely and was so small that his mother said she could have fit him into a quart jar. His father died soon after his birth, and when his mother remarried, he was sent off to live with his grandmother. He also did very poorly in school and was often teased and bullied. Then one day, the story goes, he received a crack on the head (whether by a school yard bully or an apple) and suddenly was able to perform incredible feats of logic and mathematics. No one really knows what happened to Newton, but after a clearly bad beginning he managed to become one of the most brilliant gentlemen of his time, and an influential force in physics.

He used his power of observation and deep thought to the exclusion of all else at times. Stories abound of his absentmindedness: he was sometimes found sitting half dressed on his bedside deep in thought where he had been perched perhaps for hours. He often forgot to eat or drink, and friends had to come and collect him for appointments he would otherwise be sure to miss.

Newton was responsible for finding and explaining some of the most important laws of physics. He illuminated the first law of motion to explain inertia, which is the tendency of matter once still to stay still and matter in motion to keep going in the same direction, unless acted on by an outside force. To move a body at rest, you need enough external force to overcome the object's inertia. The heavier the object is, the more force you will need. So, the second law is that the force needed to move a body is equal to its mass times its acceleration. His third law states that for every action there is an equal and opposite reaction.

Newton also figured out gravity by thinking about law number two. The old story of his being hit on a head by a falling apple and suddenly understanding gravity may not be true, but it is true that he spent a lot of time observing nature and trying to understand the laws of nature. He probably did observe an apple falling and thought about the fact that gravity is acting on that apple way up at the top of the tree. He wondered if gravity could reach all the way out to the moon. If so, the moon's orbit might actually be due to the force of gravity. He even figured out that you could theoretically fire a cannon with such force that the cannon ball would end up in Earth's orbit, a thought that would one day become rocket science!

All these laws are accompanied by a certain amount of math. Since there isn't room in a book of this scope to go into great detail, you may want to refer students to a kid-friendly website where it is put forth complete with diagrams: csep10.phys.utk.edu/astr161/lect/history/newtongrav.html. *The Handy Science Answer Book*, which is compiled by the Science and Technology Department at the Carnegie Library of Pittsburgh (Visible Ink, 1-57859-009-X, all ages), is also a good reference.

Fun activities at an official NASA site are only a click away at mars.jpl.nasa.gov/kids. Mars is less dense than Earth, so it has less gravity. The site has lots of information about gravity. For teachers looking for some low-tech ways of demonstrating the laws of physics, check out *Cosmic Science: Over 40 Gravity-Defying, Earth-Orbiting, Space-Cruising Activities for Kids*, by Jim Weiss (John Wiley and Sons, 047115826, ages nine to twelve but with many activities suitable for younger or older with adaptation). This book includes a complete materials list and careful activity guides and pointers.

(86)

Louis Braille

Birth, January 4, 1809

Our trio of interesting January 4 birthdays concludes with Louis Braille, who was born near Paris, January 4, 1809. At the age of three, he injured his eye in his father's leather shop. Infection set in and resulted in the loss of sight. When he got older, he attended Paris's Royal Institution for Blind Youths. Louis was a boy who enjoyed learning, and he desperately wanted to learn how to read. While at the Royal Institution, he heard about a military code used to send messages to soldiers at night. The message system used a series of dots punched into cardboard. Louis adapted the code to make raised letters that blind people could read with their fingers. Ironically he used the same type of tool to punch the holes as caused his original injury. Braille's system did not become popular until after its inventor's death.

Students can learn the Braille alphabet and punch their names in Braille. They can experiment with punching simple words and learning to read them. If your school district has a Learning About Disabilities program, arrange for the coordinator or one of the program's representatives to visit your room and discuss blindness. He or she may be able to bring in a Braille book, a cane, or a video about guide dogs. Can students think of places they have seen Braille print? Many children will have noticed the raised bumps on the control board in elevators.

Blind people depend on their other senses to interpret the world around them. To get students into the spirit of seeing with their other senses, place an assortment of objects your students are unlikely to be familiar with in a covered box or bag. After they feel the object inside, have them describe what they found in writing or orally. Students also can try "seeing" with their ears. Record a series of sounds: a car starting, a door opening or closing, footsteps, a sneeze, etc. See how many sounds they can identify correctly.

While your class is focusing on blindness perhaps an eye-care professional might be willing to visit and talk about eye exams and working in the eye-care professions. Try inviting a local optometrist to speak with your class. He or she could talk about how glasses and contact lenses are made.

Will your school district be conducting eye screening this month? If so (or even if not), it's a good time to talk about wearing glasses. Extol the virtues of seeing clearly and underscore that needing to wear glasses is not something to fear or be sad about. (By the way, keep your eyes on the alert for student "squinters" and refer them for eye testing.) Talk about teasing and how unkind it is. Hearken back to your celebration of Children's Good Manners Month (September).

Have the school nurse visit your class and talk with the children about eye safety. He or she might mention the danger snowballs present, since winter vacation has just ended and in some areas the ground may be snow covered. The nurse can also stress the importance of wearing safety glasses while working with certain tools and chemicals.

Two biographies about Braille that students will enjoy are: *Louis Braille: The Blind Boy Who Wanted to Read*, by Dennis Fradin (Silver, 0-614-29054-6, grades K to 5), and *Out of Darkness: The Story of Louis Braille*, by Russell Freedman (Houghton, 0-395-77516-7, grades 5 and up). Other books about being blind and how eyes work that will interest students are: *Do You Remember the Color Blue?*, by Sally Alexander (Simon and Schuster, 0-6708-8043-4, grades 4 to 9); *T.J.'s Story*, by Arlene Schulman (Lerner, 0-8225-2586-0, grades 2 to 4); *How Do Our Eyes See?*, by Carol Ballard (Raintree, 0-8172-4736-X, grades 2 to 5); and *What Do You See?*, by Patricia Lauber (Crown, 0-517-59390-4, grades 3 to 7).

For a guide to websites about Louis Braille and the Braille alphabet, go to nyise.org/braille.htm.

(87)

Carl Sandburg

Birth, January 6, 1878

Carl Sandburg was born January 6, 1878, in Galesburg, Illinois. Although Sandburg never completed high school or college, he loved literature and writing. He worked a number of odd jobs and even spent several years living as a hobo! From 1912 until the 1920s, Sandburg worked as a newspaper writer and gained fame for his poetry. He garnered literary acclaim, receiving the Pulitzer Prize for history in 1940, in recognition of his four-volume biography *Abraham Lincoln: The War Years*. In 1951, he received the Pulitzer Prize for poetry for his collection of poems titled *Complete Poems*, published in 1950. Children, however, are most likely to know Sandburg through his humorous stories, published as the *Rootabaga Stories*.

Sandburg's use of language, sense of the absurd, and ability to convey the sense of "folks chatting amongst themselves" make his stories delightful to read aloud. *The Rootabaga Stories* (Harcourt, 0-15-269062-X, grades K and up), illustrated by Michael Hague, is a lovely collection. *The Huckabuck Family* (Farrar, Straus, and Giroux, 0-374-33511-7, all ages) is a "don't miss" single Rootabaga story, illustrated as a picture book by David Small.

Students can make up lists of favorite turns of phrase or silly names used by Sandburg. They also can hunt for literary devices such as alliteration. Sandburg's poetry appeals to many age groups. Older students can read and discuss his poems relating to war, cruelty, and greed. He attacks these topics with a very hard-hitting style. Younger students will enjoy *Grassroots*, Sandburg poems illustrated by Wendell Minor (Harcourt, 0-15-200082-8, all ages), and the humor and visual nonsense found in *Poems for Children Nowhere Near Old Enough to Vote*, illustrated by Istvan Banyai (Knopf, 0-679-88990-0, grades 3 and up). Look for a copy of Sandburg's well-known "Fog."

Examine the imagery and words chosen to depict fog. Students can have fun writing their own weather poems patterned on the poetic devices used by Sandburg.

(88)

Transatlantic Phoning

Anniversary, January 7, 1927

During the holiday break, many families telephoned friends and family who live far away. January 7, 1927, was the day transatlantic telephone service was established between New York and London. This is a good time to look at the globe or a world map to see the distance and ocean between these great cities.

Survey your students and list where their families called (and from which cities they received calls) during the past several weeks. Display the world map and let students design their own world calling card "tag" that can be fastened on or near the map. One of the interesting things to discuss is the time lag that occurs during some long-distance phone calls.

Divide students into small groups. One group could calculate the distance in miles (or kilometers) from your school to the recipient of each call. Another group could investigate time zones and how they affect the hour of day between caller and call recipient. A third group could keep track of relationships: were most calls made to relatives or to family friends?

For an interesting show-and-tell, see if you can locate a telephone with a rotary dial that could be brought to your classroom. Most students are completely baffled by how one should use them to place a call. Antique models have no dial, only a hand crank on the side of the phone box (to call the operator, who then placed the call). Ask students to think about how cellular phones have changed communications in their family and their community. Has there been a big change in emergency response times to traffic accidents or other emergencies? (This might also be a good time to go over 911 calling procedures.)

If students are interested in pursuing the development of telephone technology further, they might want to read *The Telephone*, by Sarah Gearhart (Simon and Schuster, 0-689-82815-2, ages ten and up).

89

Universal Letter Writing Week

January 7-14

Around the second week of January, celebrate what may be a fading art: actual letter writing as opposed to E-mailing. Expressing ourselves clearly in writing gives us an advantage in our personal lives and in the business world. There are many different styles of written correspondence. A well-written business letter may lead to a lucrative position. Faithful correspondence helps maintain friendships when people are separated by distance. Letters may be mementos that chronicle an important event or accomplishment in someone's life. E-mails usually get deleted and will never be held in the hand of a descendent or a researcher. Receiving letters is so much nicer than getting junk mail. But the key to receiving letters is writing them.

"A Letter a Day" makes a nice theme for this week and fits in well with the language arts curriculum. Make Monday the kickoff with letter writing on a classroom level. Put all students' names in a box. Add yours if the total is an odd number. Have each student pick a name. Each student writes a letter to the student whose name she or he picked. Set a minimum number of sentences to be included in each letter. Suggest an initial comment about the weather, one thing they think the other student does well, their favorite subject in school, an activity they did over the holidays, or a hobby interest. Ask one question in the letter. Distribute letters and have students write a reply to the letter they received as homework.

Tuesday, have students write a letter to a city official in your town (prepare a list of names in advance): the mayor, a council representative, a firefighter, the person in charge of parks. Ask them to comment on things they like and dislike in the town. Wednesday, let them write a letter to a real friend, family member, or other person who lives in a different city. Avoid the famous, to increase the likelihood of a response. Monday and Tuesday's letters can be "mailed" without stamps. Drop the letters to city officials off at your town hall. Or see if the school district interbuilding mail run could include swinging by the town hall.

Thursday, start a campaign for a pen pal. World Pen Friends provides pen pals for young people ages ten to twenty in 175 countries and charges three dollars per pen pal, with group rates for classes of ten or more. Write to World Pen Friends, P.O. Box 337, Saugerties, NY 12477-0337 for information. Friday could be E-mail day, if you have access to computers. Explain how E-mail works and discuss its good and bad aspects.

A slightly different tactic can lead to good letter writing, an interesting lesson for students, and teach them something about geography as a bonus. Students will be mailing a letter at the end of the week, so they will need an envelope and a stamp for first-class postage; send a note home to let parents know of your project and need for supplies.

On Monday, have students begin work on a short biography about themselves. Open with an introduction of themselves as (the student's name), a student at (your school's name). They could include a paragraph on a hobby or a subject that fascinates them. End the letter with the following request: "Would you please send a postcard to me, here at _____ School? It can be of your town or somewhere else you think is interesting." Give the school's address and classroom number for the return address on the outside of the envelope and in the enclosed letter.

On Tuesday, work can continue during the language arts period. Consider this a rough draft. Wednesday, have students swap their completed rough draft with a classmate, who will read the draft. A writing conference that addresses clarity and content issues should follow. Ask students to be sure to make positive comments as well as critical ones.

Thursday and Friday, if needed, students should write their final copies. On Friday, each of the student informational pieces will be mailed. Prior to Friday, each student should consult with an adult at home. Together they should choose a person to mail the piece to. The person may be near or far. Make sure that by Thursday each student has the name and address of the person to whom the letter will be mailed clearly written down. Mail the letters at the end of the day.

As postcards are mailed back, tack them to a map of your state or the country and connect them to your town with yarn. Tag each string with a miles traveled note. If you want to extend the activity even further, encourage students to include a sentence in the letter they write that asks the postcard sender to mail the letter out to someone he or she knows and trusts and ask that friend to also mail a postcard to the school.

For letters using the U.S. Postal Service, ask students to bring in either the necessary stamps or the money to buy the stamps from you. Request funds to purchase stamps for students who may be unable to afford them from your school's parent organization.

Aldo Leopold

Birth, January 11, 1887

Aldo Leopold, the author of *A Sand County Almanac and Sketches Here and There*, helped redefine how biologists and conservationists regarded the natural world. Although his name does not command the immediate recognition of Rachel Carson or John Muir, you don't have to look far to find his influence on the modern environmental movement. Leopold's early commitment to establishing wilderness areas ensured that large tracts of natural areas were left undeveloped for future generations to enjoy. He recognized the need for land stewardship and wilderness preservation and the importance of predators to wildlife's natural balance. Conservation efforts to restore wolves to their historic habitats were fueled by Leopold's writings. He practically founded the field of wildlife ecology.

Leopold's appreciation of the natural world and its creatures is superbly conveyed with humor, a gentle poetic touch, and a storyteller's voice in *A Sand County Almanac and Sketches Here and There*. Since it was first published in 1949, the slim volume has sold almost 2.5 million copies. Today's students continue to savor Leopold's use of language and sensitivity in describing the world around us.

Proficient readers can read the book in its entirety. They can compare its twenty-two essays (which follow the months of the year) with Rachel Carson's *Silent Spring*. Both were regarded as ahead of their time for their view of people and their relationship to the natural world. Students could begin their own school-year almanac, writing their observations of the natural world as they see it change month by month around them.

City children may have to focus on what remnants of nature they can find, such as the changes in weather and how these changes affect them. If you really want to get students motivated, find a school in your state with a rural setting—either via a Chamber of Commerce or an Internet website—and see what kinds of bridges your students can build by sharing their observations with children who live in a completely different setting.

All students can become familiar with at least portions of *A Sand County Almanac*. They can read from "Thinking Like a Mountain" and write a companion piece to describe the hunt of the last great predators from your area. "January Thaw" imagines what a skunk's story is by following its tracks. Use Jim Arnosky's *Animal Tracker's Journal* (Random House, 0-679-86717-1), or other animal track guides and let students choose a set of tracks. They can write their own imaginings on what that animal's day might have been like, based on their own fictional "track" record. Another fine book that will motivate you to bundle up and get outside for a little fresh air this winter is *Into the Winter*, by William P. Nestor (Houghton Mifflin, 0-395-32866-7, currently out of print, but may be available at a local library).

For a look at plant life, read *Good Oak*, an eighty-year time trip that describes events that occurred during each year of the growth rings found in a section of tree cut for firewood. Students can choose a tree in the neighborhood (get help from a naturalist, or the person who planted the tree, on age estimation without harming the tree) and write about the events that occurred in your town during the tree's life.

91

The History and Physics of the Frisbee

First Introduced, January 13, 1957

Sometimes the simplest toys are the most fun. Many simple, quirky toys have been invented over the years. The Frisbee, which has had a number of different incarnations and names, was introduced January 13, 1957—and is one invention that caught on like wildfire. The name that stuck is just a new spelling of the bakery name found on the pie plates college students liked to fling at each other.

Frisbees aren't the only fad toys that have stood the test of time. Other toys include the Slinky, tiddlywinks, hula hoops, yo-yos, kites, tops, and rubber-band jump ropes.

Many people have one or more of these toys in their garage or basement. In recognition of the Frisbee, devote gym period to dusting off some of the "old standbys" and having new fun with them. Depending on the climate where you live, outdoor play may not be feasible. If so, Frisbee use may have to be regulated. Softer "Nerf" versions are available and work better for younger children and inside use.

For a history link, students could ask their parents and grandparents what toys they remember playing with as children. Their findings could be written up (or drawn) and posted on the bulletin board. Many upper elementary students are reading books, such as Laura Ingalls Wilder's *Little House on the Prairie*, that are set in bygone eras. Often, toys are mentioned in these novels. There are many nonfiction books that describe toys from the nineteenth and early twentieth centuries. Children may recall seeing pictures of children rolling hoops with sticks or playing jacks or marbles.

Many simple toys and games can be made easily. Depending upon what supplies are on hand at home, the cost may be little or none.

Here's a good opportunity for parents to help their children become resourceful and develop ingenuity. Rubber-band jump ropes, for example, are easy and cheap to make. The same with kites. Clothespin and homemade paper dolls are other easily made toys. Checkerboards can be drawn on paper with pennies (one side heads up, the other tails up) or beans used as markers.

As a fun homework assignment that will foster spending time with family, encourage students to make their own toy or game and play it with a friend or family member. Display their efforts in the classroom.

For a physics connection, why not research how a Frisbee works? What makes it fly? How do people who are really good at throwing Frisbees control where the Frisbee goes when they release it? While kids are tossing the Frisbee encourage them to be thinking about how the disk flies—you will need to introduce cool terms such as *lift, angle of attack, spin, aerodynamics*, and *Bernoulli's principle*.

If you are not a physicist yourself and are perhaps now wondering "Hey, how *does* a Frisbee work?" don't despair—there are a number of great resources that will help you. If you have never paid a visit to the Eisenhower National Clearinghouse on the World Wide Web, this would be a perfect opportunity. In fact, at the address below, you will find links to already prepared physics lessons featuring the kid-friendly Frisbee. Start at enc.org/thisweek/calendar/unit/0,1819 ,153,00.shtm. From there you can also go to a couple of "how things work" sites and a sport science site that feature the physics of the Frisbee. At one site they even recommend sanding the ridges off a Frisbee to see what effect this modification has on its flight. Newton's Apple offers a "ready-to-go" set of lessons that involve getting kids outdoors tossing the disk.

(92)

Listening to History

First Radio Broadcast, January 13, 1910

When Lee De Forest aired the first radio broadcast to a select group of people in New York City on January 13, 1910, he set the wheels in motion for a communication revolution. Bring the excitement of the momentous accomplishment into your classroom.

A visit to the public library is in order for several supplies. Find a recording of Enrico Caruso singing the role of Radames in *Aïda*, if you can. (It has kid appeal because of the Egyptian setting.) If it isn't available, another Caruso recording will do. If you locate a Caruso recording of *Aïda*, you may find the book *Aïda: A Picture Book for All Ages*, as told by Leontyne Price (Harcourt, 0-15-200405-X, grades K and up), helpful for understanding the story line.

During the library visit, look for a book that shows pictures of early radios. In the audiocassette section, many libraries have reissued recordings of historic radio shows. Look for "Sherlock Holmes," "The Shadow," or Orson Welles's "War of the Worlds," a 1938 Halloween "treat" that caused major panic.

In school, tell your students that together you are going to create a very important moment in history. Ask them to close their eyes and listen. Play the Caruso recording. When the aria ends, let them think for a few moments and then ask them to try to describe Caruso's voice. You may need to come up with some prompts. Talk about how they imagine the singer looks. Tell students that Lee De Forest, the electron tube inventor, chose the voice of Caruso and the Metropolitan Opera as the first radio broadcast. Discuss the manner of radio reception of the broadcast.

Show them a picture of Caruso and tell them about his opera career. Show students how the size and shape of the radio has changed since its early days. Share radio memories you may have.

Perhaps you listened to baseball games through an earplug while in bed late at night. Maybe you hung out at the beach or around the community pool in the summer where broadcasts were aired over the PA system. Did you ever laugh with Jean Shepherd?

Talk about how families gathered to listen to radio shows the way we gather and watch TV. Perhaps you will need to talk about how the experience differed from the passive sitting we do while watching TV. Families shelled peas, shucked corn, quilted, sewed, knitted, whittled, or did chores while they listened. The radio itself when the technology was new was seen as a mysterious and novel machine, and people saved and saved so they could own one for their family to gather around.

Many public radio stations have old shows available to purchase on tape. If you find a recording, play one of the old radio shows. Ask students what kinds of things had to be done differently to produce a radio show as opposed to a TV show: sound effects, clear voices, no relying on body language, etc. If you have access to National Public Radio you may be able to record a small segment of Garrison Keillor's "Prairie Home Companion" show, which airs (often live) on Saturdays. This show is in some ways modeled on old-time radio, complete with live music and an expert (and very funny) sound-effects person making the noises of buildings exploding, clocks ticking, ladies walking, chickens squawking, helicopters, and so forth.

Have students write and air their own radio broadcast. If you have PA system capabilities or the technical apparatus to broadcast from a separate room, that's great. But it's no problem if you don't. Create your own broadcasting booth with a setup of table and chairs. Cardboard rolls from paper towels or toilet paper can be microphones. Just anchor a tennis ball to the roll. Cover the ball with aluminum foil and the roll with black construction paper. Add a wire to the bottom, if you wish.

Divide the students into groups of four or five. To complement all areas of the curriculum, feature segments like New Developments in Science (what's your current topic?), An Interview with a Star (a student), Restaurant Report (cafeteria offerings), a short dramatic production (adapt a selection from language arts), and Sports (from recess and gym). Someone will need to provide sound effects for dramatic presentations. Students will enjoy the process even more if you record the efforts and play them back. One gang of kids used this process to invent a regular weekly "radio show" called W.O.R.M., which featured much hamming it up and some very creative writing in preparation for the weekly "newscast" and drama segments.

(93)

Poetry Break

Take time out for a daily poetry break. If you don't already have a collection of short poems to read aloud, you might want to start one. Look for poems that you can write on an index card, one per card. Keep them in a file box in the classroom and take one or two for reading during standing-in-line times like going into the gym or lunchroom.

Start the day with a poem. Read another one after lunch. You can ask students to share a favorite poem, too. Write a class poem. Doing this together helps students understand creative writing processes. After deciding on a subject, if the class if going to write a rhyming poem have students list rhyming words about the subject before you begin.

For quick poetry, explain couplets and have students write a couplet that tells something about themselves. Example: My name is Lou/My eyes are blue. If they wish, students could continue on to four, six, or eight lines.

Another poetry exercise is to play with similes. Ask students to think of a favorite color, word, food, or book. Have them describe the item in terms of a simile. Example: Blue is like a huge iceberg; *Goosebumps* books by R. L. Stine are like fingernails scratching a chalkboard.

Jack Prelutsky and Shel Silverstein have published popular collections of poetry for young readers. Also look for books by Myra Cohn Livingston, Paul B. Janeczko, Eloise Greenfield, and Paul Fleischman. Good collections containing poems that will enrich your poetry break include: *Old Elm Speaks: Tree Poems*, by Kristine O'Connell George (Clarion, 0-395-87611-7, grades K to 5); *Doodle Dandies: Poems That Take Shape*, by J. Patrick Lewis (Atheneum, 0-689-81075-X, all ages); and *The Beauty of the Beast: Animal Poems*, selected by Jack Prelutsky (Random House, 0-679-87058-X, all ages).

Pooh Day

A. A. Milne, Birth, January 18, 1882

Lovable, pot-bellied Winnie the Pooh has enchanted young readers since he made his debut in 1926. Two years later, the success of *Winnie the Pooh* was followed by *The House at Pooh Corner*. Milne modeled the books on his son, Christopher Robin, and the stuffed toys he played with. The many humorous adventures embarked upon by Christopher Robin, Pooh, Tigger, Piglet, and Eeyore took place in the Hundred Acre Wood. Many students are familiar with Pooh and his friends from Disney movies and spin-off books. Introduce them to the real thing. Begin a Winnie the Pooh read-aloud of the classic version.

Make a Pooh Day Classroom Honey Jar. Stuff it with poems written by A. A. Milne. See his books *Now We Are Six* and *When We Were Very Young* for his collected poems. Several times during the day, call a halt to class work and let a student reach into the Honey Jar and read a poem aloud.

Let groups of students write scripts from short dialogue selections from *Winnie the Pooh* and present them to the class as reader's theater. Encourage selections that focus on sensitively depicted emotional aspects of the novels: the friendship and caring among characters, helping Pooh cope with fear, the silliness of Tigger and droopy old Eeyore.

Ask very young children to draw a picture of themselves and a favorite toy. Older students can write about an imaginary adventure with one of their well-loved toys. Publish these as class books and celebrate by letting each child write an invitation to his toy protagonist, asking it to visit the classroom. The toys and students can celebrate Pooh Day with a Hundred Acre Wood afternoon tea. Serve honey on bread triangles. (Substitute apricot jelly for those who don't care for honey.)

Visit the Page at Pooh Corner website at chaos.trxinc.com/jmilne/Pooh.

95

Thesaurus Fun

Peter Mark Roget, Birth, January 18, 1779

It was a good party. No, it was a very good party. No, it was a . . . a . . . a . . . If you've ever grasped for an elusive word or synonym, it's likely you've also reached for a thesaurus. Today is the day to celebrate, honor, and observe the author of the first thesaurus.

Roget's Thesaurus is a valuable tool for older writers. The classified arrangement with its cross-referenced numbering system may be confusing for your classroom, but explanation and practice will clarify its usage. Today there are thesauri that list words alphabetically, which makes them easier for young students to use. Among them are *The American Heritage Children's Thesaurus*, by Paul Hellwig (Houghton Mifflin, 0-395-84977-2, grades 3 to 7), and *Scholastic Children's Thesaurus*, by John K. Bollard (Scholastic, 0-590-96785-1, grades 3 to 7).

Here's a Roget's Day exercise suitable for all students. Write a sentence on the board, such as, "After school, the girl walked into her house." Now, ask students to substitute another word for "walked" or any weak verb or adjective you've deliberately chosen in your sentence. Offer prompts if necessary. When you run out of classroom suggestions, use the thesaurus to show even more possible words.

A thesaurus written by the students can also be a fun yearlong activity. List words that crop up frequently in student writings (*said, then, run*). Students can suggest and illustrate alternative words on sheets of paper that can be collated into a classroom book. The prompt sentence could be, "Instead of (walk), use (skip) if you are (happy)."

You'll all have a good, wonderful, marvelous time.

96

Edgar Allan Poe

Birth, January 19, 1809

Edgar Allan Poe was born in Boston, Massachusetts, on January 19, 1809. He is known for his tales of horror and suspense and for his poetry. Many young people enjoy a good scare, and because Poe's works can deliver a fright-filled "punch" in a literary style, they are perfect for classroom use, particularly with older students. Their gloomy nature is perfect for capturing student interest and "brightening" a gray January day.

Have fun with Poe's poems by suggesting groups of students arrange specific poems for choral reading. "The Bells" has several stanzas. Each one presents a different type of bell. It has a marvelous chorus that changes slightly according to which kind of bell the stanza portrays. The bells themselves gradually change from cheery to gloomy.

"The Raven" is probably Poe's most famous poem. Not only is it fun for choral reading arrangements, but it also contains some fantastic, unusual vocabulary. *Lattice*, *beguiling*, *countenance*, *melancholy*, *seraphim*, and phrases such as "Plutonian shore" are exotic language for many students. Send them on a quest to explain the literary roots of "Plutonian shore." The same vocabulary treasures hold true for "The Bells": *euphony* and *tintinnabulation* are two examples.

Read stories such as "The Tell-Tale Heart." Students might want to try their hand at rewriting a portion of them as reader's theater or as a play script.

Incorporate music into the curriculum by asking students to choose music they feel best complements the mood of Poe's work. Music that would suit the poem "Annabel Lee" would be vastly different than that used for "The Fall of the House of Usher."

Art projects could include student drawings of how they imagine the houses in Poe's short stories to look.

One final note: Some students feel Poe is going to be boring because he has written works that are deemed "classics." However, watch those bored seventh graders begin nervously biting their nails when Poe's suspense stories are read aloud. That's when you know the story is a success!

(97)

Giving Compliments

National Compliment Day, January 22

Here's a day that will be unfamiliar to many of your students, but by celebrating it, you will generate positive feelings that extend far beyond one day.

You might start the day by writing the definition of the word *compliment* on the blackboard. Ahead of time, write one compliment about each student in your class. Type them up on the computer, then make a copy for each student. Distribute them and let the children read the compliments about themselves and their classmates silently. Ask them to think about the types of compliments you have included.

Ask each student to think—during the course of the day—of one compliment they can make about each of their classmates. The last period of the day (or language arts period) could be used to give each student the opportunity to hand write (or use a keyboard, if they are available) a compliment for each of their classmates, similar in form to the one you wrote.

The pages can be turned in and stapled together as a classroom book. Let students choose a title. Many teachers bind books that contain student work. Often, students are allowed to sign them out for a night. The compliment book could be included in this kind of circulating library and might serve as a conversation starter between parents and children. It helps parents become familiar with other children in their child's class.

Compliments are fun because positive feelings are felt by the receiver and by the giver. Do remember that kids are great falsehood detectors and that a fake compliment is worse than no compliment at all. You may want to work on the subtlety of this issue by asking students if they have ever been complimented in a way that left them wondering if the compliment was in fact genuine. Or, have they ever paid someone a compliment but really meant the opposite? This may be a subject for them to ponder in a personal journal if that is part of your classroom.

98

Women with Wings

Bessie Coleman, Birth, January 26, 1893

Ask your students to describe what they see in their mind when you say the word *pilot*, and chances are pretty good they will think of a man. Called aviatrixes in the early days of female piloting, women pilots evinced the same bravery and capability shown by their male counterparts. Women were right out there with the men in the early days of flight. In fact, a woman pilot named Bessica Raiche flew a plane her husband had built way back in 1910. In 1911 a woman named Harriet Quimby became the first woman to fly across the English Channel. She died after being thrown from her open cockpit—a fate of many early pilots as they did not have seatbelts. Anna Lowe, a Chinese American, flew in 1919, but did not have a pilot's license.

Bessie Coleman, the first black aviatrix, was denied the opportunity to become a pilot in the United States. She had her sights firmly fixed on becoming a pilot and went to France and earned an international pilot's license in 1921. Upon her return, she gained further note as a stunt pilot. *Fly, Bessie, Fly!*, by Lynn Joseph (Simon and Schuster, 0-689-81339-2, ages five to eight); *Nobody Owns the Sky*, by

Reeve Lindbergh (Candlewick, 0-7636-0361-9, ages five to eight); and *Up in the Air*, by Philip S. Hart (Lerner, 0-87614-978-6, ages nine to twelve), are three marvelous biographies about Bessie Coleman that readers will enjoy.

There were more than one thousand women who flew warplanes during World War II. See the website wasp-wwii.org for more information about the many women who qualified to fly military transport planes in the United States.

Many children have heard of Amelia Earhart. She was the second pilot to fly solo over the Atlantic Ocean. (Charles Lindbergh was the first.) The disappearance of her plane, in 1937, while flying over the Pacific Ocean, has stymied, stumped, and intrigued the world. Students could become flight investigators and research the route she took. Use a map to chart her course. Recent search investigations have proposed several likely conclusions that could be the solution to the site of her plane's crash. Different students might present the pros and cons for each conclusion. Patricia Lauber's *Lost Star: The Story of Amelia Earhart* (Scholastic, 0-590-41159-4, ages nine to twelve) will engage upper elementary and middle school readers, and Pam Muñoz Ryan's picture book *Amelia and Eleanor Go for a Ride* (Scholastic, 0-590-96075-X, ages six to nine) provides a fun historical moment for younger readers.

Sally Ride was the first American woman to travel in space. In 1983, she was a member of the crew on the space shuttle *Challenger*. (The first woman in space was Russia's Valentina Tereshkova, whose rocket ship orbited the earth forty-five times in 1963.) Sally Ride's autobiography *To Space and Back* (Morrow, 0-688-09112-1, ages eight to twelve) gives readers a glimpse into the struggles and joys of being an astronaut. Ride is also the author of several other books about space.

For a more recent look at women pilots, junior high students might enjoy researching the struggle women have had to become fighter jet and commercial airline pilots.

Denise Fleming

Birth, January 31, 1950

Denise Fleming is a popular illustrator/author of picture books for young readers. She was born on January 31, 1950, in Toledo, Ohio. Fleming makes the paper she uses for her illustrations. Pushing cotton pulp through hand-cut stencils makes the images. Her colorful illustrations are eye-catching and lots of fun. Why not share her books with some of the young readers and listeners you know?

Where Once There Was a Wood (Holt, 0-8050-6482-6, ages three to seven) describes the animals and plants that lived in an area prior to a housing development being built. As part of the social studies curriculum, students could learn what buildings preceded their school on its site. Going further back, what plants and/or animals used to live on the site? How many years ago did they live there?

Time to Sleep (Holt, 0-8050-6767-1, ages three to seven) is perfect for science units on changing seasons and on the senses. Each animal in the story uses its senses or an environmental clue to detect winter's approach. Children can make a list of what clues they can look for that signal winter's end, or the arrival of spring. What senses would they use to detect spring's arrival? What kinds of scents, sounds, and sights are they likely to notice?

Mama Cat Has Three Kittens (Holt, 0-8050-5745-5, ages three to six) is the delightful story of a cat and her kittens. The kittens all learn by imitating Mama, except for Boris . . . he's too busy napping. This is a great story for read-aloud sharing. Everyone will get a kick out of little Boris, the kitten who dares to be different.

In the Tall, Tall Grass (Holt, 0-8050-3941-4, ages three to six) and *In the Small, Small Pond*, a Caldecott Honor Book (Holt, 0-8050-5983-0, ages three to seven), are wonderful introductions to the world of nature. Have fun creating your own classroom book titled *In the Smart, Smart Classroom* or *In the Big, Big School*. As a class, write the story on large sheets of paper. Read it together as a shared reading experience.

Adventurous teachers might want to try a papermaking session. Fleming's *Painting with Paper: Easy Papermaking Fun for the Entire Family* (out-of-print; available in libraries) has instructions and suggestions for making your own colorful illustrations. Many art activity books aimed at children also show how to make paper. It is a messy but very satisfying project that can take advantage of all the scraps of paper around homes and school.

Recycling "junk" into something useful is an important task and one that children in particular really enjoy. You can also take apart a regular envelope and make a pattern for children to create their own envelopes out of homemade paper or out of recycled odds and ends. Just make sure that you have white computer labels (ask at your main office—they may have some they usually toss after printing lists) if you are using dark or printed paper. The post office needs to be able to see the address area.

Jackie Robinson

Birth, January 31, 1919

More than just an excellent baseball player, Robinson deserves recognition for grace under fire. He broke the color barrier in baseball in 1947 with the encouragement of an open-minded general manager for the Dodgers, but it was not an easy victory since his presence led to unequal treatment, name calling, physical attacks, and even death threats. The fact that he had survived a difficult time in a not-very-integrated military during WWII may have helped him, but his patience with the madness exhibited by the bigots in his life can most likely be attributed to his mother's care in his upbringing. His daughter, Sharon Robinson, has worked with Scholastic, Inc. to create a program for elementary students called "Breaking Barriers: In Sports, in Life." You may want to ask your principal or superintendent if your school district is participating in the program.

Students can be encouraged to read a biography of Robinson. There are many biographies currently available appropriate for a number of age ranges. Younger kids age four to eight can read their own book, *Jackie Robinson*, by Lola Schaefer (Pebble Books, 0736814353). Standouts on Robinson for nine- to twelve-year-olds include the biography *The Story of Jackie Robinson: Bravest Man in Baseball*, by Margaret Davidson (Yearling, 0440400198), which children often describe as a page-turner with lots of action. A work of fiction that would fit well with the theme is the highly acclaimed novel by Bette Bao Lord, *In the Year of the Boar and Jackie Robinson* (Harper Trophy, 0064401758). This tale of a young Chinese girl's emigration to the United States in 1947 is poignant and funny. Many lesson plans and discussion lists are available online to accompany the reading of this book.

You may also wish to download a well-written brief biography of Robinson and an accompanying comprehension and vocabulary test to give students after they have listened to the story twice. You can find these at projectview.org/BBHOFEFT.ELAT.est.htm. All American encyclopedias include an entry for Robinson, so students will find the highlights of his life easy to access. The Minneapolis Star/Tribune page also has links and lesson plans for Robinson: startribune .com/idea.

Older students and adults will enjoy National Public Radio host Scott Simon's book *Jackie Robinson and the Integration of Baseball*, which is a part of the respected Turning Points series (John Wiley and Sons, 047126153X, adult). Simon mentions in his book that there is a saying about Robinson: "If Robinson didn't exist, someone would have had to invent him." There has rarely been a more potent cultural icon than Robinson. Be sure your students get to know this great man.

(101)

Biographical Ideas for Black History Month

Black History Month, February

African Americans in all walks of life have made many noteworthy contributions to the success and growth of the United States. Celebrate the rich heritage found in the African American tradition.

While it's informative to learn about famous leaders, it's valuable to learn about the contributions of regular citizens, too. Many African Americans fought in the Revolutionary War, the Civil War, both World Wars, Korea, and Vietnam. Books about African American soldiers include: *Black, Grey, and Blue*, by James Haskins (Simon and Schuster, 0-689-80655-8, grades 4 and up); *Buffalo Soldiers* (a title in Chelsea House's African American Achiever Series, 0-7910-2596-9, grades 6 and up); *The Forgotten Heroes*, by Clinton Cox (Scholastic, out of print, but available in libraries); and the series *African-American Soldiers* (Twenty First Century Books). The novel *Fallen Angels*, by Walter Dean Myers (Scholastic, 0-590-40943-3, grades 7 and up), is a riveting story about young men fighting in Vietnam.

Inventors and explorers you can feature include Matthew Henson, who accompanied Robert E. Peary to the North Pole in 1909. His book *A Negro Explorer at the North Pole* gives a firsthand account of the trip. To look at his writing go to mathenson.com. At this site you can get a free download of the original book including its introduction by the famed Booker T. Washington. Students can compare his voyage (supplies, temperatures, etc.) with that of Ernest Shackleton's ill-fated trip to the South Pole. There are a number of books dealing specifically with Henson. For grades 2 to 4 you may want to use *Matthew Henson*, by Maryann Weidt (0-8225-0397-2), for preteens try *Matthew Henson: Co-Discoverer of the Pole*, by Laura Baskes Litwin (0-76601-546-7), which is a title in the African American Biography Series. Another book to refer to is *Matthew Henson and the North Pole Expedition*, by Ann Graham Gaines (1-56766-743-0). Henson's offspring are still guiding expeditions in the polar regions.

Many people know the story of Rosa Parks and the Montgomery Bus Boycott. Another civil rights story is the courage shown by six-year-old Ruby Bridges during the integration of schools in the South. Every unit on civil rights should have a copy of *Through My Eyes*, by Ruby Bridges (Scholastic, 0-590-18923-9, grades 4 and up). The cruelty she faced is almost unimaginable. The photographs are well chosen and reveal both the charm of a little girl and the ugly face of racism.

There have been many famous African American sports figures. See *Satchel Paige*, by Lesa Cline-Ransome (Simon and Schuster, 0-689-81161-9, grades 2 and up), for a gorgeously illustrated picture-book biography told with a storyteller's voice. Refer back to Jackie Robinson (Idea 100 in January). Wilma Rudolph's story of overcoming illness to become a world-famous track star will thrill and inspire any class.

There are many other books that will enrich Black History Month. The On My Own Biography series by the Lerner Publishing Group has several new early reader biographies that feature African Americans. They are entitled: *Jackie Robinson, George Washington Carver, Aunt Clara Brown*, and *Wilma Rudolph*. By various authors, all are suitable for readers ages six to nine and are available in paperback. Junior high readers should see *Ida B. Wells*, by Dennis Fradin (0-395-89898-6, Clarion, ages eleven and up), for an in-depth read about an extraordinary Civil Rights activist. *Let It Shine: Stories of Black Women Freedom Fighters*, by Andrea Pinkney (0-15-201005-X, Harcourt, ages twelve and up), is a biographical collection about women who have featured prominently in Civil Rights issues. *The Black Soldier: 1492 to the Present*, by Catherine Clinton (0-395-67722-X, Clarion, ages eleven and up), contains a wealth of information about people of color who have served in the armed forces.

(102)

African Americans in the Arts

Black History Month, February

While the previous idea looked at African American soldiers, leaders, history makers, and sports figures, this idea celebrates the many contributions African Americans have made to the arts throughout the history of the United States. Here are some suggestions that will familiarize your students with African American artists.

In language arts, older students will enjoy reading poetry and novels written by African Americans. Organize a literature study by choosing several different poets and novelists from different decades of American history. Compare thematic issues addressed in the novels and poetry. Novelists, news writers, and poets you might feature include: Jupiter Hammon (1760s), Phillis Wheatley (1770s), Samuel Cornish and John Russworm (1820s), Frederick Douglass (1840s to 1860s), Ida B. Wells (1890s), and Paul Laurence Dunbar (late 1890s and early 1900s).

Another literature focus might compare works by the writers of the Harlem Renaissance. Be sure to explain what *renaissance* means. During the 1920s, in the Harlem district of New York City, literature flourished in the black community. Langston Hughes, Countee Cullen, James Weldon Johnson, Jesse Fauset, Claude McKay, Alain Locke, and Zora Neale Hurston were prominent writers of this movement. The strong voices in their novels and poems reflect the African American experience at the end of the nineteenth century and the first half of the twentieth century. Activists and educators from this period include Booker T. Washington and Mary Church Terrell.

For reading material to support language arts studies, try *I, Too, Sing America: Three Centuries of African American Poetry*, selected by Catherine Clinton (Houghton Mifflin, 0-395-89599-5, all ages), which features the poetry of Phyllis Wheatley, Langston Hughes, Countee Cullen, and many others. To give the words impact, let students present poems orally as choral readings, scripted in different ways. Mildred Taylor's novel *Roll of Thunder, Hear My Cry* (Dial, 0-803-77473-7, grades 3 to 7) has a number of short, powerful scenes appropriate for middle school students to script for reader's theater.

African Americans have contributed to theater as playwrights and actors. Lorraine Hansberry, the author of *A Raisin in the Sun*, is the subject of a biography, *Young, Black, and Determined*, by Fredrick L. McKissack and Patricia C. McKissack (Holiday House, 0-8234-1300-4, grades 6 to 12). Also discuss Pulitzer Prize–winning playwrights August Wilson and Charles Gordone.

Clementine Hunter was an African American folk artist. Children will relate to her paintings of everyday life. For more information see *Talking with Tebé: Clementine Hunter, Memory Artist*, edited by Mary Lyons (Houghton Mifflin, 0-395-72031-1, grades 3 to 8). Lyons has also written books on African American artists Horace Pippin and Harriet Powers. Jacob Lawrence is another African American painter whose work will appeal to children. *The Great Migration: An American Story*, by Jacob Lawrence (HarperCollins, 0-06-023037-1, grades 4 to 6), reproduces his series of paintings that tells the story of the movement of African Americans out of the South. For information about Lawrence's life, see *Story Painter: The Life of Jacob Lawrence*, by John Duggleby (Chronicle, 0-8118-2082-3, grades 5 to 8).

African Americans have contributed to classical music and are responsible for the uniquely American art form, jazz. Jessye Norman, Leontyne Price, and Kathleen Battle are internationally recognized opera singers. Show video selections from operas that feature these singers. No child should grow up without hearing the rags composed by Scott Joplin, the singing of Paul Robeson, or the music of jazz artists Dizzy Gillespie, Duke Ellington, and Ella Fitzgerald. The marvelous trumpeter Wynton Marsalis excels in both the classical and jazz world. Find recordings in the library and play them for your students.

Dance, by noted African American dancer/choreographer Bill T. Jones and Susan Kuklin (Hyperion, 0-7868-0362-2, grades 1 to 4), brings the delights of modern dance to young children. Also discuss such black dancers/choreographers as Alvin Ailey and Arthur Mitchell.

There are countless possibilities for bringing African American artists to life for your students. Contact your learning center director and local public library for additional suggestions. If you live in a city of any size there are likely to be performances aimed at celebrating Black History Month—perhaps you can go see a play or a concert or a reading.

(103)

Wild Bird Feeding

National Bird Feeding Month, February

In addition to Black History Month, February is also designated as National Bird Feeding Month. Treat your students to the joy of watching birds and appreciating their contributions to our world. Many varieties of bird feeders can be made using household supplies. An inexpensive pan, with holes punched in the bottom for drainage, can be suspended with wire from a tree limb. A quick trip to the library will yield a number of "how-to" books with instructions for making simple feeders.

Birdseed can be purchased in bulk fairly cheaply. Solicit funds (with a student-written grant proposal) from your school's PTO. Ask local dealers if they will give the school an educator's discount. Keep a log of the birds that visit your feeder. Note which ones eat from the feeder and which ones prefer to eat seed that has fallen to the ground.

Being able to identify a bird is satisfying for children. They love recognizing and naming cardinals and blue jays, rather than saying "that bird." Look for Carol Lerner's *Backyard Birds of Summer* (Morrow, 0-688-13600-1, ages five to eight) and *Backyard Birds of Winter*

(0-688-12819-X, ages five to eight). Also, Peterson's Field Guides now have paperback guides for children about backyard birds and song-birds. These books contain a lot of information and helpful birding tips. Younger children will enjoy *About Birds: A Guide for Children*, by John and Cathryn Sill (Peachtree Publishers, 1561451479, ages four to eight), which has simple text featuring just one fact per page and beautiful illustrations.

If a child can identify a bird by its call, it's even more satisfying. There are many CDs and cassettes for birdcall identification. Check your library and interlibrary loan possibilities. Start with a few of the birds most frequently seen in your area. Birdsongs are a lovely way to augment and complement your music curriculum. *Songbirds: The Language of Song*, by Sylvia A. Johnson (Carolrhoda Books, 1-57505-483-3, ages seven to twelve), is a fantastic book that explains how birds learn to sing, why they do, and the physical mechanics that enable them to sing.

Some areas have raptor recovery centers. If one is near your school, you might want to call and ask if they are willing to do presentations to school groups. Many children, particularly if they live in a more urbanized area, have no idea of the size of owls and hawks. There is usually a program fee or donation request for school presentations.

The Hidden Life of Winter Plants

What happens to all the lovely green plants of summer when the cold, dry winds of winter come in the late autumn? Perhaps where you live it is warm and nice this time of year, but in much of the country whole states are blanketed in a thick layer of snow. Understanding how plants and trees manage to survive the harsh climates present for months in so many parts of the world and still manage to burst forth in green every spring will give your children a deeper appreciation for the wisdom of nature.

Many woody plants that would die if hit with a hard frost in the middle of summer are just fine by late fall when the colder weather hits. They do this by getting ready when the longer nights and shorter days send them a signal. They stop growing and begin toughening up for the cold days to come. They rest for a while. Then as it gets colder, the living material in the plants' cells will become more gel-like. Very little water ends up left in the cells, so that freezing and breaking are avoided. Many plants systematically release heat from parts of themselves before freezing actually begins. The process, called "hardening," happens little by little.

Plants have more to contend with than just freezing. Winter months are much drier than other times of the year, and most plants will now have no way of drawing up water from the soil as all is frozen and hard. They are also threatened by hard little crystals of snow scratching the plant's surface and damaging it. That's why a blanket of snow can be a very good thing—it keeps plants from getting dry and damaged. However, plants are also stressed if there is too much snow piled on top of them, or if ice accumulates on their branches. The woody plants wait out winter by going dormant. When spring comes they reverse the hardening process and begin to move water through their cells in preparation for photosynthesis and new growth.

Go outside (as a class if you can manage it) and cut a few buds from woody bushes or trees. Bring them inside and carefully cut them open to see how tightly everything is stowed away, waiting for warmth and longer days to signal it to make the changes that will result in leaves unfurling.

You can also force branches to sprout: Cut some longish branches with buds and place in a vase or tall jar and leave in your warm classroom. Change the water as needed and within a short while (perhaps as much as a week or two) the buds will begin to unfurl. If you have access to the brushy type of willow that grows in wet areas (often near roads) called "pussy willow," selecting these branches will result in the sprouting of fuzzy little buds that will delight your class and make a nice "spring is coming" display. There are a number of other trees and bushes that make colorful or interesting displays when forced to sprout inside: forsythia, witch hazel, red osier dogwood. Ask a nursery employee or extension agent what's good in your area.

Here are some drinks that can be made from winter plants. Be sure to use only plants you are sure of, because of course not all plants are safe to drink. Sumac-ade can be made from the red dry fruit of this common small tree. The malic acid in the hairs you see on the sumac is found in apples too and makes for a nice lemonade sort of beverage. Like lemonade, you will need to add sweetener. The best time to gather these fruits is after the first frost, but there may be fruit left on trees near you. Collect lots of the reddish-brown fruits, and have the children wash their hands and rinse the fruit. Children can then "bruise" them by rubbing between their hands gently. Then just toss them into a large bowl of water until a bright pinkish hue is seen. Strain through cloth or a fine strainer and add honey or maple syrup to taste. This is a drink popular with pioneer families in many regions of the country over a hundred years ago.

A nice warm tea can be made of twigs from any of the birch trees: white, yellow, or black birch will all do nicely. Be sure to ask permission before you damage anyone's trees. Break a pile of small twigs into small pieces so they will fit in a pot. Cover with water and bring to a slow simmer. Simmer for about ten minutes or until the water has darkened quite a lot. Strain the tea and add honey if desired. Birch was a traditional ingredient in root beer, so children may find the flavor somewhat familiar.

Library Lover's Month

February is chock-full of special designations, and Library Lover's Month is one of them. The library—be it public, school, or private— should be one of a student's best friends. Whether students use their library as a source of research materials or pleasure reading, a quiet place to do homework while escaping from the noisy outside world or a combination of all three, the library is a place with doors open to everyone.

Celebrate Library Lover's Month by arranging a visit to the public library. It's shocking how many school-age children do not have public library cards. See that your students know where the library is and how to get there. No child should ever be disadvantaged because he or she has no books at home and doesn't know where to get information. If walking to the library is out of the question, look into PTA-funded school bus trips.

Arrange with the children's librarian for a library tour and a story session. Budget time for the librarian to instruct older children on using the library's microfiche readers. Let the librarian know, in advance, about the need for instruction on these esoteric materials. That way she or he has time to find a high-interest old news story on microfiche. The librarian might also instruct students how to use library Internet links.

Ask the school media center director to visit your classroom. Tell him or her you would like a five- to ten-minute presentation about the materials available in the school library. This should be a "get them excited" preview. Then, during regularly scheduled class visits, ask the director to expand on each kind of material. For example, one visit could concentrate on encyclopedias and their use; another might focus on finding nonfiction materials; and a third could center on choosing a good picture book or novel. Create simple exercises that require finding specific material.

February 13 celebrates the date of the first magazine published in America. Ask the media center director to feature magazines one day. *Ranger Rick*, *Cricket*, and *Cobblestone* are three magazines many libraries have in their collections. They contain articles that are extremely useful and complement many areas of the curriculum. Check and see if the media center director has suggestions for you on how to tap into this wealth of material.

For other ideas to help commemorate this month, see *Library Celebrations*, by Cyndy Dingwall (Highsmith, 1-5797-0027-2).

(106)

Classroom "Survivor"

Robinson Crusoe Day, February 1

In 1704, following an argument with his ship's captain, Alexander Selkirk requested to be put ashore on an uninhabited island in the southeast Pacific. He remained on the island for almost four years. He was rescued on February 1, 1709. When Daniel Defoe wrote *Robinson Crusoe* in 1719, the main character's story of island survival was based on Selkirk's adventures. February 1 has now been designated as Robinson Crusoe Day. It's a fun day to celebrate with children.

Upper middle school and junior high students who are interested may want to read *Robinson Crusoe*. Some prior discussion and explanation of period writing style and language usage would be helpful. Although the day receives its name from the book, it isn't necessary to read *Robinson Crusoe* to enjoy the day. Survival, adventure, and self-reliance are themes all students can relate to.

Incorporate these themes into the language arts curriculum in several ways. One could be as a message in a bottle. Ask students to pretend they are on a deserted island. A corked bottle washes ashore. What will they use as paper and ink, and what would they write in a rescue note? Ask students who like computer or virtual reality games to write a proposal that outlines and summarizes a plot and setting for a new computer survival game. On a lighter note, students could write a survival guide for the school day, week, or year. Perhaps these could be shared with younger students as a read-aloud session.

Science tie-ins could include methods of survival in differing ecosystems. For example: what would people do in a rainforest, a desert, or Alaska? Have students break into teams if you like and report back to the class. What do they need to survive in their environment and what challenges face them? Also, while studying ocean units, students could chart a floating bottle's likely path on an ocean current—the Gulf Stream would be one possibility.

Many excellent survival stories have been written for young readers. Offer *The Transall Saga*, by Gary Paulsen (Delacorte, 0-385-32196-1, grades 6 to 8); *Climb or Die*, by Edward Myers (Hyperion, 0-786-81129-3, grades 3 to 6); *Toughboy and Sister*, by Kirkpatrick Hill (Puffin, 0-14-034866-2, grades 4 to 7); *Earthquake Terror*, by Peg Kehret (Puffin, 0-14-038343-3, grades 3 to 7); and *Invitation to the Game*, by Monica Hughes (Simon and Schuster, 0-671-86692-3, grades 6 and up), to students who are looking for great adventure. *Survival Themes in Fiction for Children and Young People*, second edition, by Binnie Tate Wilkin (Scarecrow, 0-8108-2676-3), is an annotated bibliography arranged by theme, "survival" being used in the very broadest sense of the word.

"How Far Is It to the Horizon?"

Weatherman's Day, February 5

Learning about the weather includes more than just knowing about rain, snow, fog, and sunny days. Meteorologists know lots of interesting facts, including such things as how to calculate the distance to the horizon. Curious children may ask "How far is it to the horizon?" With a little thought and a calculator, older students can answer this question for themselves.

The visual distance to the horizon is different for each observer, because the distance depends on the height of the observer. Let students prove this by seeing just how the horizon changes depending on their eye level. Outside, ask students to lie on their stomachs. With chins resting on flattened hands, ask them what they can see in the distance. Then have the students stand up. How much more can they see? If your school has several stories, go and look out a top-story window. Does the horizon appear farther?

Each student can calculate his or her visual horizon distance while standing on the ground. First, the student should measure her height (in feet) from the ground. Round to the nearest foot, if students find the math easier. Next, use a calculator to find the square root of the student's height. Use this equation: square root of student's height × 1.224 = visual distance to horizon in miles.

The equation for a student 4 feet tall would be: 2 × 1.224 = 2.448 miles. The student's visual horizon would be 2.448 miles away.

Consult a meteorological text or mathematics book for further explanation of the mathematics involved.

For further horizon fun, play the songs "On a Clear Day," composed and written by Alan Jay Lerner and Frederick Lowe, and "I Can See for Miles and Miles," recorded by The Who.

(108)

Thomas Edison

Birth, February 11, 1847

Here is a story to encourage the tinkerers in your class. Born in 1847 to a working-class family, Thomas Edison was often bored in school, and in fact was eventually banned from school by his teachers. One school even told his parents he was uneducable! His mother did not believe the school's view of her son, so she chose to school him at home. This left young Edison more time for tinkering. His parents allowed him to set up a shop and to spend lots of time observing nature. As a child he wondered if he could hatch an egg—so he sat on one for hours and hours. Left to his own devices, he even had experiments go wrong, blow up, and then had to pay for damages. Young Edison makes for a very kid-friendly topic of research or discussion.

Eventually Edison's tinkering led to more than a thousand patents. Because of his restless curiosity we enjoy lightbulbs, the telephone, movie cameras, and so on. Driven by the desire to more deeply understand an issue, he often worked around the clock. His manner of asking a question and then doing experiments to prove his theories became the "scientific method" now used by scientists around the world. Edison was also a savvy businessman and found many ways to merchandise his inventions. Unfortunately he paid more attention to inventing and less to his business partners' practices, so he often found himself in court defending his marketing claims or patents.

You can see and hear Edison himself at the Library of Congress site, memory.loc.gov/ammem/edhtml/edbiohm.html. The first page can guide you to many recordings. From the first page choose Edison's home page and from there select the Learning Page. These could be valuable resources if you choose to assign research projects for middle school (and up) students. At this site you will find questions for critical thinking, U.S. history, and arts and humanities.

Two other sites that would be appropriate for student researchers are invent.org, which is the National Inventor's Hall of Fame, and nps.gov/edis/home.htm, which is the Edison National Historic Site. This site has a number of kid-friendly features: a virtual tour of Edison's home, lots of pictures, and an interactive laboratory section where kids try to build a lightbulb or market the movie camera Edison invented.

Younger children, ages four to eight, will enjoy *A Picture Book of Thomas Alva Edison* (Picture Book Biography Series), by David A. Adler (Holiday House, 0823414140). This funny and informative book for early readers has lots of illustrations and a decent time line.

An inventor often works hands-on—if you want to do the same, you may wish to get a copy of *The Thomas Edison Book of Easy and Incredible Experiments*, by James Cook and the Thomas Alva Edison Foundation (John Wiley and Sons, 0471620904, grades 4 to 11). Set up so that students can do experiments on their own: it takes pressure off the teacher and helps unlock the creative energies in your classroom. The book is also a big help for science fair ideas.

The following books share the same title, but are from different series and are appropriate for nine- to twelve-year-olds. *Thomas Alva Edison: Young Inventor* (Easy Biography Series), by Louis Sabin (Troll, 0893758426), is fun and easy to get through. *Thomas Alva Edison: Young Inventor* (Childhood of Famous American Series), by Sue Gutridge (Aladdin Paperbacks, 0020418507), is both funny and touching. It does a good job showing that Edison worked very hard and suffered many setbacks before experiencing success.

(109)

Children's Magazines Today

First American Magazine Published, February 13, 1741

When Andrew Branford published *The American Magazine* on February 13, 1741, he scooped Ben Franklin's *General Magazine* by just three days and received the honor of having published the first magazine in America. Today, there are many magazines available to the reading public, including a number of fine publications for children.

Although a number of school libraries subscribe to a selection of magazines, they are often one of the underutilized gems of the learning center's collection. It's impossible to stay on top of everything, but a monthly browsing trip to the learning center's magazine files could yield nuggets of information that will keep the classroom curricula lively and up-to-date. Perhaps one or two of the more popular magazines could be circulated throughout the school before being shelved in the library. Staple a teacher name checklist to the front.

Many children's magazines offer related activities, as well as suggestions and questions to guide critical discussion and analysis of the articles. A hidden benefit of magazine articles is that reluctant readers appreciate the short article lengths and are more likely to accomplish the reading assignment. This is especially true of children's magazines, where authors strive for high-interest topics written in a style geared toward holding the reader's attention. Children can learn to search for magazine articles by subject in the *Children's Magazine*

Guide (Bowker-Greenwood, monthly). Ask your school librarian if the library subscribes to this index, and if she or he will help you plan a unit to introduce it to your class. Check the list of periodicals indexed and see how many of them are available in your library.

Several magazines complement the history and/or social studies curriculum. *Calliope*, for readers ages eight to fifteen, focuses on world history. Supporting materials include maps, time lines, and photographs. *Cobblestone* presents short articles about U.S. history. Each issue is centered around a single historical theme. It is intended for readers ages nine to fifteen.

Cricket (ages nine to fourteen), *Lady Bug* (ages two to six), and *Spider* (ages six to nine) are magazines that contain stories, poems, songs, games, and book reviews that will interest young readers. Young writers interested in having their work published can contact several publications, including: *Stone Soup: The Magazine by Young Writers and Artists* (Stone Soup, P.O. Box 83, Santa Cruz, CA 95063); *Merlyn's Pen: The National Magazine of Student Writing* (Merlyn's Pen, Inc. P.O. Box 910, East Greenwich, RI 02818); and *Potluck Children's Literary Magazine* (potluckmagazine.com).

Nature magazines for children include *Ranger Rick* (ages six to twelve); *National Geographic Kids* (formerly known as *World*, ages eight to fourteen); and *Chickadee* (ages six to nine). Explore the scientific world with these titles: *Odyssey* (ages eight to fourteen) features cutting-edge stories about earth and space science; *Click* (ages three to seven) features science-related topics for the very young. *Scientific American* has a new science magazine, *Explorations*, that is great for bringing parents, teachers, and children together over science issues. Each issue features a pullout section called "Dragonfly" that focuses on a particular child doing scientific research. There is also a teacher's guide to go with each issue. Visit Explorations.org for more information or call 800-377-9414 for a free issue and teacher's guide.

Zillions: The Consumer Reports for Kids will interest the budding financial consultant, children interested in learning money management skills, and those interested in product evaluation.

The Weekly Reader Corp. (3001 Cindel Drive, Delran, NJ 08370; weeklyreader.com) and Scholastic, Inc. (2931 E. McCarty Street, Jefferson City, MO 65101-3710; scholastic.com) are two organizations that publish a number of magazines that complement school curricula. Write or see their websites for their current offerings. Boomerang offers a monthly magazine on cassette tape that covers a very diverse set of topics and features children's voices almost exclusively. It has received numerous awards including the Parent's Choice Award. It can be played on headphones for students who finish work early and is appropriate for a wide range of ages from early elementary to middle school (800-333-7858; boomkids.com).

Finally, *Book Links*, a Booklist publication of the American Library Association, is a magazine for teachers that works to connect books, libraries, and classrooms. Each bimonthly issue offers articles linked to specific curriculum areas, such as geography, science, and the arts. Ask at your media center or library.

(110)

Valentine's Day

February 14

Where did this odd celebration come from? Well, the truth is, what we do now with candy and cards and flowers has little to do with the early days of the Romans' festival of love. Those ancient Romans loved to party; they loved games and festivals and feasts. They also believed in love and honored it with a special festival called *Lupercalia*. Cupid was honored in ancient Rome and Greece (where he was known as Eros), because he was the son of Venus, the Roman goddess of love and beauty, and he had a magical way of bringing lovers together that came to be represented by a bow and arrow. (Thus the arrow through the heart symbol so common today on Valentine's cards).

You can stick with making Valentine's cards on this day, or you can take a science and math tack. Start with the heart. The heart has been seen by Western cultures as the seat of love for many hundreds of years. Other cultures favor different parts of the body. Can you imagine what we would be making today if our ancestors thought the spleen was the romantic location of love in the body? You can test your students' knowledge of the heart with some fun "IQ" tests available online at http://sln.fi.edu/biosci/activity.html#healthyheart. You can print out tests on the heart, blood, smoking, and asthma. You may also want to open a textbook to a good photo of a human heart and compare that to the construction-paper versions that are probably in evidence in your class today.

There are lots of fun games to be found at online lesson plan sites that make use of "conversation hearts" candy pieces. Mona Grayson, a teacher, offers a fun idea for teaching longitude and latitude or plotting coordinates called Valentine's Battleship. All you need is copies of a ten-by-ten paper grid and some candies. Label the lines up from the bottom starting with A, B, C, and so on. Label the horizontal axis from left to right starting with 1, 2, 3, and so on. Kids pair up, each with a grid of his or her own and five candies. Place a barrier (like a folder or large book) in between so they can't see each other's grids. Students place their candies on intersections of lines on the grids, and then take turns calling out coordinates to guess the location of their partner's candies. A "hit," or correct guess, means they get to take that piece of candy. The object is to get all the candies, but tell them not to eat the playing pieces! You can assure the kids they will get other candies after the game that are fresh from the box and have never been handled.

Another fun activity featuring candy can be used to reinforce estimation, comparison, addition, subtraction, and graphing skills. Hand out individual boxes of candy and blank pieces of paper to work on, but tell students they should not open the boxes yet. First ask students to estimate the amount of candy in their box. Ask how many tens and how many ones are in that number. Then ask students to empty their box and count the actual number of candies. Have students calculate the difference between the actual number and what they previously estimated. If you wish you can offer a prize for the closest guess.

Next students sort the candy by message, and then by color. Create a sheet to find differences or sums using the number of colored hearts. You can ask them yellow minus orange, or pink plus yellow, for instance. You can also have them do less-than or greater-than problems.

Using the same procedure you could also provide a graphing sheet to graph hearts on a bar graph by color or message. Another idea is to create a pie graph by gluing the hearts around a paper plate by color. Color in the pie graph wedges to match the candy color. Use percentages and discuss. What is the most common color in the classroom's candy collection? If your students have better ideas for the hearts' messages, they can send the suggestions in to the company (see candy box for address), as they do change the messages from time to time to keep up with new sayings.

(111)

Galileo Galilei

Birth, February 15, 1564

Give the science curriculum a February boost by celebrating Galileo's birthday, February 15. Although Galileo didn't invent the telescope, he improved the lens and began stargazing. His observations of planetary motions converted him to Copernicus's theory of a sun-centered solar system, a personal discovery that led to heresy charges by the Roman Catholic Church. In 1610, he discovered four moons that circle Jupiter.

If possible, borrow a telescope. Ask students to write how it changes their perception of distant objects. With parental coordination, organize an evening in the classroom when students can look at the stars through the telescope. Ahead of time, choose one or two constellations (the Big Dipper is an easily spotted one) that students can search for. Many cultures have myths about the formation of constellations. Students can write their own explanations.

Planetary mobiles really brighten up a classroom, as do dioramas. Making constellations with cellophane and construction paper is another colorful classroom decoration. Scratchboard-style crayon artwork (with black crayon covering an underlayer of colors) is also fun.

Pisa, Galileo's birthplace, is a quick geography and science link. The Leaning Tower is a landmark with world recognition. Students can research what has caused the tower to lean.

Involve the class in a discussion of Galileo's imprisonment in later life for adhering to beliefs he held. *Starry Messenger*, by Peter Sis (Farrar, Straus and Giroux, 0-374-37191-1, grades 2 to 6), is another literature connection.

NASA has chosen to honor Galileo by naming a spacecraft after him. In 1995 the spacecraft *Galileo* entered the orbit of Jupiter after taking six years to journey there. It continues to orbit, studying several of Jupiter's moons. Older students will want to visit NASA's Galileo website at jpl.nasa.gov/galileo/index.html. The site also has a Galileo Education Resources page for K–12 teachers at jpl.nasa.gov /galileo/education.html.

(112)

Japanese American Internment

Roosevelt Signed Order for Japanese American Internment, February 19, 1942

President Franklin D. Roosevelt signed Executive Order 9066 on this date in 1942. This order resulted in the internment of Japanese Americans who lived along the United States' western coast into concentration camps located in several western states. The excuse for this action was that Japanese Americans were thought to be a potential threat to the security of the nation while it was fighting Japan during World War II. For many years, the subject was not discussed and was excluded from mention in history textbooks. In recent years, concerned people have worked to educate others about this important period of our nation's history.

Classroom discussion could center around the political and social climates that provided the seeds that led to internment. Older students can debate what constitutes a government's reasonable right to protect its citizens from internal threat versus overreaction and abrogation of a citizen's rights. They could compare concentration camps established at different times in history. The United States government forcibly removed many Native American tribes to concentration camps and then onto reservations where they were required to live. Millions of people were imprisoned in the Soviet Gulags from the late 1920s up into the 1950s. In the 1990s, concentration camps were established by each of the warring factions in Bosnia-Herzegovina.

Junior high school students might do a literature comparison of World War II concentration camps. Compare and contrast: *The Devil's Arithmetic*, by Jane Yolen (Puffin, 0-14-034535-3, grades 5 to 9); the biographical *Journey to Topaz*, by Yoshiko Uchida (Creative Arts, 0-916870-85-5, grades 4 to 12); and *Beyond Paradise*, by Jane Hertenstein (Morrow, 0-688-16381-5, grades 7 to 10), the story of an American girl imprisoned in a Japanese-run camp in the Philippines.

Students can research the United States government's efforts to provide remuneration to those who were interned and their families. The troubles of interned families did not end when they were allowed to go home. Many found their homes destroyed by fearful or angry neighbors, some found their jobs taken by others, and a number of formerly prosperous ranching and farming families in Southern California returned to find their land had been stolen from them while they were gone.

Other literature connections include: *The Children of Topaz: The Story of a Japanese-American Internment Camp Based on a Classroom Diary*, by Michael O. Tunnell and George Chilcoat (Holiday House, 0-8234-1239-3, grades 4 to 7), and the fictional *The Journal of Ben Uchida*, by Barry Denenberg (Scholastic, 0-590-48531-8, grades 6 to 9).

113

Washington, D.C.

Washington Monument Dedicated and Presidents' Day, February 21

The area in Washington, D.C., known as the Mall contains familiar architectural monuments, especially those dedicated to presidents. Unfortunately, many children do not have the opportunity to visit our capital city. The year 2000 was the two hundredth anniversary of the federal government's move from Philadelphia to the new city of Washington. In 1800, President John Adams and his family moved into the White House, Congress met for the first time in the new Capitol building, and the Library of Congress was founded. Start your class on a geography and history field trip to D.C. without actually leaving the room.

Divide your students into four groups, each representing a compass direction. Designate each wall as a direction of a compass. Through research, artwork, and photographs, let your students bring the Mall in Washington, D.C., to your room. Students on the west wall would focus on the Lincoln Memorial, the Vietnam Veterans Memorial, and the large reflecting pool. The south group works on the Franklin Delano Roosevelt and Thomas Jefferson Memorials. Those in the north group do the Washington Monument (which is actually in the center of the Mall) and the White House. There is also a new sculpture in the center of the Mall honoring nurses who served during war times. Members of the east group research the United States Capitol and the Library of Congress.

Small groups can give presentations to the class on the history of these buildings and biographies of the people they commemorate. Students can look for depictions of these memorials. For example, the Lincoln Memorial is on the penny and the five-dollar bill. The White House is on the twenty-dollar bill. Presentations might feature important events that took place during the years the presidents governed or events that have occurred in each building.

Learning center directors can steer you toward the many books available for young readers. Congressional representatives are usually glad to send a map and other information about the city (particularly tourist attractions) to a class that writes and requests them. If you have Internet access, the Library of Congress is online at loc.gov, the White House at whitehouse.gov, and you can tour the Capitol at senate.gov.

(114)

George Frideric Handel

Birth, February 23, 1685

George Frideric Handel was born in 1685, in Halle, Germany. He loved playing music, especially the clavichord, the harpsichord, and the organ. By the time he was twelve, Handel was the assistant organist at the Halle Cathedral.

Although his father advised against pursuing a career in music, Handel persisted. He studied in Hamburg, where he and a friend often participated in operas. (Handel played harpsichord in the orchestra pit.) In 1706, Handel toured Italy, studying and performing music and also writing short operas for friends. After several years in Italy, he moved to England, where he was determined to succeed as a musician and to persuade English audiences to love opera as much as he did.

While Handel loved opera, he is best remembered for his other compositions. He composed one of his most famous instrumental works, *Water Music*, in 1717 for a floating party held by King George I. An orchestra played the music as they sat in a barge drifting down the River Thames. This piece, while not directly related to the hydrologic cycle, would be fun to include as background music for units about water.

In 1749, Handel composed *Royal Fireworks Music*, another instrumental piece, to celebrate the end of the War of the Austrian Succession between England and Germany. The various sections of the piece represent the cacophony of battle and war, the gentle quiet of peace, and the people's jubilation at the end of the war. This is marvelous music to use in art class. While listening to a section, have everyone draw pictures, lines, or just shapes to represent the feelings that the different sections of music evoke inside them. Afterward, share with the students what Handel envisioned for each section.

Handel's most popular piece, *The Messiah*, written in 1741, is an oratorio, or a piece written to tell a story, which is usually religious. Performed by soloists, choruses, and an orchestra, an oratorio is similar to an opera without costumes, scenery, or acting. The "Hallelujah Chorus," from *The Messiah*, is a thrilling piece of music and one of the classics of western music. If you play it for your class, note the manner in which each vocal section blends with and amplifies the phrasing of the previous "voice." Discuss the tradition of standing while the piece is being played.

Handel's music is widely available on CDs and records. Check your local library. A new picture book about Handel's life by M. T. Anderson is titled *Handel: Who Knew What He Liked* (Candlewick Press, 0-7636-1046-1, ages eight to twelve). Kevin Hawkes has provided humorous illustrations of Handel's life. For a straightforward biography see Mike Venezia's *George Handel* (Children's Press, 0-516-44539-1, ages six to ten).

(115)

Three Flags

Fiesta of the Mexican Flag, February 24

Your students may be perplexed if you spout the word *vexillology*, which means the study of flags, but they'll love some time to look at all the beautiful flags of the world and begin to understand the symbolism behind their features.

Perhaps your class has already studied the Stars and Stripes and understands the meaning behind the number of stars and the colors reflected there. But introduce them to three flags from around the world . . .

Show them the striking flag of our neighbor, Mexico, with a story that will thrill them. This flag features three bands of green, white, and then red. Green symbolizes hope, white symbolizes purity, and red symbolizes union. But the most noticeable aspect is the center medallion on the white field that depicts an eagle with a snake clasped in its beak perched on a cactus. In Aztec legend, the city that is now Mexico City was on a site decreed by the gods, who told the Aztecs to look for a sign: the eagle devouring a serpent. When the Aztecs saw such a sight on an island in the middle of a lake, they knew the prophecy was come and built a marvelous city—filling in the lake bed to create their main metropolis.

Each February 24 is a day to honor the Mexican flag that was adopted with Mexican independence from Spain in 1821 (much as our June Flag Day honors "Old Glory").

Brazil has a colorful flag that also features a striking centered medallion. On a field of green—symbolizing its lush rain forests—is a yellow diamond (yellow on many international flags symbolizes mineral wealth). In the diamond is a blue globe with a constellation of stars and a banner with the slogan "order and progress." The constellation is one that can be seen over Brazil.

A final flag to introduce to your class is more recent, as it is the flag of Nunavut, the land of the Inuit people of Canada (see Idea 135 in April). This flag features a yellow field butted against a white field centered by a stone monument in red. At the top right corner is a deep blue five-pointed star. This star represents the North Star, which has for millennia guided mariners and travelers. The stone monument is a similar guiding feature. The yellow, white, and blue represent the riches of the land, sea, and sky while the red of the monument represents Canada (whose own flag with the red maple leaf should be recognizable to students). The government of Nunavut has an informative website at gov.nu.ca.

Of course, there are hundreds of flags to investigate, and it would make a fun unit to assign flags to small groups for research. Many websites feature flags of the world and their symbolism. Or, have your class research your state flag (and city flag if you have one). What does it look like? What are the symbols in it? When was it adopted?

Flag Lore of All Nations, by Whitney Smith (Millbrook, 0761318992, ages nine to twelve), offers a good research source for such a project.

116

The Irish Heritage

Irish American Heritage Month, March

House Joint Resolution 401 calls for a presidential proclamation establishing March as Irish American Heritage Month. Irish immigrants were one of the many groups of people who have contributed to the building of this country. Beginning in the late 1840s, more than two million people left Ireland, many of them moving to the United States.

The majority of the Irish immigrants fled Ireland because of the Great Irish Famine. Several times between 1845 and 1850, a blight struck Ireland's potato crop and destroyed it. Loss of the potato, the main food crop, added to possible neglect by the British government, resulted in starvation and disease that killed one million people.

In recent years, the potato famine and the impact it had on Irish immigration has been the topic of several books for young people. *Nory Ryan's Song*, by Patricia Reilly Giff (Random House, 0-385-32141-4, ages twelve and up), is an excellent and gritty slice-of-life novel about young Nory and her struggles to keep her family from starving while Papa is working far from home. The book begins in

1845 and the reader's fear of the spreading blight grows along with Nory's fears as time passes.

The Grave, by James Heneghan (Farrar Straus and Giroux, 0-374-32765-3, ages twelve and up), is a gripping historical time-travel fantasy in which Tom falls into a grave in 1974 Liverpool and "wakes up" to find himself in Ireland in 1847. There he struggles to help a family remain together and survive. His success or failure will have tremendous impact on the future.

So Far from Home, by Barry Denenberg (Scholastic, 0-590-92667-5, ages twelve and up), is one of the entries in Scholastic's terrific Dear America series. A young heroine begins a new life at Lowell, Massachusetts, in 1847, working as a mill girl. Mill life enables her to eke out a living and make a life for herself far removed from the tragedy of the potato famine. However, working in the mills was hard, dangerous work. The emphasis in this book is on the Irish immigrant experience in this country.

Two nonfiction books also shed light on the potato famine and Irish immigration. *Black Potatoes: The Story of the Great Irish Famine, 1845–1850*, by Susan Campbell Bartoletti (Houghton-Mifflin, 0-618-00271-5, ages nine and up), contains primary source materials about the famine. *Irish Immigrants 1840–1920*, by Megan O'Hara (Capstone, 0-7368-0795-0, ages seven to eleven), contains photographs and information chronicling the immigrant experience. For social studies lessons, you might want to compare and contrast the experiences of Irish immigrants with those of present-day immigrants.

In a lighter vein, Saint Patrick's Day is celebrated on the seventeenth of this month. Two books will give your students information on the story behind this popular holiday: *Saint Patrick's Day*, by Gail Gibbons (Holiday House, 0-8234-1173-7, ages five to eight), and *Saint Patrick's Day*, by Janet Riehecky (available in libraries, ages five to nine).

117

Women's Rights

Women's History Month, March

There have been two movements for women's rights in this country. Elizabeth Cady Stanton and Susan B. Anthony were among the early crusaders for women's rights in the nineteenth century. Like many in the women's suffrage movement, they were both abolitionists, believing that the institution of slavery should be abolished. Their ideas that women should have voting rights, equal educational opportunities, and the right to own property were radical and hotly contested. It was not until 1920 that women finally won the right to vote with the passage of the Nineteenth Amendment to the Constitution.

The first Woman's Rights Convention was held July 19, 1848, at Seneca Falls, New York. After learning about the convention, middle grade students can make posters and banners that they might have carried if they were representatives attending the first convention. Ask your students to draw political cartoons about women's suffrage. Real examples of these can be found at the Smithsonian collection online at www.si.edu.

Stanton and Anthony pioneered many women's rights issues. Junior high students can research, then compare and contrast them with issues raised during the equal rights movements of the 1960s and 1970s, the second wave of the women's movement. Betty Friedan and Gloria Steinem figured prominently in that movement. Now that women had the vote, what were the issues raised by the equal rights movement? What does the word *feminism* mean? Did the equal rights movement only benefit women, or were there benefits for men as well? Students might want to read back issues of *MS* magazine. They can also survey women in their families and find out how the movement has affected their lives. In what way, if any, did they participate or benefit? Many women of your classroom's grandmothers' generation joined "consciousness raising groups." Perhaps you can find a woman to come in and talk about this time of her life.

Women's fashions have changed in many ways throughout history. Discuss how wearing trousers changed women's lives. Compare and contrast historical conceptions of beauty with modern ideas. The Chinese tradition of foot binding, the European custom of removing a rib or two to achieve a tiny waist, and today's craze for body piercing, tattooing, and henna decoration are topics that will interest students.

(118)

Women Who Shaped Our World

Women's History Month, March

There are many excellent biographies about influential women who lived in the past. Call Women's History Month to your students' attention by borrowing a collection of biographies from your school's learning center or the public library. Let students decide how to group and arrange the books. They may sort them by historical era or by topic areas. Women you might consider including are: Mary Cassatt, Rosa Bonheur, Beatrix Potter, Laura Ingalls Wilder, Rachel Carson, Sojourner Truth, Marie Curie, Sandra Day O'Connor, Wilma Mankiller, Jane Addams, and Florence Kelley. Have students develop a bulletin board time line of women's history.

Encourage students to identify influential women who have excelled in a subject area they find interesting. In small groups, students can introduce each other to the women they find. For example, a child who loves sharks could acquaint the others with Eugenie Clark, a marine biologist and pioneer in the study of sharks.

Middle school students can research and write "news flash" style headlines that announce women's historical firsts. Suggestions might feature Valentina Tereshkova, the first woman astronaut, or Elizabeth Blackwell, the first American woman to receive a medical degree. An amusing project for small groups of older students is to write a classroom TV talk show (à la "Oprah"), during which famous women confront their critics. Each group should have a host, an influential woman, a critic, and two or three enthusiastic audience members who can ask questions and put in their two cents.

Develop a unit on "The Women in Our Lives." As a class, create a list of good interview questions. Have children interview women in their families. Keep the focus on what life was like for the person being interviewed. Questions might include asking about favorite foods, the kinds of clothes they wore, fashion fads, household chores, and jobs held in the past.

Encourage the children to bring in family history stories about women from past generations. Invite parents to bring old photos and/or memorabilia pertaining to those women to the classroom. To prevent damage or loss, ask them to share the material with the students, answer student questions, and then take the items home. Several parents could be scheduled concurrently to speak to small groups rather than the whole class. Each small group can jot down short notes during the meetings and later give a quick recap of the high points to the whole class.

There is a wealth of children's literature about famous women and their contributions to the sciences, the arts, and politics, but *Seven Brave Women*, by Betsy Hearne (Morrow, 0-688-14502-7, all ages), is an outstanding book that celebrates the importance of contributions that fall outside the category of fame. This picture book describes seven generations of women in one family who demonstrated bravery by conquering the challenges of everyday living.

Young Oxford History of Women in the United States, edited by Nancy Cott (eleven volumes, Oxford University Press, 0-19-508830-1, grades 6 and up), is an excellent survey of American women's history.

119

Classy Music

Music in Our Schools Month, March

March is designated as Music in Our Schools Month—a time to celebrate the educational value of music. Many of the ideas in this book concern famous composers, but there are many ways to bring music into your classroom, even if you don't sing or play an instrument.

One fun way is to link recorded songs with literature. Here are a few fun ideas: "Wild Thing," recorded by the Trogs, with *Where the Wild Things Are*, by Maurice Sendak (HarperCollins, 0-06-025492-0, grades K to 3); "Tar Beach," recorded by John Sebastian, with *Tar Beach*, by Faith Ringgold (Crown, 0-5175-8031-4, grades K to 3); "What a Wonderful World," recorded by Louis Armstrong, with *What a Wonderful World*, by G. D. Weiss and Bob Thiele (Atheneum, 0-68-980097-8, all ages).

On a folksy sing-along note, link "Take Me Out to the Ballgame" with *Teammates*, by Peter Golenbock (Harcourt Brace, 0-15-200603-6, grades K to 3); "Frog Went A-Courting" with *Frog Went A-Courtin'*, by John Langstaff (Harcourt Brace, 0-15-230214-X, grades K to 3); and "I Know an Old Lady Who Swallowed a Fly" with any of the several children's book versions. Even hearing-impaired students can relate to music. See *Moses Goes to a Concert*, by Isaac Millman (Farrar Straus, 0-374-35067-1, grades K to 4), for a story about deaf children going to a concert.

To expose students to the classics, recordings are available of Sergei Prokofiev's symphonic fairy tale *Peter and the Wolf* (read aloud one of the many versions of this fairy tale), Saint-Saëns's *Danse Macabre* (read aloud Cynthia de Felice's *The Dancing Skeleton* [Aladdin, 0-68-980453-9, grades K to 3] before playing this), and Maurice Ravel's orchestration of Mussorgsky's *Pictures at an Exhibition* (perfect for students to draw their ideas of what the pictures might look like).

Invite students to bring in selections of music they enjoy. Set guidelines as to what is appropriate for classroom use. Consult with the learning center director to see if the school owns some music collections. You could designate one week as Rock 'n' Roll, a second as Classical, a third as Children's Songs, and a fourth as World Music. Use the music as background during silent reading periods or during attendance taking. Each week the students can vote on a "song of the week."

As always, try to encourage parents with musical expertise to visit the classroom and share their love of music. Invite students who play instruments to talk about their instruments and play a tune or two. Perhaps some musically inclined students would like to compose a song or a rap.

A daily music break gives all of us a few moments to relax, reflect, and examine ourselves. Music provides an opportunity to slow down the hectic pace of today's life. The way you bring music into your students' lives doesn't matter as much as the fact that you do it. Everyone relates to music—you just have to find the right kind. It will enrich students' lives in ways you could never imagine.

This Little Piggy . . .

National Pig Day, March 1

It's time to *pig out*! There's something about pigs that makes us smile. Try saying Porky Pig, Wilbur, Babe, and Arnold Ziffle (remember him from the TV show "Green Acres"?). You'll probably be smiling before you're finished. Kick off a National Pig Day celebration with the following quiz. See how many students can fill in the blanks correctly. (You may have to leave some out for very young children.) Students can have fun making their own quiz for a different animal.

As sloppy as a _____

_____ barrel politics

A _____ in a poke

_____-back ride

A greedy _____

_____-headed

And _____ may fly

_____ wild

Casting pearls before _____

You can't turn a _____'s ear into a silk purse.

Regardless of the reasons, pigs are attention grabbers and worth sneaking into the curriculum. You might want to consider a short pig unit. The wide variety of pig books makes it possible to use a whole language approach. There are even several pig math books.

Middle and junior high school educators may be leery about incorporating a pig novel into a literature group. Don't be. Any initial resistance to animal fantasy quickly wears off when the plot and characters are well developed, especially in a novel such as *Charlotte's Web*. Charlotte and Wilbur's friendship is one of the most endearing (and enduring) tales in children's literature. Unfortunately, by the time most children reach middle school, *Charlotte's Web* has dropped out of sight. That's a shame. Middle school and junior high years are the time when children begin struggling with who they are. They are ultraconscious about friends and the meaning of friendship.

In reading class, dust off copies of *Charlotte's Web*, by E. B. White (0-06-440055-7, HarperCollins), and let the children read it (again). Middle school age students are the perfect age for recognizing emotional nuances and appreciating White's clever use of language, two things many of them probably missed if they read the book as a primary student. Pose provocative questions about friendship and its responsibilities and group discussions will take off. Also, because children already know the story line and are comfortable with the characters, you can dig into the novel and use it to teach literary elements including setting, characterization, plot, irony, and theme. (See also Idea 32 in October.)

Two books that will leave students chuckling are: *Swine Divine*, by Jan Carr (Holiday House, 0-8234-1434-5, ages five to nine), and *Swine Lake*, by James Marshall (HarperCollins, 0-06-205171-7, ages six and up). Both are filled with puns that would be great to stimulate similar creative writing projects.

When Pigasso Met Mootisse, by Nina Laden (Chronicle Books, 0-8118-1121-2, ages five to nine), is a clever way to introduce modern art and pigs.

Pigs will also fit nicely into the science curriculum. For farm animal units get a copy of *Life on a Pig Farm*, by Judy Wolfman (Carolrhoda Books, 1-57505-237-7, ages seven to twelve). It has great pictures. For a geological unit see Tomi Ungerer's *The Mellops Go Spelunking* (Roberts Rinehart, 1-57098-228-7, ages five to nine) for a light-hearted exploration of a cave. Other Mellops adventures include *The Mellops Strike Oil*. On a more serious science note, ask your reference librarian to help you locate recent articles on pigs' assistance in medical research that impacts humans. Pigs are very much like us, and thus their organs are valuable to researchers and transplant recipients alike.

And in case you're stuck on quiz answers, here are some clues: *pig, sow, pork, piggy, swine,* and *hog.* When the hard hog work is done, why not relax with a game of Pig Mania? It's a fun and challenging gambling game that will build math skills (the game points go up and down quickly so children have to add and subtract their scores) and involves tossing little piggies instead of dice. This game may be in kids' game closets already, see if you can borrow it.

Newspaper Fun

Newspapers in Education Week, First Full Week in March

A lifelong habit of reading the paper can be started with this week-long introduction to newspapers. The newspaper was once the only source of real news, but now many of us get our news via electronic media. Thus, very few of your students may have had any experience with reading a paper. If this is the case be sure to start with the basics. See the sponsors of Newspapers in Education Week at naa.org, for details. The *Star Tribune* newspaper (Twin Cities, Minnesota), offers a website just for teachers: startribune.com/education/classroo.shtml. Here is how they suggest you start:

- Teach the sections of the paper from front to back.
- Teach students to follow an article from one column to the next and from the front page to the "jump" page.
- Show how to scan a newspaper from left to right and then top to bottom.
- Have students sign their copy of the paper in a designated place. This will encourage tidiness and help avoid confusion if students are allowed to take their copy home.
- Allow five to ten minutes for students to read by themselves so they will be more ready to take instruction.
- If you want students to pay attention to just one section, ask them to place the others in their desks or under their chairs.
- Younger students may find it easier to handle a paper that has been stapled in the upper left corner or down the left-hand side like a binding.

This week is devoted to bringing newspapers into children's lives. It's a great opportunity to focus attention on print as an important informational medium. You can start in a number of ways. Many local papers are glad to donate free copies for educational use. (More than seven hundred newspapers around the country sponsor Newspaper in Education Week.) A classroom subscription assures regular reading. Sometimes parent-teacher organizations will provide a school year's subscription to the Learning Center. Add the newspaper to the "reader's corner" of your classroom so students can browse the paper when they have finished in-class assignments.

Collect items that pertain to curriculum content areas—science, particularly medicine, environmental concerns, and space exploration—to supplement textbook information with up-to-the-minute discoveries. Have students clip articles and start subject files they can refer to during the balance of the school year. Discuss what makes an attention-grabbing headline. Start a collection of new words and their definitions. Look for grammatical and spelling errors. Make opportunities for students to share the news they've read about with each other.

Each day during the week focus on a different section of the newspaper. The Home/Family section, which often contains the comics, is a good attention grabber for Monday morning. Survey students for what features within this section they read most frequently. You can do the same survey-style response to rank favorite comic strips. Have students chart the results as a bar graph for math.

On Tuesday, you might choose to feature the first section and focus on headline styles. It's also a good opportunity to learn percentage and area. Do this by measuring the page and then comparing the relative area occupied by featured stories with that occupied by advertisements.

Devote Wednesday to sports. Before doing so, poll the class to determine what their favorite sports are. Rank them numerically. When looking at the sports section, see if the coverage given various sports reflects the interest of the class. If it doesn't, as a language arts activity (and a lesson on consumer input) students could sum up their findings in a letter to the sports editor of the newspaper and ask what determines how much page space a particular sport is given.

On Thursday, take a look at the business and advertisement sections. Explain what the stock report figures mean and why they interest so many adults. Note what kind of want ads the paper features. Students could have fun writing their own mock ads that would feature toys or sporting equipment they wish they could sell. By Thursday, the class has had time to look at several sections in depth. Have them find out which sections contain the most advertisements for consumer goods and how the ads change to reflect the nature of the section.

Hopefully, during the week students have taken note of the main stories. On Friday, focus on the editorial pages to see how quickly, if at all, people have responded to the breaking news of the earlier days. Each student should try writing a letter to the editor about a subject that concerned him or her. Many editorial pages have Web addresses, so you won't need stamps and envelopes. But students should use a writing process that includes revision before E-mailing a letter. Read one or two columns by featured editorial writers and discuss how their views complement or disagree with those of the students.

If you are willing to give producing your own classroom newspaper a try, get a copy of *Creating a Classroom Newspaper*, by Kathleen Buss and Leslie McClain-Ruelle. It is published by the International Reading Association and offers a great deal of practical advice. (IRA publication number 274-448. To order, call 302-731-1600 or visit the IRA online bookstore at bookstore.reading.org.)

122

More Newspapers in Education

Newspapers in Education Week, First Full Week in March

Reading newspapers fosters literacy and stimulates interest in current events. The latest scientific research is usually first-section news. Articles about health and space exploration are far more up-to-date than classroom textbooks and are important curriculum supplements. Coverage of political events can be used to stimulate interest in government. Voter apathy is becoming widespread; helping students become aware and informed is one way to combat this trend.

Newspapers often feature interviews with people who are making the news. Children should be encouraged to analyze the kinds of questions that were asked to elicit the responses reported in each article. They can learn to formulate effective interview questions, which avoid yes-or-no answers. For example, asking, "What kind of sports do you like?" versus "Do you like sports?" Let students pair off and interview each other. They also might want to try interviewing people in the community.

Bring in an article from a tabloid. Discuss what draws our attention to that kind of writing and why we read it. Ask students to dissect the article and search for unsupported statements and vague references. Ask them to cite the author's evidence. Alert students to the use of unspecific "they" references, or "experts say" as a source of information. Elect a student moderator to conduct a classroom discussion on the difference between gossip and fact. Encourage students to explore how events in their lives get distorted and turned into harmful and painful gossip.

Play with the comics section during art class. Discuss the different kinds of comics depicted. Examine artistic technique and textual content. Some comics are very simple drawings, while others are much more detailed. The situations that occur in some strips reflect family life, while others explore social issues. Some are just plain silly. Talk about what makes a good comic strip. Contrast the comic section with editorial cartoons. Make collages of headlines, sporting events, financial news, and other themes that interest students. Students may wish to bring in an example of their favorite comic strip.

Ask students to research old newspaper issues on microfilm and see how the funny pages and editorial cartoons have changed over the years. At the same time, have them note top stories of the day and the prices of merchandise advertised in the paper. Compare and contrast them with today's stories and prices. Most public libraries have a microfilm reader, some with copying capabilities. Learning to use microfilm and microfiche readers allows students to expand and develop their research skills.

Call attention to the ratio of advertising and reported news. Some papers are heavily weighted one way or the other. Students can compare the quality of reporting in each case.

Students can clip stories from newspapers at home. At school, they can create and maintain a weekly or monthly bulletin board that features stories voted on by the class as the craziest, scariest, saddest, best headline, etc. of the week or month.

Pick up copies of several newspapers and let your imagination run wild. There are lesson plan idea nuggets galore. The cost is minimal and the satisfaction immense.

Some newspapers have devoted a part of their websites to materials for the classroom. At the New York Times Learning Network (nytimes.com/learning), for example, there is a lesson plan every day suitable for grades 6 and up .

(123)

Dr. Seuss

Theodor Geisel, Birth, March 2, 1904

Theodor Geisel, more familiarly known as Dr. Seuss, was born March 2, 1904, in Massachusetts. At first he worked doing commercial art, and during World War II he was involved in creating propaganda for the United States. He began his career as a children's author with the story *And to Think That I Saw It on Mulberry Street*. The story of how this story finally made it to print is pretty amazing: he submitted it to twenty-seven publishing houses before it was accepted by a publisher. Dr. Seuss went on to publish many much-beloved and outstanding books for young children including *Hop on Pop, The Cat in the Hat, How the Grinch Stole Christmas*, and *Horton Hears a Who*, just to name a few.

Geisel illustrated and wrote all his works. Using great rhymes and silly words he managed to amuse children and adults alike. Read his works aloud and see if children can sort them into categories. Some of his books teach reading, and others have important messages about paying attention to folks of all sizes, the environment, the dangers of doing nothing when action is called for, and even about nuclear war. Some members of your class may wish to adapt a book into a play. A number of Dr. Seuss books work well for a reader's theater approach. Children could also write a story of their own as individuals or teams, using the rhythm and rhyme of Dr. Seuss, and then create imaginative illustrations to accompany the writing.

In 1984, Geisel received a Pulitzer Prize "for his contribution over nearly half a century to the education and enjoyment of America's children and their parents." He died in 1992, but his works live on in books, TV specials, and films.

Celebrate the good doctor's birthday by having some fun with one of his slightly lesser known titles, *The 500 Hats of Bartholomew Cubbins* (Random House, 0-394-84484-X, ages six to ten). This zany story of a boy with an endless supply of hats connects beautifully with the art curriculum. After a read-aloud session of the story, students can make their own hats and then hold a parade down the halls of the school. Encourage students to collect bits and pieces of materials from home or the outdoors in advance. Leaves, string, and other odds and ends lend a distinctive air to millinery creations. Older students might prefer drawing their versions of fancy hats. These can become quite elaborate and make a fascinating bulletin board or hallway display.

Further connect this story with other books about hats. *Caps for Sale*, by Esphyr Slobodkina (HarperCollins, 0-06-443143-6, ages five to seven), is a great choice, and *The Hatseller and the Monkeys*, by Baba Diakite (Scholastic, 0-590-96069-5, ages four to eight), is an African retelling of the same folk story, filled with colorful illustrations. If you celebrated Abe Lincoln's birthday last month, you could have a reading of *Abe Lincoln's Hat*, by Martha Brenner (Random House, 0-679-84977-7, ages six to eight). Ann Morris's *Hats, Hats, Hats* (Morrow, 0-688-12274-4, ages four to seven) is a lovely nonfiction photo essay book featuring hats from many cultures.

(124)

Our National Anthem

"Star-Spangled Banner" Becomes Official U.S. National Anthem, March 3, 1931

The words to the "Star-Spangled Banner" were written by Francis Scott Key during the War of 1812. On September 13, 1814, while the British bombarded Fort McHenry, Key was detained overnight on a truce ship in Baltimore Harbor. The next morning, the sight of the American flag still flying over the fort inspired him to write several poetic verses about the flag. The anthem's melody is from an old English drinking song, popular in the late seventeen hundreds, which had also served as the melody for other patriotic songs of early America. In 1931, the U.S. Congress officially approved the "Star-Spangled Banner" as the national anthem. President Herbert Hoover signed the bill the same day.

In addition to singing or playing a recording of the song, print out (or have students write) the four verses. Discuss the words and meaning of each verse. Elementary students are often confused about what the words to the first verse are. Reading them helps sort out the meaning.

Compare the "Star-Spangled Banner" with "America the Beautiful," by Katherine Lee Bates. Hold a class vote on which song the students like best and why they feel the way they do. A multicultural approach to North American national anthems makes a nice musical contrast. Play the national anthems of Canada ("O Canada") and Mexico ("Himno Nacional de Mexico"). Talk about the kinds of emotions different anthems evoke.

To further celebrate music (since March is also Music in Our Schools Month, see Idea 119), have some "state spirit" and find out if your state has an official state song (some do). If yours doesn't, your class could write the words for one. Start by brainstorming important features of your state. You might include some state symbols, such as the state bird, flower, etc.

For an even more relevant song, invite the high school band to pay a visit to your school. Chances are the high school has a school anthem. (But make sure they know you want the anthem, not the football fight song!) Encourage your students to appreciate the school spirit that such anthems inspire. Let the students write verses for a school song about your school. Middle and junior high students interested in music might try their hands at writing melodies; a music teacher might lend a hand.

(125)

Whoop It Up
for Whooping Cranes

Whooping Crane Spring Migration, Early March

At one time or another in their lives, most people have a dream in which they can fly. And the image of a fledgling leaving its nest is often used as a metaphor for young adults ready to begin lives away from their parents' home.

Watching birds fly can be inspiring. By placing food at feeders, wild birds are easily enticed to backyards and even school yards. Many sparrows and pigeons already make school buildings their homes. Sparrows often nest around light fixtures and alarm bells.

In recent years, the plight of the rare and endangered whooping crane has received national attention as well as federal legislation protecting it. The whooping crane is one of the rarest birds in the United States. This tall, graceful bird reaches an adult height of four to five feet (depending on the age you teach this may be many kids' height). Its long black-tipped white wings have a wingspan of six to eight feet. Whooping cranes and the more common sandhill crane are the only two species of crane that are native to the United States. Worldwide, there are fifteen species of cranes.

Scientists' efforts to save whooping cranes include removing one of the two eggs from nesting females (under normal circumstances only one chick usually survives) and artificially incubating the egg in the laboratory, where it can be protected from predators. Raising captive populations of whooping cranes and also establishing new wild populations have succeeded to some extent, but the whooping crane is still very rare.

Teaching sandhill cranes raised in captivity how to migrate is one of the goals of certain biologists and aviators. A pilot flies an ultra-light aircraft and leads young sandhill cranes from "nesting" areas in the north to Florida, a crane wintering habitat. The film *Fly Away Home* tells the story of a similar experience with Canada geese. If the Florida program proves successful, biologists hope to implement a similar plan for young whooping cranes.

The International Crane Foundation has an excellent website where you can hear the odd sound made by these incredible creatures. Check it out at savingcranes.org and be sure to visit the teacher center where you can download or order activity packets. Offerings may change, but the current packet is designed to be used before or after a field trip to a crane center but can also be adapted to general classroom use. Level I: "Chick Chat" is an introduction to cranes and includes puzzles, a coloring book, and a puppet. Level II: "Cranes, Kids and Wetlands" introduces cranes, their biology, and their ecosystems. Level III: "Cranes, Communities and Cultures" includes information from Level II as well as a focus on the role of humans. Level IV: "Crane Conservation" shows studies in crane behavior, the importance of genetic diversity, as well as the link between the activities of people and the survival of the species. You will find lots of other great stuff at this site too!

To learn about whooping crane conservation in the United States, contact the Whooping Crane Coordinator, U.S. Fish and Wildlife Service, P.O. Box 1306, Albuquerque, New Mexico 87103, or on the web at endangered.fws.gov/i/b/sab6t.html.

Many states are making efforts to restore displaced birds to their traditional native habitats. In Illinois, scientists were recently thrilled when they lured sandhill cranes back to an area of restored prairie. Encourage students to find newspaper and magazine articles that call attention to the birds in your area. How are people interacting with wild birds? Are there problems, or do birds and people seem to get along?

Carolrhoda Books' Nature Watch Series has an excellent book about cranes. *North American Cranes*, by Lesley Du Temple (1-57505-302-0, ages eight to twelve), contains information about the life cycles of these elegant birds and ecological threats to their survival. The National Audubon Society website (audubon.org) has much information on this and other birds.

126

Spring Tides

If you and your students live near the ocean, you may already be familiar with the topic of tides. Sea levels usually rise and fall in a predictable manner twice a day, a pattern known as tides. The study of the movement of water can be very interesting and can help inform students in a way that will make further study likely.

The gravitational pull of the moon and sun create heaping of water in the ocean. Think of water being pulled up toward the moon or sun as if a net was cast and pulled up toward the sky. The spring tide occurs when the sun and the moon are aligned with the earth at a new and full phase of the moon (it has nothing to do with the season of spring but comes from the German word *springen*—"to rise up"). Because they are both pulling together, this generates bigger-than-average tides. A lunar tidal wave travels a complete circuit around the confines of the ocean basin, sort of like a racetrack. It takes a lunar day to complete the cycle, which is twenty-four hours plus fifty minutes.

The other side of the spring tide is the neap tide, which happens when the moon is in its first quarter. This is generally a smaller and weaker tide. Here the moon and sun are pulling at right angles to each other. It takes about 14.75 days, a little more than two weeks, to move from spring to neap tide. The tidal differences between these two times can vary by about 30 percent. Students will appreciate a diagram or picture at this point. You may have one handy in a textbook, or there is a really nice illustration on page 9 of *The Incredible Journey to the Depths of Ocean*, by Nicholas Harris (Peter Bedrick Books, 0-87226-601-X, grades 5 to 8).

Older students can benefit from the math and science involved in predicting tidal behavior. You can find tidal predictions, real-time observations, and historical data from around the country at this government-sponsored site: opsd.nos.noad.gov/co-ops.html. Star Gardens offers activities for younger and older students at pbs.org

/oceanrealm/intheschoo/school8.html. Here students can use tidal tables to plot curves, and create a tidal calendar. A good site for middle schoolers is coast-nopp.org/toc.html, which also features a tide-tracking activity.

Of course, if you live near an ocean, you could calculate the next spring tide and then plan a class outing to observe a spring tide in action. Ask students to bring small notebooks, pencils, and rubber boots. You should bring a measuring tape, some garbage bags, and a stopwatch. Have students break into teams to predict how far the surf will come in or out while you are there, based on what they have studied about the action of tides.

If you need to occupy the class while awaiting the movement of the waves you can have them go on a "trash treasure hunt" on the beach and parking lot. Litter is a serious danger to sea life, and a group of children can make a big difference in just a few minutes. Perhaps the winning group of estimators or trash collectors could be allowed to choose their seats on the way home. The team whose estimate is off by the most can pick up any trash on the bus and haul it to a proper receptacle at school.

(127)

The Artist Inside You: Michelangelo

Birth, March 6, 1475

Michelangelo di Lodovico Buonarroti Simoni, born March 6, 1475, is an artist whose first name is recognized by almost everyone. While Michelangelo had a particular love of sculpting, he also painted spectacular pictures and was interested in architecture. One of his most famous works is the painting on the ceiling of the Sistine Chapel in Rome.

Art in the classroom lets creative students showcase and develop talents beyond academic abilities, which helps them gain self-confidence and earn peer respect. Celebrating Michelangelo's birthday offers many art possibilities for the classroom. March is also Youth Art Month. Pictures of Michelangelo's paintings and sculpture can be used to set up a mini art gallery. Students of all ages can experiment with clay, paint, ink, charcoal, chalk, and crayons and produce their own work. Older students may want to explore sculpture with soap (flakes and bar carving), wire, and papier-maché.

Freedom to choose among various media gives each student a greater chance of personal satisfaction. The truly adventurous may want to experiment by painting while lying on their backs, the way Michelangelo did while working on the Sistine Chapel. You can even have them work on the inside of large cardboard appliance boxes—these may be donated by parents or your local appliance sellers.

Completed student artwork can be displayed in the classroom or in display cases throughout the building, simultaneously celebrating Michelangelo's birthday and Youth Art Month.

Michelangelo is especially noted for his portrayal of the human body. His human figures are restrained, yet show considerable animation because Michelangelo made a practice of studying anatomy. This dovetails nicely with science curriculum units on the human body. Make the connection between muscle structure and how Michelangelo uses it to give life to their figures. Encourage students to draw a picture of their own hand, showing how their bones and muscles stand out.

For a look at Michelangelo's playful side try *Michelangelo's Surprise*, by Tony Parillo (Farrar Straus Giroux, 0-374-34961-4, preschool to grade 3). Mike Venezia's *Michelangelo* (Children's Press, 0-5164-2293-6, grades K to 2) is a biography and contains illustrations of Michelangelo's paintings and sculptures. This book is from the Getting to Know the World's Great Artists series. *Muscles*, by Seymour Simon (Morrow, 0-688-14642-2, grades 3 and up), nicely complements the science connection.

128

Deaf History Month

March 13 to April 15

The "baby boomers" are getting older. And with age come joys (grand-parenting) and woes (bifocals). Many children will have older family members and friends who may be experiencing some hearing loss. This can be frustrating for all concerned. The last half of March and the first half of April are specially designated for learning about deafness.

Older children can understand the phrase "enunciate clearly." Lessons on sound wavelengths are really helpful at the middle school and junior high levels. As part of the science curriculum, you might study sound waves and how they move. (Sound waves must travel through a medium of some kind.) Also, let students research what sound ranges a person is likely to lose first. (High frequencies such as bird calls, a higher-pitched child's voice, and the beginning conso-nants sounds of "s," "t," or "p.")

Older children can also think about how hearing loss may distort a person's perception of a conversation. For example, a question like, "Do you like the speeches?" might be answered with, "Yes, I like peaches." Both parties may chuckle when the confusion is sorted out. But it's sad if neither party realizes the problem is hearing related. The "off-base" response may be mistakenly interpreted as a sign of senility.

Try incorporating a lesson in rhyme for younger children. This blends in well because it can be combined with Poetry Month (April), or used as a preparation before it. Start by choosing a simple word, such as *cat*. Talk about the difficulty people with a hearing loss might have hearing this word. Discuss how mishearing the first letter eas-ily creates a completely different word. List words that are formed by changing only the first letter of *cat*.

In small groups or pairs, do the same exercise with words of two or more syllables, which the students have chosen. Students should write the initial word at the top of each sheet of paper and list the rhyming words below. When reading the lists aloud, you can define the word *rhyme* and ask if anyone can think of a kind of writer who would welcome lists like the ones the students have just completed. The neat thing is, in addition to gaining a better understanding (and hopefully, more tolerance) of the stress of hearing loss, the class will have generated its own *Classroom Rhyming Dictionary*, which can be bound and distributed for use during Poetry Month. Think of several catchy titles for the new book and let the class vote on which one they want to use.

For a historical focus, you might want to discuss Ludwig van Beethoven (1770–1827) and play some of the music he wrote. He began going deaf in his early thirties and continued to compose beautiful new music after becoming completely deaf several years later. You might also feature music performed by Evelyn Glennie, a present-day percussionist who happens to be hearing impaired.

Teachers looking for lesson plans won't be disappointed with offerings on the web. Try pbs.org/wnet/soundandfury/lesson1.html for starters or use an advanced Google search with these words: *science, deafness, lesson plan*. Or you can use: *history, deafness, lesson plan*. You get the idea. There are many, many excellent teaching tools for those wishing to include deafness information in their classes. You may also wish to have a deaf person and an interpreter visit your class. If you go this route, be sure to have a classroom discussion ahead of time to generate questions, and include reminders of how to be a polite audience. If you live in a large city you may also be able to invite a trainer of companion animals to bring in a dog who is learning to assist a person with hearing loss.

(129)

National Agriculture Week

Annually, the Week That Includes the First Day of Spring

The beginning of spring marks National Agriculture Week. In an era when fewer and fewer kids are growing up on farms, it is becoming ever more important for teachers to help impart the understanding of how food is grown, sold, and ultimately ends up on our tables.

You can observe this week with an experiment. Have students plant three bean seeds early in the week before National Agriculture Week. The first will be placed on top of several layers of damp paper towels in the bottom of a paper cup. The towels must be kept moist, so water them daily. The second seed should be planted in soil and watered as necessary. The third seed should be planted in soil and be watered and fed with a plant fertilizer. Students can hypothesize about the results.

During Agriculture Week the seeds will sprout. Students can measure, draw, and note changes they observe over the next few weeks. Have them answer the question, Do fertilizers make a difference? For ideas about other plant-related activities, see *Garden Wizardry for Kids*, by L. Patricia Kite (Barron's, 0-8120-1317-4, grades 4 to 6), which describes more than three hundred projects.

A geographical focus could include mapping the areas of the country that supply your region with the meat and produce your students eat. *Harvest Year*, by Cris Peterson (Boyds Mills Press, 1-56397-571-8, grades K to 3), uses maps and photographs to show that every month something is being harvested somewhere in the United States. What is the most important agricultural product grown in your state? Other topics to explore this week include: getting food to the marketplace; family farms versus large corporate farms; and organic farming versus use of herbicides and pesticides. Books like *The American Family Farm: A Photo Essay*, by George Ancona and Joan Anderson (Harcourt Brace, 0-15-203025-5, grades 4 to 6), will help introduce farming to urban children. *Farms Feed the World*, by Lee S. Hill (Carolrhoda, 1-57505-075-7, grades K to 3), describes different types of farms. *Becoming Felix*, by Nancy Hope Wilson (Farrar Straus Giroux, 0-374-30664-8, grades 4 to 7), is a novel about a family's struggle to maintain their farm.

A related holiday in March is the birthday of Cesar Chavez (March 31), a Mexican American who founded the first union for farm workers in the United States. *Cesar Chavez: A Photo-Illustrated Biography*, by Lucile Davis (Bridgestone, 1-56065-569-0, grades 2 to 4), and *Farmer's Friend: The Story of Cesar Chavez*, by David R. Collins (Carolrhoda, 1-57505-031-5, grades 4 to 7), are two biographies with information for young readers.

A discussion of world hunger would be an appropriate side issue for older classes this week. Ask students why there is hunger in the world and post the list of answers. Most people (including adults) do not realize that more than enough food is grown every year to feed everyone on the planet, but that wars, politics, and economics create major distribution roadblocks so that food does not always get where it is most needed. Discuss how communities and individuals can make changes that would impact hunger in your town and in the world at large.

⬭130⬭

Lois Lowry

Birth, March 20, 1937

Two-time recipient of the Newbery Award, Lois Lowry wrote books that are among the most widely read (and loved) books in children's literature. *Number the Stars* (Bantam, 0-440-40327-8, ages nine to twelve), one of her Newbery Award books, is a riveting tale of Denmark during World War II. Supplement this book with *Darkness Over Denmark*, by Ellen Levine (Holiday House, 0-8234-1447-7, ages ten and up), a nonfiction account of young people in Denmark during WWII.

Lowry writes equally well when the setting is contemporary. Her talent for writing realistic and funny contemporary dialog makes her Anastasia Krupnik books shine (and those about Anastasia's brother Sam, too). *A Summer to Die* (Bantam, 0-440-21917-5, ages twelve and up), another of Lowry's contemporary novels, is an outstanding story of a young girl's relationship with her terminally ill older sister. Give this book to Lurlene McDaniel fans.

Lowry's novel *The Giver* (Bantam, 0-440-21907-8, ages twelve and up), her second Newbery Award book, may be her best known. She explores what determines the value of human life in a technologically advanced, futuristic fictional society. A junior high literature group could have a challenging and totally engrossing discussion comparing the societies and relationships in *The Giver* with those in Monica Hughes's *Invitation to the Game* (Simon and Schuster, 0-671-86692-3, ages twelve and up). Hughes's book is a futuristic survival story, and its dark, rough society will provide many points of comparison and contrast with the seemingly idyllic society found in *The Giver*.

Readers who love both these books may want to read Lowry's *Gathering Blue* (Houghton Mifflin, 0-618-05581-9, ages twelve and up). It is a story of a parallel society, set in the same time as *The Giver*, but this novel focuses on artistic repression in a culture where technology is almost absent.

For biographical material on Lois Lowry, see Gale's *Something About the Author* series, available in most libraries. It contains many anecdotes about Lowry's life and several photographs. *Lois Lowry*, by Lois Markham (Creative Teaching Press, 0-8816-0278-7, ages eight to twelve), is a "stand-alone" biography.

⟨131⟩

Randolph Caldecott

Birth, March 22, 1846; Youth Art Month, March

Randolph Caldecott was born in Chester, England, on March 22, 1846. He is remembered for his lively illustration of children's books. Caldecott's work drew the attention of the general public to the charm and value of illustrated children's books. During the seventeenth and eighteenth centuries, children were regarded as little adults, and were expected to help the family by working at home, and often by the age of eight were working jobs in factories, farms, shops, or mines.

By the latter part of the nineteenth century, society's views had altered and childhood was starting to be accepted as a playing and learning time. Caldecott's artistic style was well suited to the new concept of children's literature as a pleasurable, rather than didactic or educational, experience. His humorous pictures held great appeal for young readers.

The Caldecott Medal is awarded in the United States by the American Library Association to the illustrator of the most distinguished picture book for children published in the preceding year. The award was named in recognition of Randolph Caldecott's contribution to the field of picture books and children's book illustration.

Caldecott's illustrations can be found in many collections published by Frederick Warne, including *The Randolph Caldecott Treasury*. Although they may be out of print, they should be available in public library collections. *Randolph Caldecott: The Children's Illustrator*, by Marguerite Lewis (Highsmith, 0-913853-22-4, grades 2 to 7), is a biography.

March is also Youth Art Month. One way to celebrate this month and Caldecott's birthday is by focusing on children's book illustration. *What Do Illustrators Do?* by Eileen Christelow (Clarion, 0-395-90230-4, grades 1 to 4), provides a nice overview of how illustrators work. Pat Cummings has edited a three-volume collection, published by

Simon and Schuster, titled *Talking with Artists*. Barbara Elleman's *Tomie dePaola: His Art and His Stories* (Putnam, 0-399-23129-3) is a retrospective study of the work of the popular children's book author and illustrator. *A Caldecott Celebration: Six Authors Share Their Paths to the Caldecott Medal*, by Leonard Marcus (Walker, 0-8027-8656-1), focuses on how six children's illustrators created their award-winning books.

Ask students to bring in their favorite picture book (perhaps even one from when they were tots) and to tell why they liked the pictures in it. To begin your celebration of illustration, choose a selection of Caldecott Medal books from various years. Arrange them in chronological order around the front of the room. Ask students, as a class, to talk about the illustrations in each book, starting with the oldest example. Note their comments on the overhead or blackboard. One of the changes students will note is the development of the four-color printing process and how it altered the look of picture books. *Color*, by Ruth Heller (Putnam, 0-399-22815-2, grades 2 to 6), will be helpful to explain the process.

Next, explore different artistic media and styles. Categorize a selection of books by medium: paint, pencil, collage, printmaking, photography, and computer-generated art. Another way to categorize is by choosing a selection based on artistic style, including representations of realistic, cartoon, impressionistic, and abstract illustrations. Let students create their own artwork by making classroom books to reflect each artistic style.

Talk about representing emotion or physical movement in illustration and how the different styles may be used effectively. Above all, stress that art and illustration should engage readers and make them want to become involved in the reading/looking experience. For a larger connection to the art world, students may compare artistic styles found in children's book illustration with famous works by the grand masters of the art world at large.

(132)

Make Up
Your Own Holiday

Make Up Your Own Holiday Day, March 26

Here's a chance for your students to create their own holidays. Let imaginations run wild and design the perfect holiday. Perhaps you can interest students in designing two holidays: one could be their own personal celebration; the second could be curriculum oriented. Is there a time of the year that seems short in holidays?

For math, students might designate the day by the current topic under instruction. They might create a character who invented addition, subtraction, etc. Make up a silly interview with him or her and find out why the person invented those math functions.

For social studies, chose a famous local historical figure and give him or her a holiday, including suggestions for all the trimmings such as food and festive events. Choose music that would be appropriate to the time period to create atmosphere.

Declare the day "Our Classroom Rules Day" and let students write short poems, raps, or jump rope chants that tells why your class is the best in the school.

Each student can draw or write a poster that describes his or her special holiday. They should include the background of the holiday and any traditions, foods, or special celebrations (fireworks?) that they would like to see accompany it. They should explain why the day has been set aside as a holiday. What activities do they suggest people do in observation of this day? Students might want to make greeting cards that celebrate their holidays.

Stimulate ideas by discussing some of the special events mentioned in this book. Discuss different traditions that are associated with various holidays and how they are celebrated in different regions of the United States or the world. You might also consider bringing in a few general holiday books that feature multicultural events. To explore similarities and differences around the world, a great choice is the book *Children Just Like Me: Celebrations!*, by Anabel Kindersley (DK Publishing, 0789-420-279, ages eight to twelve).

(133)

Earthquake!

Earthquake Strikes Alaska, March 27, 1964

On March 27, 1964, the worst earthquake in recent U.S. history occurred. Thousands of earthquakes take place every day all over the world, but most of them are too minor to be sensed without technical equipment like a seismograph. However, in the last decade, major earthquakes in southern California, Japan, and Turkey have shown how dangerous quakes can be.

Ask your students where the worst earthquakes in the United States have occurred, and they will probably say California. Actually, Alaska has been the site of some of the world's worst earthquakes in terms of magnitude. The U.S. Geological Survey's National Earthquake Information Center has loads of information about quakes. Go to neic.cr.usgs.gov and click on General Earthquake Information.

Looking at a list of the worst earthquakes of the past century or decade, your students might notice that the quakes with the highest scores on the Richter scale don't necessarily cause the largest number of deaths. Brainstorm about why more people died in the Mexico City earthquake than in the worst earthquake of the twentieth century in Chile. Discuss such things as population density and the quality of building construction. Compare the San Francisco quake of 1989 and the one in Turkey in 1999. These are both densely populated areas. Why the difference in the number of people killed? If any of your students has a parent who is in the field of building inspection or construction ask if he or she will talk about building codes.

With older students, discuss the Richter scale and the fact that it is not arithmetic but logarithmic. That means an earthquake of 8 on the Richter scale is not twice as strong as one that is a 4 on the scale but is several hundreds times stronger. The National Earthquake Information site has information explaining this.

Discuss earthquake safety with your students; even if you don't live in an area that is prone to earthquakes, your students may vacation or ultimately live in such a place. For more information, go to the Red Cross site at crossnet.org/disaster/safety/earth.html. This website is also available in Spanish.

There are many good books on earthquakes. Here's a list to get you started: *Earthquakes*, by Seymour Simon (Morrow, 0-6880-9633-6, preschool to grade 3); *Quakes!*, by Catherine McMorrow (Random House, 0-679-96945-4, grades 1 to 5); *Earthquakes*, by Sally M. Walker (Carolrhoda, 0-8761-4888-7, grades 4 to 7); or *Earthquakes and Volcanoes*, by Lin Sutherland (Readers Digest, 1-5758-4380-3, grades 4 to 7).

(134)

Joseph Haydn

Birth, March 31, 1732

Joseph Haydn was born on March 31, 1732, in Rohrau, Austria. While a young boy, he sang as a soprano in the choir at Saint Stephen's Cathedral in Vienna. Later, he worked as a music teacher. He studied music with Nicola Porpora, an Italian composer.

In 1760, Haydn was hired by the Hungarian Esterházy Princes. Haydn served as their resident composer for thirty years, providing the music for their church services and for their entertainment. During his career, Haydn composed hundreds of works that included vocal music, orchestral pieces, two dozen operas, and chamber music. Haydn died on May 31, 1809.

While working for Prince Nikolaus, Haydn and the other court musicians resided at Esterháza, the family's royal retreat. The musicians were not allowed to bring family members along with them. This caused familial strife as the days, weeks, and months wore on keeping the musicians away from their homes. The musicians reported their grievances to Haydn, who spoke with Prince Nikolaus. Nikolaus turned a deaf ear to the musicians' requests to go home. In response, Haydn wrote his Symphony no. 45, named *The Farewell Symphony*. In this piece, the musicians leave the stage one at a time, each blowing out a candle as he departs. At the symphony's end, the stage is left dark and deserted. Supposedly, the tone of the music and the empty stage conveyed the message to Prince Nikolaus. He ordered the court to pack up and return to their normal homes.

Anna Celenza has written a fun and informative children's picture book that explains the background of Haydn's life and the story behind *The Farewell Symphony*. Her book, entitled *The Farewell Symphony* (Charlesbridge, 1-5709-1406-0, ages five and up), comes with a CD that contains the symphony and another of Haydn's works.

Celebrate Haydn's birthday by sharing his symphony and a really neat story with your students. It's a lot more interesting than singing "Happy Birthday."

(135)

Meeting the Inuit

Nunavut Created, April 1, 1999

Take this opportunity to help your class understand an important group of people who live in the snowy reaches of this continent and in Greenland—the Inuit. Start first with the issue of the name. *Inuit* means "the people" and is much preferred over the term *Eskimo*, which was a name given the Inuit by a group of what Canadians call "First People," a term equivalent to "Native American" in meaning in the United States. The Athabaskan people called the Inuit "raw meat eaters" in their tongue, and arriving Europeans soon followed suit. Therefore, start by asking students to toss the term *Eskimo* in the trash heap of old, not-so-nice names for people and start with a new and better name. Ask for a brainstorming session to see what they think of when they think of the Inuit. Perhaps they will think of igloos, dog sleds, rubbing noses instead of kissing, and so forth. All these things still exist, but are now accompanied by little houses made of modern materials, snow machines (snowmobiles), and western-style handshakes. Most Inuit live in two worlds.

This is an exciting time to be Inuit. In April of 1999 the government of Canada and the people of the large areas to the west and north of Hudson Bay finally signed an agreement making Nunavet (which means "our land") a native-controlled territory of approximately 250,000 square miles in Canada. The people will be able to make important decisions on how this land is administered and will have more opportunity to rediscover their heritage. Greenland released the Inuit in their country to home rule in 1979, after which point the Inuit withdrew from the European Union.

Who are these people? The ancestors of today's Inuit have been hunting and fishing the icy reaches of the Arctic for thousands of years. They divided eventually into two main groups: the Yupik, who live in Siberia and western Alaska; and the Inupiaq, who occupy eastern Alaska, Greenland, and parts of Canada. The rest of the world and the dwellers of the far north had little contact until the landing of Erik the Red, a Viking, on Greenland in 983 A.D. Other early explorers also visited in the sixteenth century but did not stay. The people continued in their traditional ways, following game and fishing until quite recently. Caribou, whale, seal, walrus, birds, fish, and berries all played important roles in the native diet.

Contact in the last 150 years or more with European explorers, missionaries, and settlers caused many problems for the Inuit. New diseases and foods ill suited to the climate decimated some populations. Missionaries converted people to different religions, thereby destroying the traditions of song, dance, and story that carried the history of the people as well as the ways of doing important tasks like hunting, building shelters, and relating to others. Recently, pollution from city populations far away has spread into the formerly clean Arctic making some animals and fish toxic to eat. Despite all of this the Inuit continue, and many are working to be sure the coming generations learn the important languages, songs, and skills that will help them thrive well into the future.

Inuit people live in a part of the world where it is hard work just to stay alive. They are hardworking people but also love to play games, socialize with friends and family, make music, and have fun. Have you ever seen a picture of an Inuit blanket-toss game? It is like a trampoline except your friends toss you up in the air on a leather blanket. Some old games have changed little in thousands of years and are easy to play in a classroom. Here is a variety to get your class having fun. Inuit people sometimes play string games. Do any of your children know the string figure we often call "witch's broom"? It is very close to one *ajarraaq* (string puzzle) that the Inuit know as "the tent." Many games are a test of strength and skill, and some of them are really tough. Leg wrestling is a lot like arm wrestling except the contestants lie on the ground head to toe, side by side. They hook legs and see who can pull the other person's leg to the floor.

Another test of skill that is always good for a laugh often involves husbands and wives, but can be played with any team. Traditionally, the men stand a certain number of paces away from the women, who hold up a sewing needle. The men each have a piece of thread. They race to their wife and try to thread her needle. Much merriment ensues as the men tend to have a pretty hard time with a task the women would be handy at. The first man to thread the needle wins.

For the next game you will need a sawed-off broom handle about twelve inches in length. Pairs of students should stand close to each other, each on a piece of tape marking where his or her feet are to stay. The two students each grab an end of the handle and pull or push, trying to make the other contestant lose his or her balance and step off the mark or release the stick. The winner should have the stick at the end but not have left the foot marker.

Balls made of seal bladders, jacks made of bones from a flipper, and many other toys were created from materials close at hand. Today's Inuit kids are likely to have rubber balls and Frisbees and such, and still excel at games of speed and agility. Recently computer distance learning has been introduced into some of the truly isolated villages, so now students will be playing many of the same computer games students in the lower parts of the continent enjoy.

For an interesting and easy craft project, try making eye protectors, which were worn before the advent of sunglasses to protect eyes from snow blindness. If you have a nice sunny day you can even go outside and see how they work. Take any stiff paper or lightweight cardboard and have students fashion a small strip and attach string to go around their head. Have them mark slits that will be made for each eye. The teacher can cut the slits if students are too young for tricky cutting. Eye slits need to be less than one-quarter inch wide and just a little longer across than the eye. During the summer in the far north the sun shines almost all day and night, and anyone traveling on the bright white snow pack will experience sunburn on exposed skin and may even have temporary blindness from the glare of sun on snow and ice.

An excellent guide to the Inuit called *What Do We Know About the Inuit?*, by Bryan and Cherry Alexander, is part of the well-constructed What Do We Know series by Peter Bedrick Books (0-87226-380-0, grades 5 to 8). Another book that tells interested students quite a lot about the Inuit is *Exploring the Polar Regions*, by Jen Green (Peter Bedrick Books, 0-87226-489-0, grades 5 to 8). The government of Nunavut has an informative website at gov.nu.ca.

136

April Foolin'

April Is Humor Month

There's nothing like a good story. And if it's a humorous one . . . why then it makes our hearts lighter. Tall tales have a larger-than-life quality that can't help but bring a smile to our faces. The exaggerations found in tall tales cross over into the outlandish, and that makes them all the more appealing. Why not feature tall tale read-alouds in your classroom this month? There are a number of picture books that students from kindergarten through high school will enjoy. Junior high and high school students may groan at first, but they'll secretly be entertained. And collections of tall tales from lands other than the United States are becoming more widely available.

It's easy to find tall tales that will blend right into curriculum content areas. American history is chock full of figures who have become larger than life. *The Narrow Escapes of Davy Crockett*, by Ariane Dewey (out of print, but available in library collections, ages eight to ten), and *Pecos Bill*, by Steven Kellogg (Penguin, ages six to eight), chronicle the adventures of two well-known American folk legends. *Will Rogers: Larger than Life*, by Debbie Dadey (Walker, 0-8027-8681-2, all ages), features the adventures of one of America's best-loved humorists. For a tall tale about a woman see Anne Isaacs' *Swamp Angel* (Penguin, 0-14-055908-6, all ages).

Heat Wave, by Helen Ketteman (Walker, 0-8027-7577-2, all ages), and *Chinook*, by Michael O. Tunnell (out of print, but available in library collections, all ages), are two way-out tales that will complement weather units.

Collections that contain selections suitable for reading aloud include: *McBroom's Wonderful One Acre Farm*, by Sid Fleischman (Morrow, 0-688-15595-2, ages eight and up); Mary Pope Osborne's *American Tall Tales* (Knopf, 0-679-80089-1, ages nine to twelve); and *Cut from the Same Cloth: American Women of Myth, Legend, and Tall*

Tale, by Robert San Souci (Putnam, 0-698-11811-1, ages eight and up). After reading aloud several tall tales discuss what elements they have in common. Most tall tales, while "over-the-top," are not mean-spirited in nature.

Have fun writing tall tales as a small-group exercise—it spreads the humor. You might suggest students try creating a group of tall tales that feature prominent early settlers of your area, well-known regional landmarks, imaginary area crops, or local industry.

Many more tall tale books are available in your public library. Oddly enough, most of them will be found in the nonfiction stacks. Ask your librarian.

(137)

Math Fun

Mathematics Education Month, April

Focus on incorporating fun math activities into the daily classroom routine. Primary students can create ongoing addition problems centered around the date. For example:

April 1 = 1 + 0; April 2 = 1 + 1 or 2 + 0; April 14 = 7 + 7, 10 + 4, 8 + 6, etc.

Challenge students to see how many different sums they can find for each day. The same exercise can be extended as multiplication problems for third and fourth grade students.

Explore numbering systems used by different cultures. *The History of Counting*, by Denise Schmandt-Besserat (Morrow, 0-688-14118-8, grades 5 to 8), discusses and presents the history of several different counting systems. *How Tall, How Short, How Faraway?*, by David Adler (Holiday, 0-8234-1375-6, grades 1 to 4), also looks at number systems, but is intended for a much younger audience. It encourages experimentation, measuring, and calculation. *Math Games and*

Activities from Around the World, by Claudia Zaslavsky (Chicago Review Press, 1-55652-287-8, grades 3 to 7), is a multicultural collection that even offers activities from ancient Egypt.

Talk about base two or binary counting and how computers use this system to encode information. Students might want to try converting familiar numbers—their age, weight, or birth date, etc.—into base two numbers. Try keeping score in gym class in a new numbering system. *Reader's Digest*, in conjunction with many educational experts, has a big, colorful, and very engaging book called *How Math Works: 100 Ways Parents and Kids Can Share the Wonders of Mathematics* (0-7621-0233-0, all ages). It has information and activities on all sorts of aspects of math including different cultures, different base systems, and quite a lot of history. If your school doesn't own it, perhaps you could request it via interlibrary loan. It is a perfect book to have on hand as you celebrate math.

Huge numbers don't have to be intimidating. *On Beyond a Million*, by David Schwartz (Bantam, 0-385-32217-8, grades 1 to 5), helps explain exponential notation and the importance of zero as a placeholder. Older readers will find *G is for Googol*, by David Schwartz (Tricycle, 1-8836-7258-9, grades 5 and up), contains many terms and definitions used in higher levels of math.

Playing games with numbers is a great way to cure "math block." *25 Super Cool Math Board Games*, by Loraine Egan (Scholastic, 0-590-37872-4, grades 3 to 6); *Math Games for Middle Schoolers*, by Mario Salvadori (Chicago Review Press, 1-55652-288-6, grades 6 to 9); *Logic Posters, Problems and Puzzles*, by Honi Bamberger (Scholastic, 0-590-64273-1, grades 3 to 6); and *Counting Caterpillars and Other Math Poems*, by Betsy Franco (Scholastic, 0-590-64210-3, grades K to 2), are all books that incorporate different levels of the math curriculum and emphasize having fun with math.

138

More Fun with Math

Mathematics Education Month, April

Make enjoyable math activities the focus this month. Primary students can work as partners and take turns acting as storekeepers and customers. Give students play money to "purchase" items they would regularly use for the day in class: paper, books from the classroom library, scissors, or paste. Prices should reflect amounts that will lead to the most student success, depending on the purpose of the lesson. In first grade, prices might be the face value of coins. For higher levels of interaction, set amounts at prices that will require making change.

Use data from attendance records and cafeteria lunch choices to work with bar graphs and percentages. The same can be done with class polls on favorite foods, singers, stories, or school subjects.

Calculators provide hours of entertainment. *Calculator Riddles*, by David Adler (Holiday House, 0-8234-1186-9, grades 3 to 7), is informative and fun. Adler gives a key to turning numbers into letters so you can encourage students to invent their own riddles. Here is a quick example: "What is Little Bo Peep's middle name?" Answer: 10 times 10 divided by 125 equals "BO." You get this answer by turning the calculator upside down so that numbers appear as letters. This is a very fun way for students to learn their way around the calculator, and it may even give you the opportunity to explain what the symbols mean to younger children so that they aren't so mysterious.

Language arts blends into the math curriculum when you incorporate books like *Hickory Dickory Math: Teaching Math with Nursery Rhymes and Fairy Tales*, by Cecilia Dinio-Durkin (Scholastic, 0-590-06541-6, grades K to 2), *Marvelous Math: A Book of Poems*, selected by Lee B. Hopkins (Simon and Schuster, 0-68-980658-2, all ages), and *Mother Goose Math*, by Emily Bolam (Viking, 0-67-087569-4, preschool to grade 2). Have students write and publish a classroom book of math poetry. For additional book suggestions, consult *Read Any Good Math Lately? Children's Books for Mathematical Learning*, by David J. Whitin and Sandra Wilde (Heinemann, 0-435-08334-1), and *Math Through Children's Literature: Making the NCTM Standards Come Alive*, by Kathryn L. Braddon, Nancy J. Hall, and Dale Taylor (Teacher Ideas Press, 0-87287-932-1).

Divide students into groups and ask them to brainstorm about the places they use math without realizing it. Examples could include the room's clock, a pizza, and shoe sizes. If you have any reluctant math learners turn them toward a very funny and educational math activity book called *I Hate Math*, by Marilyn Burns (Little, Brown and Co., 0-316-11741-2, all ages). It features delightful illustrations and terrific ideas for kids to use to stump the grownups in their lives (so you better read it first!), and even a way to get out of drying dishes.

The Math Forum is a website with links to math education materials for teachers at all levels at forum.swarthmore.edu. One feature of this site is MathMagic, a project that uses E-mail to help students engage in a problem-solving dialogue with children at another school. MathMagic posts challenges in each of four categories (grades K–3, 4–6, 7–9, and 10–12). A team of students works via E-mail with a team at another school to solve the problem. Go to forum.swarthmore.edu/mathmagic to learn more.

Four Weeks of Poetry

National Poetry Month, April

To have a monthlong celebration of poetry, categorize poetry into four thematic groups, one for each week. The first week, focus on the elements of poetry. Explore topics like meaning, rhythm, sound patterns, figurative language, and sensory images. Robert Frost's "The Road Not Taken" is a thought-provoking poem for discussing meaning. Sound patterns include rhyme, onomatopoeia, alliteration, and consonance. There are many examples of these scattered throughout poetry collections. Try David McCord's "Song of the Train" for a great example of a speeding train. Figurative language—the use of similes and metaphors, personification and hyperbole—and sensory images also are found in many collections. Read through several volumes of children's poetry; personal taste will help you find poems that best illustrate these elements for your students.

The second week focus on story poems (long narratives that tell a story). Narrative poems students usually enjoy include "The Shooting of Dan McGrew" and "The Cremation of Sam McGee," by Robert Service; "The Highwayman," by Alfred Noyes; and "The Raven," by Edgar Allan Poe. All of them are lovely for reading aloud or arranged as choral readings. *The Illiad* and *The Odyssey* are suitable for upper junior high and high school readers, but it may take some students a while to work through them.

During the third week read humorous poetry. This lighthearted look at poetry ties in beautifully with April is Humor Month. Shel Silverstein, Jack Prelutsky, Edward Lear, Bruce Lansky, and David Harrison have written collections of humorous poetry for children. Share them with each other in the classroom. Talk about what makes them funny. Suggest students read them aloud with their families. Encourage students to recall humorous family moments and then write them up as a silly poem. Calvin and Hobbs books usually contain at least one or two funny poems Calvin writes on the topic of his stuffed tiger Hobbs. Ask kids if they own any of these collections, or borrow from your library so you can read them aloud.

For the fourth week feature different kinds of poetry on successive days. Topics could include haiku, limericks, nursery rhymes, and concrete poems. Or you might want to feature poems about different subjects—trees, flowers, math, animals, science, etc.

Several noteworthy new books of poetry for children are: *Relatively Speaking*, by Ralph Fletcher (Orchard, 0-531-33141-5, grades 3 to 9); *Old Elm Speaks*, by Kristine O'Connell George (Clarion, 0-395-87611-7, grades K to 5)—see reference in next section for more details; *Touch the Poem*, by Arnold Adoff (Scholastic, 0-590-47970-9, grades 2 to 7); *Flicker Flash*, by Joan Graham (Houghton, 0-395-90501-X, grades 1 to 4); and *Classic Poetry: An Illustrated Collection*, selected by Michael Rosen (Candlewick, 1-56402-890-9, grades 5 and up).

(140)

Poetry Wind Sock

National Poetry Month, April

Poems. Words that touch your heart, resound inside your head, tickle your funny bone, or maybe bring a tear to your eyes. Poems may be highly personal and may often reflect the poet's intimate relationship with the subject. The best poetry takes the reader to a new level of understanding and pushes him or her to look at life—an object, an emotion, an experience—in a new and different way.

Memorizing poetry can be a special part of the experience. Memorizing need not be a chore, especially when the child finds a poem that means something to him or her. *Poetry by Heart*, selected by Liz Attenborough (Scholastic, 0-439-29357-9, all ages), contains simple rhymes for young listeners and more complicated, classic poems for older readers. All are easily committed to memory and are fun to share. If your local high school has a forensics team, see if students who are competing in the poetry division could visit your class to talk about memorizing and performing poetry at contests.

In addition to memorizing a poem, one of the best ways to "keep" a poem is by letting it sail away. Let each student create a poetry "wind sock." First, make a number of poetry books available to your students. Ask each student to find a poem he or she likes. Next, make the wind sock. Use small brown paper lunch bags. Reinforce the bottom of the bag with a rectangle of cardboard glued to the inside. Cut a hole through the center of the rectangle and the bottom of the bag for air flow.

Anchor string around the cardboard rectangle in at least two places. Students can then decorate the outside of the bag with a painting or drawing that illustrates the poems they have chosen, or just colorful artwork. Cut the open edge of the bag into narrow strips to create the wind sock effect.

Have each student copy his or her poem on a small piece of light-colored construction paper. Let students decide on the shapes—they don't have to stick with plain old rectangles! Glue the poem to the space near the top of the wind sock (the end where the string pokes through).

Take them outside on a breezy day. As students move with out-stretched arms, the breeze will lift the wind socks like low-flying kites. Take turns reading the poems aloud and talk about the images children see when each poem is read. Encourage students to memorize one of the "flying" poems they have heard and enjoyed.

(141)

Go for the Goal

Now that your school year is coming to an end it may be a good time to revisit your classroom goals from August. Have you achieved most of what you hoped? If not, what went awry? Encourage students to think back (or look back if their ideas were recorded) to what they were hoping to accomplish this school year. Perhaps it is time to set new goals. Host a goal-setting workshop in your class this week.

First of all make sure everyone really understands what a goal is. Remind students that a goal should be something specific they want to do that is achievable, personally meaningful, and realistic. A goal should have some sort of completion time attached to it. Goals work best if they are written down. Writing a goal down helps clarify it and makes it more solid in the writer's mind. Goals should be simple. If the goal is too complex, help the student break the goal into defined pieces that go in some sort of order.

Goals are easier to achieve if the goal setter identifies certain times for specific activities that will foster attainment of the goal. For instance, if a student wants to have no cavities by her next dentist visit, she might decide to spend an extra five minutes each night and morning on brushing and flossing, or to carry a toothbrush and brush after lunch. Students must understand that planning is the key to success in many arenas.

Another key for success in attaining goals, once they are recorded, is to see if it is the kind of goal someone else might have too. The "buddy system" makes working toward goals fun. Having a friend working on the same issues also makes it more likely for a person to stick with his or her efforts. The buddy system is a key factor in many lifestyle changes, for instance, because making changes is hard for human beings and we all need extra support when we reach for a goal.

If you and your students have recorded previous goals, take some time to monitor the progress. Monitoring should go on periodically and not be left to the end since goal work should allow for mishaps, mistakes, missteps, and so forth. Each time there is a setback there is an opportunity to rethink the methods being used to reach the goal. Take advantage of every problem to talk about the goal and what can be done to get back on track. The universe is always generous in providing shake-ups, mayhem, and chaos . . . what we do from there is up to us.

Middle schoolers and up will enjoy this slim volume because in addition to good basic goal information it is filled with interesting anecdotes: *Winners for Life: A Teenager's Guide to Success Using the Proven Power of Goal Setting*, by Donny Anderson and Linkie Seltzer Cohn (Winners for Life, 096505400, young adult). Many teachers swear it is magic for teens. Also a popular choice for teens is this book: *What Do You Really Want? How to Set a Goal and Go for It*, by Beverly Bachel (Free Spirit, 1575420856, young adult).

(142)

Marvelous Metrics

Anniversary of Adoption of Metric System in France, April 7, 1795

The United States is the only industrialized country in the world that hasn't switched to the metric system. Though Congress passed the Metric Conversion Act in 1975, this system has been implemented only to a limited extent in the United States. Don't leave your students clueless when it comes to the metric system; as the world shrinks we will need to be prepared to use and understand the metric system, if only when we are dealing with other countries as business partners or when on holiday.

Converting height into centimeters always amuses children, whose size suddenly seems astronomical. Calculate and post classroom dimensions, measure desktops, have a recess ten-meter dash or meter high jump. Sports fans can figure the metric height of a basketball backboard, a football field, or a baseball diamond.

Have fun with food measurements. Convert the ounces from soda cans and milk cartons into liters. Conversely, convert a liter soft drink bottle into ounces. Many food products today note both the customary and metric measure—have students look for examples at home and in the supermarket.

Car speeds zoom into high numbers when expressed as kilometers per hour. Don't forget about Celsius degrees. What happens to the boiling and freezing points of water? What is a normal human body temperature? Here is one place where our goofy system of measurement actually seems to be better: the Celsius scale on thermometers is less accurate than the temperature expressed in Fahrenheit degrees.

Many Americans do use the metric system in their jobs on a daily basis. Discuss some occupations that use the metric system (engineers, chemists, and some factory workers, for example) and why.

Get older students involved in a critical thinking debate on the pros and cons of switching to the metric system. After the debate, hold a classroom vote on "Should the United States fully convert to the metric system or not?"

You can also have fun with word play. Does an inchworm become a centiworm? What happens when you give someone an inch? Is this the end of the Quarter Pounder? For easy reference, post the conversion formulas in several easy-to-spot locations. Next to the classroom clock is a great place since eyes frequently turn in that direction.

The website of the U.S. Metric Association provides a table of metric units and equivalents and other useful information at lamar.colo state.edu/~hillger.

(143)

Stars in the Sky
and Stars in Their Eyes

People have been fascinated with stars and the sky for thousands of years. The Chinese charted star positions in the 1300s B.C. The Babylonians had charted heavenly bodies by 450 B.C. Mayan astronomers created an accurate calendar based on the sun about A.D. 300. Students can find examples of these ancient charts and compare them with today's sky maps and calendars.

Copernicus proposed the theory of a heliocentric (sun-centered) universe in 1543 A.D. Later Galileo was tried for heresy when he accepted this theory. Students could debate the issue as it might have occurred at the time, and then present evidence that the planets in our solar system revolve around the sun. This topic lends itself to newspaper editorial stories that students can publish in class.

Studying the moon and its phases is another research project, which extends into two- and three-dimensional art. Representing the planets in our solar system makes a great classroom art project. A wonderful interactive website on the planets is Nine Planets: Multimedia Tour of the Solar System at seds.lpl.arizona.edu/nineplanets/nineplanets/nineplanets.html. Many students enjoy learning about constellations and comparing explanations of the night sky's patterns from various cultures. Stargazing can be a fun evening homework assignment. Students will appreciate this information when they can wow their parents by pointing out constellations in the night sky.

Books to help you get started include: *The Planets in Our Solar System*, by Franklyn Branley (HarperCollins, 0-06-445178-X, grades 1 to 4); *Can You Catch a Falling Star?*, by Sidney Rosen (Carolrhoda, 0-8761-4882-8, grades 3 to 6); Seymour Simon's planet series (published by Morrow); *The Planet Hunters*, by Dennis Fradin (Simon and Schuster, 0-689-81323-6, grades 5 to 9); *Spacebusters: The Race to the Moon*, by Philip Wilkinson (Dorling-Kindersley, 0-789-42961-6, grades 1 to 4); and *One Giant Leap: The Story of Neil Armstrong*, by Don Brown (Houghton Mifflin, 0-395-88401-2, grades K to 4). Fiction includes the Commander Toad easy readers series by Jane Yolen for ages five to eight and the Alien Secrets series by Anita Klause for grades 4 to 8.

There are many great astronomy websites; for example, Astronomy for Kids at frontiernet.net/~kidpower/astronomy.html and NASA's StarChild site for children at heasarc.gsfc.nasa.gov/docs/StarChild/StarChild.html.

Reading a Road Map

The ability to read a road map is a necessary survival skill in today's "age of cars." More people are on the road than ever before. Knowing where you're going and how to get there are definite assets, and even in the age of global positioning tools, nothing beats a map.

Young primary students can become familiar with map reading by drawing simple diagrams of the classroom and the hallway outside the room. You can create classroom "streets" by pushing desks together into patterns that simulate streets and avenues. Give each street (row) a name. Avenues can be wider and run from the front of the room to the back.

Older students can make their own maps of the streets that surround the school. Students can choose a nearby shop or building and locate it on their map. Have another student write directions to that location by reading the map. Explain the importance of orienting the map to your current direction of travel, and knowing where the four points of the compass rose are located.

Create a map that includes the roads to the nearest school in your district. Include landmarks a driver would see on the way. Or map the route the food truck takes when it carries food from the district's distribution area to your school's cafeteria. Older students can map the bus route from their home to the school. Pretend they had to give directions to the driver as though he or she was brand-new and unfamiliar with the route.

Get a road map of your state (often available free at interstate rest stops). Pick a town fifty miles or more away. Let groups of students choose the roads they would travel to reach the town. If you have Internet access, introduce your students to the Mapquest website (mapquest.com). Have them type in the street address and town for your school and examine the resulting map. Show them how to zoom in for greater detail or zoom out to put your school on a larger map. Then let Mapquest design a map from your school to the town chosen earlier. Compare it to the routes students have chosen.

Vary the theme by choosing two routes. One should be the most direct, the other could be a scenic route. What sights would be included on the scenic route, and why?

Another fun map activity, with a nod to local history, is to search the public library or the town hall for old street maps. Look for maps older than seventy-five years. It's interesting to note what streets were not around in the past. On maps older than 150 years, students may find that some of the streets had different names. Names from colonial times are often highly descriptive, such as Swinefield Road or Whiskey Lane.

Children's books that feature map making include *Mapping Penny's World*, by Loreen Leedy (Henry Holt, 0-8050-6178-9, ages six to nine); *Maps in Everyday Life*, by Martyn Bramwell (Lerner, 0-8225-2923-8, ages ten to fourteen); and *Me on the Map*, by Joan Sweeney (Crown, 0-517-88557-3, ages five to eight).

Your local American Automobile Association (AAA) may be able to give you some outdated road maps to feature in your class. Just look for them in the phone directory or online.

(145)

Some Like It Wild Week

National Wildlife Week, Third Week in April

This is a week to draw attention to the wide variety of wildlife (and their habitats) found throughout the United States. National parks provide much-needed room for wildlife to roam. Student groups could present reports about national parks from different areas of the United States. Compare and contrast the kinds of habitats and wild-life found in national parks such as Acadia, the Everglades, Carlsbad Caverns, Death Valley, Canyonlands, Denali, and Hawaii Volcanoes. These diverse climates and terrains support many different animals. Information can be found at the National Parks Service website: nps.gov.

Conservation issues are often highlighted in newspaper and magazine articles. Students can discuss and debate recent challenges to the Endangered Species Act. Coastal development and the destruction of wetlands are major threats to wildlife. Research and discuss construction practices that help and harm wildlife. The U.S. Fish and Wildlife Service's Endangered Species website at fws.gov/r9end spp/endspp.htm has information for both teachers and students.

Students might find researching and reporting on unusual forms of wildlife interesting. Sea horses, armadillos, wolverines, manatees, and Gila monsters are a few examples. Facts about and artwork of the researched animals could be displayed on a bulletin board. Another board could focus on things we do that harm wildlife and what we can do to help.

Even really young children like to know they can make a difference. Did you know those plastic six-pack holders are very dangerous to wildlife? They should be cut up so that birds, fish, and small creatures don't get their necks stuck in the holes. Plastic bags floating in water look just like jellyfish and thus kill many marine creatures that try to eat them each year. Talk about how garbage can go astray and kill or harm animals. If weather allows, go out and collect garbage near your school—look alongside fences where wind will leave all manner of things. Gloves are recommended. Perhaps your class can sponsor a bulletin board to remind others in the school of the part they play in keeping wildlife alive. The litter you collected can be made into a collage for maximum visual impact.

Older students can debate the issue of wild animals being reintroduced into areas they formerly occupied. There are many sources for information on the reintroduction of wolves. *Wolf Wars*, by Hank Fischer (Falcon Press, 1-56044-352-9), is a good teacher resource that explores the subject in depth. Students will enjoy *There's a Wolf in the Classroom*, by Bruce Weide and Patricia Tucker (Carolrhoda, 0-87614-958-1, grades 3 to 7). Information is presented as a visiting wolf program. For additional sources and classroom activities see the *Book Links* magazine article "Wolves: Fact and Fiction" in the September 1998 issue and National Geographic's website at nationalgeo graphic.com/resources/education/geoguide. Upper elementary and middle school classrooms may want to participate in the Journey North program, which tracks spring's journey north via wildlife migration at learner.org/north.

146

Understanding an Ecosystem

An ecosystem is a very important concept to understand, and there are many ways of making something as complex as an ecosystem understandable to young children. First you may want to write a definition: "An *ecosystem* is made up of living and nonliving things and includes all the interactions between them." Make a list of living things like worms, bugs, animals, fish, people, and so forth. Now make another list with items like temperature, sunlight, and nutrients.

Take some time to list the ecosystems near your school. Are there forests, streams, lakes, prairies, oceans, or other important ecosystems? In each of these change is always occurring. Plants grow and die, animals reproduce, and so on. Each part of the system impacts the others. Two important processes are energy flow and nutrient cycling. These connect the living and nonliving parts of an ecosystem. During the energy flow process living plants capture the sun's energy using photosynthesis. Each plant stores this energy in its tissues. When the plant is eaten or dies these organic molecules are released and may be used as energy by other living creatures. This energy gets used when animals breathe or eat or run around. They use up some of the trapped sun energy leaving less for whatever creature becomes the next consumer in the food chain.

Unlike energy, which gets used only once, nutrients get used over and over. They cycle through both living and nonliving parts of the ecosystem. Plants get nutrients from the air, the earth, and water. They become part of the plant's tissues during the process of photosynthesis. These nutrients get passed along through the food chain from plants to animals to bigger animals. Nutrient cycling couldn't happen without the activities of many players: earthworms, bacteria, and all manner of tiny living things such as fungi help create nutrients from the building blocks around them.

Biodiversity is a term that represents all the kinds of plants and animals that make up an ecosystem. When you take out one part you impact the rest because they are all dependent upon each other in some way. (A good example is the early settlers' and farmers' attempts to wipe out all wolves and coyotes in the Midwest—the deer population soared because there weren't as many being killed by the hunting animals. Now most states in the Midwest sponsor deer hunting seasons to keep these herds in check.) Clearly people are an important part of an ecoystem. We affect ecosystems and are also affected by them. For instance we need wetlands to help clean the water that will eventually become our drinking water.

Humans make an impact wherever we go. Because of our wants and needs we build buildings, log out trees, take minerals from the earth, build roads, and grow food. These needs sometimes have a negative impact on an ecosystem, leaving people in a quandary about how to deal with the conflicts between the perceived needs of people and the ecosystems that support them. It is not uncommon to find many different people trying to solve these problems: groundwater specialists, animal scientists, foresters, government regulatory agencies, and nonprofits all benefit from working together to preserve ecosystems.

Here is a variation on a game suggested by the Western Regional Environmental Education Council (they offer a Project Wild workshop—for more information call them at 301-493-5447). The Habitat and Wildlife game requires two equal groups of kids. One group will represent the habitat aspects of an ecosystem. Each of them will choose one of these to be: food, water, shelter, or space. The other group will be wild animals. Each child should pick in his mind a need from the list above. On your mark the lines of children will begin to whisper what they have to offer if they are in the habitat line, and the other group will whisper their needs (they cannot change once they begin to whisper). Students will mill around until they find a match from the other group. Once this happens both the habitat and the wildlife will rejoin the wildlife line (because the animal's need was met, it can now reproduce and make the animal population higher). If a wildlife critter finds no habitat match for his or her need, he or she joins the habitat group (because its need was not met the animal dies and goes back to the earth in the nutrient cycle).

Repeat the game several times, letting children change their need or offering, and each time making a note of the fluctuation in the animal population. Ask students to think about what would be likely to happen to the habitat in the ecosystem if the population of wildlife were to grow and grow. If some of the critters were prey and some were hunters (predators), what would happen to their populations if the other group grew or shrank.

Other fun activities are available from *Exploring Environments: A Handbook of Environmental Exercises*, which is produced by the Staten Island Institute of Arts and Sciences (phone 718-727-1135).

(147)

First Modern Olympics

Started April 6, 1896

Looking ahead to the Olympics, students can have fun celebrating the birth of the first modern Olympic Games in Athens, Greece, in 1896, especially if you generate enthusiasm and fact-finding missions before April 6.

Students should research the original Olympics and find out what sports were included. (There were only nine, so this isn't a big project.) Compare them with the number of sports included today. The Sydney Olympics in 2000 saw the debut of tae kwon do and the triathalon as Olympic sports. Are there any new events planned for the upcoming games? Also discuss the role of women in the history of Olympic competition. Until fairly recently women were not allowed to compete.

Students interested in specific sporting events can seek out winning statistics for their sport at intervals of every three Olympics. Consult *Chronicle of the Olympics* (Dorling-Kindersley Publishing, 0-789-42312-X, all ages) for statistics from the games from 1896 through the winter games in Nagano, Japan, in 1998. Plot the results on graphs and discuss why the results change: better training, better nutrition, better equipment, or changes in the playing field?

As an art project have students design posters to represent the nine original sports in the first modern Olympics. These can be presented and displayed on April 6.

Older students can have fun writing proposals for new sports to be added to the Olympics. Students could choose silly events—sumo snowboarding—or more realistic ones—skateboarding. Many new sports have been suggested: how about Olympic surfing or rollerblading? Ask them to make a commercial advertising the debut of the new sport. Some students could imagine what a 2096 Olympics might be like.

(148)

Ocean Wonders

National Week of the Ocean, Second Week of April

If you have ever looked at pictures of the Earth taken from satellites or space vehicles, you may have been struck by how blue our planet looks. The waters of our five oceans—the Atlantic, Pacific, Indian, Arctic, and Antarctic Oceans—are responsible for its stunning blue color. Oceans cover about 70 percent of our planet's surface and hold 97 percent of Earth's water.

The deep-sea floor of Earth's oceans are our last unexplored frontier. New technology now enables scientists to map and "visit" great depths via sounding devices. Small, specially equipped submarines transport scientists to depths close to seven thousand feet. Fascinating creatures, such as six-foot-long tube worms and giant clams, survive in dark water. Tiny microbial life teems in the waters near hydrothermal vents. Scientists now estimate that millions of species inhabit ocean waters deeper than ten thousand feet.

Ocean life is truly diverse. Curriculum units about oceans can easily center around several different ocean environments. Have students set up an ocean environments bulletin board. Microscopic phytoplankton are the base of the ocean's food chain. They convert sunlight into energy. Larger organisms gain that energy when they gobble the phytoplankton. Find pictures of phytoplankton, and let students observe and redraw them. Create a phytoplankton bulletin board to represent the view as it would be seen through a microscope. Reefs, beaches, tide pools, marine mammals, dark-water dwellers, and frigid waters are other ocean environment bulletin board ideas. Cardboard-box ocean environment dioramas are a smaller-scale and individualized alternative.

Create a classroom "ocean surround." Affix fish and seaweed cutouts to the windows and walls. Suspend ocean creatures on nylon thread from the ceiling. Some students may want to bring in and display shell collections. Protect them from poking fingers. If your school has microscopes and you have shell pieces, their patterns can be very fun to see close up.

Make a connection to poetry for the month of April by writing ocean poems and collating them into a classroom book. Students might write from a fish or ocean mammal's perspective. Write concrete poems to represent shell or wave outlines.

The health of Earth's oceans is threatened in several ways, including overfishing (removing too many fishes from a specific area), coastal development, underwater mining, and pollution. Middle school and junior high students can investigate these topics and hold debates to explore the environmental and economic pros and cons for each. They can write letters to elected officials and ask what efforts the present Congress and Senate are making to ensure healthy oceans in the future.

Many excellent books are available about oceans and their inhabitants. Here are some that will get your students started: *The Oceans Atlas*, by Anita Ganeri (Dorling Kindersley, 1-56458-475-5, grades 3 to 8); *Dive! My Adventures in the Deep Frontier*, by Sylvia A. Earle (National Geographic, 0-7922-7144-0, grades 4 to 8); *Exploring the Deep, Dark Sea*, by Gail Gibbons (Little, Brown, 0-316-30945-1, grades 2 to 4); *Sea Soup: Phytoplankton*, by Mary Cerullo (Tilbury House, 0-88448-208-1, grades 3 to 6), and *Sea Soup Teacher's Guide*, by Betsy T. Stevens (0-88448-209-X); *Sea Horses*, by Sally M. Walker (Carolrhoda, 1-57505-317-9, grades 3 to 8); and *Gentle Giant Octopus*, by Karen Wallace (Candlewick Press, 0-7636-0318-X, grades K to 2).

(149)

Charles Willson Peale

Birth, April 15, 1741

Charles Willson Peale, born April 15, 1741, was one of the most famous portrait painters in Colonial America. In his early life, in Maryland, he apprenticed as a saddle maker. He was fascinated by art, especially drawing, and firmly believed anyone could learn to draw. Peale sought advice from John Singleton Copley, one of the world's premier portrait painters, and later studied in London with Benjamin West, a renowned painter of historical subjects. (For a good picture-book biography about Benjamin West, see *The Boy Who Loved to Draw: Benjamin West*, by Barbara Brenner [Houghton Mifflin, 0-395-85080-0, all ages].)

Many famous early American leaders sat for Peale, including George Washington, Benjamin Franklin, Thomas Jefferson, and John Adams. Peale was married three times and had many children. His sons Raphaelle, Rembrandt, Rubens, and Titian (named after famous artists) all became painters as well. In art class, have students search for books that contain photographs of the work of the famous painters for whom Peale's sons were named. Compare paintings by the masters with those by the Peale family. Discuss how styles and subjects differed.

In the late 1780s Peale established a natural history museum in his home at Philadelphia. Open to the public, his displays included many curiosities of the animal world. One display that stunned visitors was the huge mammoth skeleton from upstate New York. Two wonderful books have recently been published about this discovery. *The Mystery of the Mammoth Bones and How It Was Solved*, by James C. Giblin (HarperCollins, 0-06-027493-X, ages ten and up), and the picture book *The Great Unknown*, by Taylor Morrison (Clarion, 0-395-97494-1, ages five and up), explain and explore the topic, and would be a great complement to a unit on fossils.

Other visitors to the museum were startled and delighted by Peale's trompe-l'oeil (photographically realistic) painting of his sons Titian and Raphaelle. See Michael O. Tunnell's *The Joke's on George* (Boyds Mills, 1-56397-970-5, ages six and up) for a delightful story about George Washington and this painting.

Peale perfectly complements units on the American Revolution. His family moved to Philadelphia in 1776, and lived in the midst of the Revolutionary fervor. Peale served in the militia and painted miniatures of many officers. See *The Ingenious Mr. Peale: Painter, Patriot, and Man of Science*, by Janet Wilson (out of print, but available in libraries), for an engaging biography for students age ten to fourteen. Older students may enjoy *The Poison Place*, by Mary E. Lyons (Aladdin, 0-689-82678-8, ages twelve to fifteen), a novel that explores a possibly mysterious and dark side of Peale.

(150)

Bonding with the Bard

William Shakespeare, Birth (1564) and Death (1616), April 23

William Shakespeare was one of the world's greatest dramatists. His flair for language and his acute perceptions about human nature continue to enthrall and enchant audiences hundreds of years after his death. A recently discovered portrait dated 1603 may be the only existing picture of the playwright painted during his lifetime. (For information about this painting see the *Chicago Tribune*, "Shake-up in the Art World," May 17, 2001, section 5, page 2, or the *Globe and Mail*'s [Canada] front-page story of the discovery in the May 11, 2001, issue.)

Recent movie versions of Shakespeare's plays set in modern times, plus the release of the movie *Shakespeare in Love*, have stimulated a new interest in the Bard, especially in young people. Many people contend, however, the plays should be presented orally, as they were intended to be heard, and not just read. (See the article "I Tell Kids That Shakespeare Was the Original Rapper," by Julia Keller in the *Chicago Tribune*, May 13, 2001, section 7, page 1, for one high school teacher's success with a new approach to Shakespeare.) Excerpting short sections from several well-known plays and having students act them out may be a good approach to catch the interest of students unfamiliar with the plays and reluctant to delve into reading them.

Adaptations of plays for younger actors include a series of Shakespeare's plays published by Firefly Books. The books, all written by Lois Burdett, feature plays such as *Macbeth, Hamlet,* and *Twelfth Night.*

A first introduction to Shakespeare's work can be found in *To Sleep Perchance to Dream: A Child's Book of Rhymes,* illustrated by James Mayhew (Scholastic, 0-439-29655-2, ages three and up). This picture book features short selections of some of Shakespeare's most famous lines. *Tales from Shakespeare* (Candlewick, 0-7636-0441-0, ages eight to twelve), and *Bravo, Mr. William Shakespeare!* (Candlewick, 0-7636-1209-X, ages eight to twelve), both by Marcia Williams, present several of Shakespeare's plays in a cartoon-style picture-book format with short plot summaries. They are lots of fun and great for whetting literary appetites.

In addition to the plays, William Shakespeare himself has been the subject of a number of novels for young readers. *Shakespeare's Scribe,* by Gary Blackwood (Dutton, 0-525-46444-1, ages twelve and up); *The Shakespeare Stealer,* by Gary Blackwood (Dutton, 0-14-130595-9, ages twelve and up); and *The Playmaker,* by J. B. Cheaney (Knopf, 0-375-80577-X , ages twelve and up), all have Shakespearean England as their backdrop.

Nonfiction for younger readers includes several entertaining books. *William Shakespeare and the Globe,* by Aliki (HarperCollins, 0-06-443722-1, ages eight and up), is a wonderful account of the building, use, and later restoration of the Globe Theater. A "Shakespeare's Vocabulary" list at the end of the book is a good source of words for a Shakespearean spelling bee or spelling word list. *Shakespeare's London,* by Julie Ferris (Kingfisher, 0-7534-5234-0, ages seven to eleven), takes children on a historical sightseeing tour. *Shakespeare for Kids,* by Margie Blumberg (Chicago Review Press, 1-5565-2347-5, ages eight to twelve), includes period-related activities that students can do as they celebrate Shakespeare's work. *The Bedside, Bathtub, and Armchair Companion to Shakespeare,* by Dick Riley (Continuum,

0-8264-1250-5, all ages), contains plot summaries, the historical context of Shakespeare's works, and a discussion of whether Shakespeare really wrote his plays. Short chapters make it a good candidate for browsers, and it can help you as a teacher gain background before presenting Shakespeare to your class.

(151)

Mapping the World

First Identification of "America" in a Book, April 25, 1507

Research reveals that large numbers of American students are unable to locate the United States on a map or a globe, and that we rank far down the list when compared to students in other countries' knowledge of basic world geography. Geographical awareness is important in our world of instantaneous global communication. An event that occurs in a town halfway across the world is reported on TV and radio within minutes of its happening. Citizens with a better understanding of geography make better decisions when it comes to forming political opinions.

It's a good idea to know, at least in general, where momentous events have taken place. Keep a map of the world displayed in your classroom. Ask students to search the first section of the newspaper or listen to the evening news for the locations of leading stories. Make arrow-shaped cutouts large enough to write an event, town, and country location on. Pin the labeled arrow with its tip pointing to the geographical location on the world map. Change cutouts weekly, or when the need arises. You can coordinate events with the curriculum. Feature the locations of hurricanes, tornadoes, or earthquakes on your map and connect them with weather units, and so on.

Map skills are crucial (see Idea 144, "Reading a Road Map"). One way to help students understand maps is by making a map relevant to their own lives. Have students pin stars on the map to show where they were born and where their parents or grandparents have lived. Label each star with the name of the relative, his or her classroom connection, and the town's name. In the case of ancestors who immigrated, feature a boat with names listed on it in the appropriate ocean. The same can be done for present-day relatives who may have arrived by airplane.

To develop further map-reading skills, students can plan a trip to locations accessible by car. Using a road atlas, they can trace and write out the route they would travel if they were to make a visit to a relative's home or another place they would like to go. On a local scale, have students map the streets they use while traveling from home to school.

Older students may want to participate in *National Geographic* magazine's Geographic Bee. Information about school participation in the nationwide bee can be found at nationalgeographic.com/geographicbee. This involves a series of tests at the school level. Winners are then tested at the state and national levels.

Me on the Map, by Joan Sweeney (Random House, 0-517-88557-3, grades K to 2), introduces the basic concept of mapmaking. Sorting states and their capital cities can be a daunting task. *The Scrambled States of America*, by Laurie Keller (Henry Holt, 0-8050-5802-8, grades K to 4), is a humorous story about states switching places, filled with facts and geographical fun.

Maps have been used as navigation tools for many years, long before America was even thought to exist. *Mapping the World*, by Sylvia Johnson (Simon and Schuster, 0-689-81813-0, grades 4 to 8), gives an overview of how maps drawn throughout history reflect people's perception of the world. The U.S. Geological Survey, which maps the United States, has lesson plans on its website at usgs.gov/education/learnweb/index.html.

(152)

Terrific Trees

National Arbor Day, Last Friday in April

There's nothing like a walk in the forest on a cool, crisp day, or listening to the leaves rustle in the wind as you snuggle in bed. Unless, it's leaning against a tree trunk and savoring the shade on a hot summer day. And what about climbing up into a tree and feeling as though you are on top of the world? Then again, there's nothing like the thrill of building a tree house (and using it for a clubhouse with your friends). And of course, the marvelous crackles that occur when you jump into a pile of leaves.

Celebrate Arbor Day by enjoying the trees in your life. Let students work in small groups. They could share some of the trees they have enjoyed at various times of the year. For example: pussy willow "fuzzies," maple tree "helicopters," oak trees and acorn "fingertip hats," sycamore tree "itchy balls," or maybe evergreens and pine cones.

As a science project, list and describe the trees found in your school's neighborhood. Students could collect a fallen leaf and press it, or they could draw the leaf. Paste the leaf (or drawing or crayon rubbing) on a sheet of paper and write facts about the tree beneath it. Bind the book into a classroom "Trees Around Our School" book.

If you really like to plan ahead, make this a project introduced in September and have students keep a monthly journal about a particular tree and how it changes each month. Their observations can be in a factual or poetic vein. By the time Arbor Day rolls around, they each have a booklet to assemble. Each student will have a neat end-of-the-year science journal and a writing project as well.

If possible, you might want to approach the PTO or school administration and find out if they have plans for an Arbor Day planting at your school. Participate in that by researching the kind of tree being planted. If no project is planned, suggest planting a tree. If no funds are available, and your class has permission and would like to plant a tree, call a few local growers. Many times by the end of April (in some regions of the country) growers can see they have overstocked certain varieties and may be willing to donate.

For a social studies project, let students contact the municipal building via letters or phone calls. Have them discover which department handles trees and if that department has a list of the oldest trees in your community. If possible, get a picture of the tree. Students can research and write the tree's perspective of the social changes it has "seen" during its lifetime.

Writing projects could include writing a poem or prose piece about a student's favorite tree. *Old Elm Speaks*, by Kristine O'Connell George (0-395-87611-7, Clarion, grades K to 5), and *My Favorite Tree: Terrific Trees of North America*, by Diane Iverson (1-8832-2093-9, Dawn, ages five to twelve), are wonderful for stimulating ideas.

There are lots of fun art projects your students can do with leaves. One is to make leaf prints by dipping a leaf in paint. For a twist, have students print the leaf with the stem pointing toward the top edge of the paper. Then, have them add crayon or marker lines to incorporate the leaf into an article of clothing. You can also use leaf prints to form a border on large paper that students can use to "frame" a tree drawing.

There are many books worth having in your classroom for an Arbor Day celebration. *Tree Trunk Traffic*, by Bianca Lavies (Penguin, 0-14-054837-8, ages five to nine), has great photos of creatures that live in seventy-year-old maple tree. *A Log's Life*, by Wendy Pfeffer (Simon and Schuster, 0-689-80636-1, ages five to nine), is a beautiful paper collage presentation of the life cycle of a tree and the life it supports as the tree grows, falls, and then decays. *A Tree is Growing*, by Arthur Dorros (Scholastic, 0-590-45300-9, ages eight to twelve), chronicles the growing stages of an oak tree. Although this focuses on the oak, there are gorgeous line drawings of many other leaves as well.

(153)

National Book Month

Make plans now to celebrate National Book Month in your school. One great way to celebrate is to choose one book per grade level and designate it as "The book everyone's talking about." (Some cities have citywide "book clubs," where all residents are encouraged to read a designated title. For example, in Chicago, in 2001, *To Kill a Mocking-bird* was chosen for the citywide read.)

Encourage every child to read the book chosen for his or her grade. Pick a schoolwide book discussion time toward the end of the month. The time could be fifteen minutes for primary grades and thirty minutes for older students. Everyone drops everything and the designated books are discussed. The whole school should be talking about books at that time. You might want to have several discussion-starter comments or questions to get the ball rolling, or you could ask students to write one question or comment they have about the book.

The books for discussion should be chosen well ahead of time, to make sure the learning center copies are available for circulation. Contact the public library to see if copies could be loaned to the school for an extended period. Also, contact the PTO and see if funds could be made available to purchase extra paperbacks to have on hand. Many children may wish to buy their own copy, but it's important to have books available for those who are unable to do so. Check with a local bookstore and see if a discount is available when purchasing multiple copies.

Some book suggestions listed by grade level are:

Kindergarten: *Full Belly Bowl*, Jim Aylesworth; *Tops and Bottoms*, Janet Stevens (both are picture books)

First grade: *Daniel's Duck*, Clyde Bulla; *My Brother Ant*, Betsy Byars (both are early readers)

Second grade: *Donavan's Word Jar*, Monalisa De Gross; *Tornado*, Betsy Byars

Third grade: *Beany and the Dreaded Wedding*, Susan Wojciechowski; *Surviving Brick Johnson*, Laurie Myers

Fourth grade: *The Warm Place*, Nancy Farmer; *The Good Liar*, Gregory Maguire

Fifth grade: *Because of Winn Dixie*, Kate DiCamillo; *Secret Letters From 0 to 10*, Susie Morgenstern

Sixth grade: *The Wanderer*, Sharon Creech; *The Well*, Mildred Taylor

Seventh grade: *Gold Dust*, Chris Lynch; *Running Out of Time*, Margaret Haddix

Eighth grade: *Esperanza Rising*, Pam Muñoz Ryan; *The Dark Side of Nowhere*, Neal Shusterman

Don't forget to check the National Book Foundation website (nationalbook.org) to find out the current winner of the National Book Award for children's books.

(154)

Twisting in May

May, the Most Dangerous Month for Tornados

According to one study, May is the most likely month for tornados in the United States, averaging a whopping 329. That's just statistics of course. If you live in the East you're more likely to have tornado weather in April. If you live in the southern plains states you see a peak in May, but the northern plains and Great Lakes get the worst tornado weather in June.

Weather units can be part of the science curriculum at any time of the year. Many elementary and younger middle school students are frightened by the thought of tornados. And since in the United States, April, May, and June are the prime tornado season months, this might be a good time for a little classroom research.

One way to help children begin working through fears about tornados is to educate them on exactly what occurs during a tornado and also to recognize the kinds of weather patterns that might lead to the development of a tornado.

Books that complement information already included in science curriculum materials include: *Tornado*, by Stephen Kramer (Lerner, 1-5750-5058-7, ages eight and up); *Tornadoes*, by Seymour Simon (Morrow, 0-688-14846-5, ages eight to eleven); *Storm Chasers: Tracking Twisters*, by Gail Herman (Grosset and Dunlap, 0-448-41624-7, ages seven to nine); *Twisters!*, by Lucille Penner (Random House, 0-679-88271-5, ages seven to nine); *Eyewitness Hurricane and Tornado*, by Jack Challoner (DK Publishing, 0-789-45242-1, ages nine to twelve); *Disaster Science*, by the editors of Klutz Press (1-57054-251-1, ages nine and up), which includes lots of great tornado photos and facts; and *Do Tornadoes Really Twist?*, by Melvin and Gilda Berger (Scholastic, 0-439-14880-4, ages seven to eleven).

Novels and picture books that feature tornados include *Twister on Tuesday*, by Mary Pope Osborne (Random House, 0-679-89069-6, ages seven to ten); *Twister Trouble*, by Anne Schreiber (Scholastic, 0-439-20419-4, ages seven to ten); *Twister*, by Darleen Beard (Farrar Straus Giroux, 0-374-37977-7, ages five to eight); *One Lucky Girl*, by George Ella Lyon (DK Publishing, 0-7894-2613-7, ages five to eight); and *Tornado*, by Betsy Byars (HarperCollins, 0-06-442063-9, all ages).

The National Weather Service (NWS) has information for children on tornados and other severe weather hazards on its website at crh.noaa.gov/mkx/owlie/owlie.htm. Older children may want to use another NWS webpage at nws.noaa.gov/om/brochures/tornado.htm.

To extend the tornado theme into other areas of the curriculum, use the slang term *twister*. In gym or at recess, play the game Twister. A durable Twister game cloth is easily made by painting colored circles on a plain white sheet.

In language arts, have fun with tongue twisters. Make up your own weather-related tongue twisters or use a book such as *Six Sick Sheep: 101 Tongue Twisters*, by Joanna Cole (Morrow, 0-688-11068-1, ages five to ten), to get you started.

Twisters are also appropriate for music (and by association, gym). Have a twist enthusiast teach your students how to do the twist. A recording of Chubby Checker's "The Twist" is a good starting tune. "Twist and Shout" and "Twisting the Night Away" are two additional songs that complement the tornado theme. Recordings of The Beatles' version of "Twist and Shout" are easily found in libraries, and a group called the Sugar Beats has a recording that contains "Twisting the Night Away." It has a number of other fun rock songs, adapted for children, on it as well.

155

Egg-Cellent Fun

National Egg Month, May

Have some "egg-cellent" fun turning your classroom into a giant incubator. First explain what an incubator is and how it works. Focus on its nurturing aspect. Talk about how a classroom is a place for incubating ideas. Put a giant construction paper egg on the bulletin board. Leave the top edge open so idea slips can be inserted. Solicit student ideas for creatively spelling words, solving math problems, finding out answers to questions. You might also include egg-related trivia facts such as the smallest, largest, or heaviest eggs. Have students write ideas, facts, or even egg poems on slips of paper and put them inside the egg pocket. Designate a time each day, perhaps 10 A.M. because it has three egg-shaped zeros in it, to pull one idea from the pocket and share with the class.

For silly egg fun, brainstorm with students on idioms that contain references to eggs. The term "goose egg" instead of zero, saving a "nest egg," and "don't put all your eggs in one basket" are a few examples. Write silly stories that offer explanations of how these phrases were invented. Have fun making egg puns by converting words with "ex" to "egg" (like "eggs-it") and drawing pictures to illustrate the pun.

See if you can get someone to donate ladybug or praying mantis egg cases to the classroom. Students can observe and record changes in appearance and length of hatching time. When the eggs hatch, let the insects go free in nearby gardens. *What About Ladybugs?*, by Celia Godkin (Sierra Club, 0-871-56549-8, grades K to 3), is a picture-book story about how ladybugs are beneficial to gardeners. *The Backyard Hunter*, by Bianca Lavies (Puffin, 0-14-055494-7, grades K to 3), discusses the life cycle of praying mantises.

Sea turtles are on the threatened species lists. Nesting and egg-laying habits and how people are working to protect the turtles is a fascinating research topic.

Sea turtles travel hundreds of miles to lay their eggs on specific beaches. *Into the Sea*, by Brenda Z. Guiberson (Henry Holt, 0-8050-2263-5, grades K to 3), is a beautifully illustrated story of a sea turtle's life. Students can research how turtle, shark, frog, and butterfly eggs differ from those of birds.

If you choose to focus on the familiar chicken egg, perhaps you can hatch some chicks. Many classrooms have made their own or purchased egg incubators, obtained fertilized chicken or duck eggs, and successfully hatched babies. (Local 4-H Clubs or Farm Bureaus may be able to provide informational materials.) If you choose to do this kind of activity, plan well in advance what is to happen to the chicks or ducklings after they hatch.

Students can research the nutritional benefits of chicken eggs and how they can be judiciously included in our diets. *Everyone Eats Eggs*, by Gillian Powell (Raintree, 0-8172-4759-9, grades 2 to 6), contains nutritional information about chicken eggs, a multicultural look at the ways eggs are prepared, and lots of egg trivia.

Students may enjoy drawing cross sections of eggs and labeling the parts. If you extend an egg unit to include amphibians, reptiles, and mammals, you will have quite a wide range of egg forms to compare.

Blowing out the insides of chicken eggs (from the store) and then painting them in patterns inspired by Ukrainian Easter eggs is an imaginative art project.

For further information about eggs and birds, see Lerner Publications' Birder's Bookshelf series for grades 4 to 7. This enjoyable four-book series by Dean Spaulding explores feeding, housing, watching, and protecting birds. For tadpole information try *Lily Pad Pond*, by Bianca Lavies (Puffin, 0-14-054836-X, grades K to 3).

(156)

May Day

May 1

Since ancient times, May Day has been celebrated as a festival to welcome back spring after winter's long presence. In England during medieval times villages were decorated with flowers, songs rejoicing in the beauty and bounty of the growing season were sung, and a maypole was erected in a public area. Colorful ribbons dangled from the top of the maypole. Dancers grabbed hold of the ends and danced, their steps weaving around the pole. By the dance's end, the maypole was completely wrapped in colorful ribbon.

May baskets have long been a tradition in many countries. These tiny paper baskets, made and distributed by children, are filled with flowers and anonymously hung on a neighbor's doorknob. Although May baskets are more popular in Europe, particularly Great Britain, some neighborhoods in the United States celebrate the custom.

Students can make a simple classroom May basket and fill it with good wishes. Get a small empty cardboard box. Add a cardboard handle. Each student can design and cut out a tiny flower. Cover the box with the students' flowers. Ask each child to think of a positive thought that would make a person feel good if someone were to say it to him or her. Students can write their good wish sentences on a small square of paper. Use some paper from the recycling box, if you have one. Preview all the sentences before the first drawing in case some are inappropriate. If numbers are low, add your own sentences so that everyone will have a turn picking a May wish from the box.

Put all the wishes in the box. Explain that each morning during the month of May, a student will reach in the May basket and select one of the May wishes and read it to the class. After reading the wish, let the student write it on the board.

Another approach to the same idea is to write the wishes on colored paper cut into flower shapes. Make a bulletin board that initially features brown dirt. Each day, a student reads a wish and then "plants" the flower on the bulletin board, where others can read it during the month. By the end of May, you'll have a full flower garden.

Crazy Crystals

Crystalline structures are an important area of scientific study, can be lovely to look at in natural rocks, and can also be made right in your classroom with very few special materials. You will need to find a special powder, potassium alum, for this activity. Ask at your local high school's science department for local purchasing options or check with a pharmacist or a photo supply shop. You may also be able to borrow the appropriate size glass containers from the high school if you call in advance.

For each set of two crystal candles, you will need the following:

50 grams of potassium alum
a tall narrow jar (300 cc preferably)
cotton yarn
nuts or washers
a pencil or twig
water
an enamel saucepan (can be shared between teams)
a hot plate or stove

Completely dissolve 50 grams of potassium alum in enough very hot water (approximately 250 cc) to not quite fill your tall narrow jar. Place two strands of yarn a little longer than the jar to a pencil or twig that can rest across the mouth of the jar. Use a washer or nut to weigh down the end in the jar so the yarn hangs nice and straight. Place the jar in a safe place where it won't get bumped or jiggled and leave it for the whole day or even overnight. Remove the crystals carefully. Rest them gently on paper bags or other paper to dry. These lovely (but nonedible!) crystalline structures can be hung in your windows as sparkly decorations or sent home with the children.

Many more ideas, some much more complex, are available in many books aimed at the "do-it-yourself" market of homeschool parents and students who like to cook up science at home. Ask at your local library or media center for reference books with complete directions. If you plan ahead you may even be able to use crystals to make holiday gifts this winter.

(158)

Observing the Weather

National Weather Observer's Day, May 4

We've talked about bad weather—twisters—but there's a whole lot more to learn. May 4 is National Weather Observer's Day, so why not deputize your class as apprentice weather observers?

Take a good day to go outside and get a good look at the weather. There are a number of ways to incorporate observing the weather into various areas of school curricula. (If the actual date falls on a weekend, the classroom activities will have to take place on the day before or after. But that's OK. A short weekend assignment can include family or friends from outside the classroom.)

Go outside for five to ten minutes, depending on the age of the students. Emphasize how accurately scientists must make observations. Have students list as many words as they can to describe the weather. Ask them to notice air temperature relative to the classroom temperature. Bring a thermometer out with you and take the actual temperature. Take the temperature twice: once in the sun and again in the shade. Notice cloud patterns, if any, and the color of the sky. Is there any wind? If so, describe it. If it's raining, students may need to look out the window. Have a small can or bottle handy to collect raindrops for a specific period of time.

These observations can be carried out for a second time, as a homework assignment. Now, the students will be "experts," so they can be the teachers who direct family members and friends in carrying out the exercise. Let each student make a quick list of descriptive words found in their observations from home. Share them in class during language arts as a minilesson on word choice and writing to create vivid images.

Some weather words—*contrail*, *rainbow*, and *dog days*, for example—are rather exotic. Another way to incorporate weather words into language arts is by letting children write a fun, short paragraph to define what they think one of the words may mean. Later, let them use the dictionary to look up the technical definition. Some children may wish to write a short poem based on their weather observations. Others may wish to draw a picture that shows their favorite kinds of weather.

In math, older students can create math problems using the temperature recordings they have observed. Convert Fahrenheit temperatures to Celsius. Create a subtraction or addition problem to discover how many degrees warmer or colder the outside air is compared to the classroom's temperature and the temperature recorded in the sun versus that from the shade.

A longer lesson might introduce line graphs. To do this, students would have to use newspaper archives or the Internet. Let them compare and graph recorded temperatures for January 4, February 4, March 4, April 4, and May 4. List the five months on the horizontal X axis and a suitable temperature range on the Y axis. How much has the temperature changed during the five months? How might this data vary if you lived in another part of the country? What if you lived in Australia?

Also, measure how much rain you collected in the can. Calculate the volume of the can and the volume of raindrops you collected and the rate at which the rain fell. Then calculate how much rain (at the same rate) would fall in ten hours, twenty-four hours, etc.

Some useful books include: *Weather Sky*, by Bruce McMillan (Farrar, Straus and Giroux, 0-374-38261-1, ages eight to twelve); *I Call It Sky*, by Will C. Howell (Walker, 0-8027-8677-4, ages five to eight); *Hurricanes: Earth's Mightiest Storms*, by Patricia Lauber (Scholastic, 0-590-47406-5, ages eight and up); *Tornadoes*, by Seymour Simon (Morrow, 0-688-14846-5, ages seven to twelve); *Weather Forecasting*, by Gail Gibbons (Simon and Schuster, 0-689-71683-4, ages five to eight); and *Weather Words and What They Mean*, also by Gibbons (Holiday House, 0-8234-0952-X, ages five to eight).

---

(159)

Pied Piper of Hamelin

Robert Browning, Birth, May 7, 1812

The great English Victorian poet, Robert Browning, was born in May 1812. Of interest to children is Browning's poem about the Pied Piper of Hamelin. You might introduce your students to the poem and to the legend—myth or reality?

The Pied Piper legend of Hamelin, Germany, became widely known after Robert Browning wrote his work recounting the story of the strange man whose music spirited away the town's children.

As legend has it, the town of Hamelin was infested by rats. Desperate to rid themselves of the rats, the mayor agreed to pay a wandering piper a certain sum of money if he got rid of them. After the piper's music lured the rats away to a watery death in the Weser River, the mayor reneged on the deal. In response, the piper played another tune that lured the town's children into following him out of town. They followed him into a cave inside Koppen Hill and were never seen again.

It appears that the story's roots may lie partially in truth. In the 1280s, the Bishop of Olmütz sent an agent to Hamelin to recruit the youth to settle the area of Moravia. A second explanation suggests the children may have been taken as part of the Children's Crusade. A third possibility, although rather far-fetched, reports that the children were kidnapped by robbers. Whether the story is fact or fiction is irrelevant. It's a great tale with a grim moral about what happens to people who make promises and don't keep them.

Older children will enjoy reading Browning's poem. Younger children will enjoy picture-book versions of the poem or story. Two out-of-print versions to look for in your library include one illustrated by Donna Diamond and a retelling by Barbara Bartos-Hoppner. Kate Greenaway's illustrated version (Dover, 0-486-29619-9, all ages) is available in stores as is a retelling by Robert Holden (Houghton Mifflin, 0-395-89918-4, all ages). The illustrations in Holden's book are by Drahos Zak. These odd, quirky drawings will appeal to kids with an offbeat sense of humor and older students as well. It would be fun to compare several versions and let the children decide how different illustrations set the story's tone.

A fun writing exercise would be to do your own version of the Pied Piper of _____ and fill in your town's name. Create your own problem and select a piece of music that the students think would entice them to follow.

(160)

Introducing Local History

National Historic Preservation Week,
Second Full Week of May

Many people in today's society do not live in the town where they grew up. Unlike generations before ours, who often remained in the same area for years, job opportunities sometimes carry us far from our roots. Those who have lived in one area for many years may be aware of their town's heritage, while others may be too busy to take notice. Regardless of where you come from, learning about the heritage of the town you live in makes you part of that community.

Children can become involved with historic landmarks in many ways. One way is to notice the architecture of the buildings that occupy the oldest part of town. Features like rooflines, cornices, and building materials often provide clues to the period in which the building was constructed. Students could compile an architectural directory of the styles they see in different areas of town. A tour book format, with numbered "stops," makes a useful guide. Another possibility is a series of "Can you identify this building?" flash cards, each depicting a historic landmark.

The local history section of your public library should have information about the history of existing landmarks, as well as those that have been lost to progress. Each student can choose a building and research the people who built it and how the building's use may have changed over the years. Encourage students to raise their eyes and look for clues on buildings. For example, the original occupants sometimes had their names chiseled into stonework high on the facade; some buildings have old signs painted on the side.

If you live along a waterway, groups of students can research specific time periods and present to the class information about the boats that used the water during each era. Some towns still have old water mills and dams visible.

Many towns preserve old cemeteries. If possible, visit one and note the names of the people who are buried there. See how many names the students can connect to buildings they have researched. Tombstone inscriptions are often interesting and can tell stories of their own. Suggest students look for deaths during specific wars or multiple deaths during a short period of time that could be indicative of disease (the 1918 flu epidemic, for example). Students may want to try their hand at tombstone rubbings. Use thin paper and charcoal, fat crayons with the paper peeled off, or chalk. Take care not to mar stones or nearby plantings in any way. Discuss the need to be respectful when visiting a cemetery.

If possible, arrange for a class trip to famous local landmarks, especially living history displays or ongoing archaeological digs. A wealth of fascinating cultural information may be close at hand. *Breaking Ground, Breaking Silence: The Story of New York's African Burial Ground*, by Joyce Hansen (Holt, 0-8050-5012-4, grades 5 to 8), is a marvelous example of archaeological investigation. Invite the town historian to visit your classroom and talk about historic buildings and settlement patterns. Check and see if landmarks from Native American, Spanish, or French settlements existed in your area.

By preserving old buildings and getting to know the people who built them and lived in the area before we did, we become involved in our town's history. It forges a connection between us and our past and helps us become aware that we have a stake in the town's future.

(161)

Biographer's Day

May 16

Samuel Johnson (1709–1784), an English writer, and James Boswell, a Scottish author, met in London on May 16, 1763. Little did they know that one result of their meeting would be a brilliant biography. In 1791, Boswell published *The Life of Samuel Johnson*, considered by some critics to be the finest biography ever written in the English language. You might consider observing this day by introducing biography as a genre and asking students to begin reading a biography of their choice. There are lots of biographies available today—and more are being written all the time—many of which are as captivating a read as a novel.

Borrow a copy of *The Life of Samuel Johnson* from the library and choose several passages where you feel Boswell has captured Johnson's wit, wisdom, or a personality trait—perhaps a bit of a letter or a recounted dialogue.

Discuss with students what makes a good biography. You might want to mention that some biographies are fictionalized, for example, *Carry On, Mr. Bowditch*, by Jean Lee Latham (Houghton Mifflin, 0-395-0688-19, grades 8 to 12). In this fictionalized biography, Latham creates the dialogues that occur between characters in the book, based on facts discovered during the research process.

Authentic biographies, on the other hand, contain only information that has been documented. This could be through letters, eyewitness accounts, speeches, and audio- and videotapes. *Abigail Adams*, by Natalie Bober (Aladdin, 0-689-81916-1, grades 8 to 12), is an excellent example of an authentic biography for older readers.

Let students work in pairs as a biographer and a biographee. Ask them to make a list of questions that will serve as the starting point for the interviews that will follow. After one set of questions has been answered, the students should switch roles with the present biographer becoming the new biographee. Students may want to focus on one particular aspect of a person's life, for example sporting prowess or a favorite hobby. The biographer should concentrate on capturing the dynamics and essence of the biographee.

Recently published biographies that will interest a wide range of students include *Mary Anning: Fossil Hunter*, by Sally Walker (Lerner, 1-57505-425-6, ages six to nine); *Aunt Clara Brown: Official Pioneer*, by Linda Lowery (Lerner, 1-57505-045-5, ages six to nine); and *A Voice from the Wilderness: The Story of Anna Howard Shaw*, by Don Brown (Houghton Mifflin, 0-618-08362-6, ages six to nine), all for younger readers.

Upper elementary students will devour *Satchel Paige*, by Lesa Cline-Ransome (Simon and Schuster, 0-689-81151-9, ages eight to ten); *Lou Gehrig: the Luckiest Man*, by David Adler (Harcourt, 0-15-200523-4, ages seven to ten); and *Richard Wright and the Library Card*, by William Miller (Publisher's Group West, 1-8800-0057-1, ages seven to ten).

Junior high readers will find the collection of short biographical chapters in *Let It Shine: Stories of Black Women Freedom Fighters*, by Andrea Pinkney (Harcourt, 0-15-201005-X, ages eleven and up), very informative. Soccer fans will enjoy *Go for the Goal*, by Mia Hamm (HarperCollins, 0-06-019342-5, ages twelve and up). *Fireflies in the Dark: The Story of Friedl Dicker-Brandeis and the Children of Terezin*, by Susan Goldman Rubin (Holiday House, 0-8234-1461-2, ages eleven and up), is a heartrending account of a woman's attempt to keep hope alive in a World War II detention camp.

Enslow Publishers and the Lerner Publishing Group are two companies with comprehensive lines of biographies. Their biography series are available at several different reading levels.

(162)

Hold Your Own Geography Bee

The finals on the National Geographic Bee are held in Washington, D.C., early in May. Why not hold your own classroom Geography Bee to complement the national version? As discussed earlier in the month, American students appear to be way behind their counterparts all over the world in ability to understand where things are.

You can have several variations on the geography bee theme. A straightforward "typical" bee, similar to the National Geographic Bee, is one possibility. However, several variations will allow you to incorporate more students and are likely to be more fun.

Team play fosters cooperative learning skills. Divide students into groups of three or four. Instruct each team to choose a name for themselves. They can respond as a team to questions that pertain to geographical connections to the curriculum. Consultation among team members would be allowed, and the spokesperson for each team could rotate to a new team member each round.

A variation on team play would be to assign a geographical feature as a specialty to each team. For example, team specialties could be rivers, mountain ranges, states, etc. Ask other teams to generate the questions that will be posed to opposing teams. The asking team must be able to supply the correct answer. See which team can answer the most questions correctly.

A few truly motivated (or competitive) students may wish to offer a classroom challenge against another classroom. Structure the rules on this version to resemble those on "Who Wants to Be a Millionaire?" Choose a student to be Regis. Classmates from each class can be the "phone" resources à la the TV show.

You can play a game of *Geography: Near and Farther* with upper elementary, middle, and junior high students. Start by thinking of a geographical location or a state. Let students play a version of Twenty Questions to find the answer. Restrict questioning so you will respond only with the words "Near" or "Farther." For example: if you live in New York, and your mystery location is California, questions might be, "Is it nearer than Nebraska?" "Is it farther than Mississippi?" The student who guesses the correct location gets to think of a new location and be the "teacher." This one is fun as a quick game while waiting in line, etc.

For very young primary students, hold a local Geography Bee. After explaining the term, think of well-known local "hot spots," and provide clues to help students recognize them. They could be places inside the school building, local lakes or rivers, even playground equipment. The goal is quick student recognition, so make your clues strong ones.

(163)

World Turtle Day

May 24

American Tortoise Rescue has chosen this date to foster awareness of turtles, tortoises, and their habitats worldwide. Only one reptile—the turtle—has a shell. There are about 250 species of turtles found on Earth. About 40 species are tortoises, turtles that only live on land. These four-legged reptiles carry their homes, made of plates of skin tissue, with them wherever they go. Most turtles can pull their head, tail, and legs inside the shell for protection. Sea turtles cannot.

Turtles have lived on Earth for millions of years. Fossils of turtles have been found dating to at least 185 million years ago. One species of fossil sea turtle grew to a length of twelve feet. Today, turtles are much smaller. The world's longest turtle, the leatherback, grows to lengths between four and eight feet. The Galapagos tortoise grows to four feet. Tortoises can live to be more than one hundred years old.

In 1975, the U.S. Food and Drug Administration banned the sale of most species of turtles as pets. Prior to that, red-eared and painted turtles had been popular sale items in pet stores. However, it was found that many of the turtles carried the bacteria that cause salmonella, a serious health concern for humans.

Turtles can be a fun addition to the language arts curriculum. Introduce students to the old proverb "Slow and steady wins the race." Ask them what it means. Then read the Aesop's fable "The Tortoise and the Hare." Compare the fable's moral with the proverb. Students could rewrite the fable and feature turtle and rabbit species native to your area and set it in modern times. What would the animals see and pass while running their race? What diversions in your town would capture the rabbit's attention?

Other books that will complement the language arts curriculum include the funny *Road Signs: A Hare-Y Race with a Tortoise*, by Margery Cuyler (Winslow, 1-8908-1723-6, ages five to seven), which although listed for young readers will delight upper elementary and middle school students with its many puns. *Old Turtle*, by Douglas Wood (Pfeifer-Hamilton, 0-9385-8648-3, all ages), is a cautionary tale about the place people hold in the world and our responsibilities to the natural world. The Franklin turtle series, all written by Paulette Bourgeois and published by Scholastic, are very popular with primary students. Franklin and his friends cope with many of life's concerns that children experience as they grow up.

Enhance science units with studies on sea turtle migration and the efforts to save sea turtle species from extinction. *Into the Sea*, by Brenda Z. Guiberson (Holt, 0-8050-2263-5, all ages), is a gorgeous picture book that chronicles the life of a female sea turtle. The text is beautifully written and will appeal to older students as well as young listeners. *Interrupted Journey: Saving Endangered Sea Turtles*, by Kathryn Lasky (Candlewick, 0-7636-0635-9, ages eight to twelve), is a nonfiction account of a boy who participates in sea turtle rescue. As the story continues, the turtle is cared for by veterinarians and turtle rescue biologists until it can be released back into the wild. Great photographs and information about turtle rescue programs make this a must addition to library shelves.

Sea Turtles, by Frank Staub (Lerner, 0-8225-3005-8, ages six to nine), and *All About Turtles*, by Jim Arnosky (Scholastic, 0-590-48149-5, ages five to ten), are books on the life cycle of turtles. Staub's book contains color photographs, while Arnosky's are watercolor and pen illustrations.

Information about all types of turtles can be found on the Web at octopus.gma.org/turtles. A site for sea turtles is located at turtles.org.

164

Introducing Jazz

International Jazz Day, May 24

Jazz is often heralded as the only musical art form to originate in the United States. While jazz began gaining popularity in the late eighteen hundreds, its roots are much earlier and can be found in African rhythms, African American music, and in music played by bands in America. Some of its musical forms have roots in European music traditions as well, but jazz grew its own unique style in the United States. Dixieland jazz bands were recorded as early as 1917.

The best way to bring jazz into the classroom is by listening to it. The end of the school year is a time when attentions start wandering. Playing some jazz will give everyone a chance to wiggle, tap, and jive their prevacation excitements out. All students should become familiar with at least a few of the wonderful jazz tunes. See if students can tell a "hot" jazz piece from a "cool" one. Jazz has evolved into many overlapping styles, and some like it hot and some like it cool, some like it Latin and some like it Middle Eastern.

There are many fine jazz musicians and a wide variety of recordings from which to choose. Keep things interesting by varying artists and instrument sounds. Use different songs to create background mood.

Duke Ellington played the piano and composed jazz. He greatly influenced the direction of jazz and was one of the founders of big band jazz. Ellington's "Mood Indigo" is a haunting orchestral piece that marvelously blends orchestral instruments. Don't miss his "Take the A Train" and "East St. Louis Toodle-oo" either. International Jazz Day is also the anniversary of Ellington's death, on May 24, 1974.

Charles Mingus brings the bass to life and is known for his atonal style. Play his piece "Fables of Faubus." Its brilliant intonation and memorable melodies show anger at racial bigotry and mock Orval E.

Faubus, the governor of Arkansas who, in 1957, called out the Arkansas National Guard to block integration of Central High School in Little Rock. Play this and use it for a discussion starter on how music can be used to express emotion and to reflect political or societal issues.

Don't forget Ramsey Lewis. Born on May 27, 1935, in Chicago, Illinois, Lewis has won three Grammy Awards for his work. A piano player, his work moves back and forth between jazz and easy listening pop music.

The drum set takes center stage when the sticks are held by the likes of Max Roach and Art Blakey. For Latin jazz drumming look for recordings by Tito Puente. All of these artists recorded work with many people. Lionel Hampton is another percussion virtuoso, but his instrument is the vibraphone, familiarly called "the vibes." His mallets seem to fly along the vibraphone keys.

Charlie Parker, nicknamed "Bird," played the saxophone and composed music as well. He is credited, along with Dizzy Gillespie, for the rise of bebop. He was a master at improvisation, and his work is wildly different from his contemporaries. Check out Parker's "Ornithology" and "Confirmation." Read aloud Chris Raschka's picture book *Charlie Parker Played Be-Bop* (Orchard Books, 0531-059-995, ages six and up) and see if children catch the unique rhythmic writing style that mimics Parker's own music.

Don't miss Miles Davis and his soaring trumpet. His "Kind of Blue" ranks among the most popular jazz tunes of all time, and "So What" is popular, too. Everyone should hear them.

Wynton Marsalis plays the trumpet and has recorded many pieces. In addition to playing, he also composes and, in 1997, was the first jazz composer to win a Pulitzer Prize in music. He won for his work on "Blood in the Fields," which was commissioned by Jazz at the Lincoln Center, where he is currently the music director. Some of his other honors include nine Grammys. If you want to know what he is up to right now, see his Web page: WyntonMarsalis.net. But before students start reading about this creative genius, let them hear him at work. This man can really blow his own horn! An easy place to start is Columbia Jazz's recording *Popular Songs: The Best of Wynton Marsalis*. Any media center is likely to have a large selection of Marsalis's work available for you to borrow. While you are there see if they have the four-part video, book, and CD series for kids created by Wynton Marsalis (2002). It is called *Marsalis on Music,* and is available from Sony Classical Film and Video. Because the price tag is close to three hundred dollars, it is likely to be a borrow-only item for most teachers. If you can get your hands on it and make some time for viewing, you will have one of the best-informed classes in your school!

These are only a few of the scores of talented musicians who have brought jazz to music's forefront. Include some of your own favorites. If your local high school has a jazz band, see if several of the players could visit your school for a short jazz assembly. Elementary students love visits from the "big kids," and it's a great way to generate interest in the district's band program. See if any well-known jazz players came from your area and play their works, or if you can arrange it, why not have an artist visit and play some jazz for your class.

(165)

Amelia Jenks Bloomer

Birth, May 27, 1818

Amelia Jenks was born in Homer, New York, in 1818. An educated woman, she worked as a teacher before she married David Bloomer, a newspaper editor from Seneca Falls, New York. The couple moved to Seneca Falls, and several years later, Bloomer altered the course of women's fashion.

Seneca Falls was the site of the 1848 Women's Rights Convention. Prominent spokeswoman Elizabeth Cady Stanton lived there. Stanton's quest for women's rights influenced Bloomer's life. In 1848, when the Ladies' Temperance Society was formed, Amelia Bloomer served as one of its officers. You may need to talk about what the word *temperance* means—have someone volunteer to look it up. Stanton began the journal *The Lily*, which was the first newspaper edited and run entirely by a woman. *The Lily* informed its readers on women's issues and the suffrage movement. Bloomer believed in women's rights and served as the town's deputy postmaster to demonstrate that a woman had the right to fill any position as long as she could serve it capably.

While she worked tirelessly for suffrage, the issue that pushed Bloomer into the public eye was an article she wrote about women's clothing. She loved a new French outfit worn by a visiting cousin. A short skirt worn over baggy pantaloons offered women freedom from the heavy, constricting long dresses they normally wore, allowing them to try the new craze of bicycling. Bloomer's article was an overnight sensation, and the startling new garment rocked the nation. Some women's rights advocates and women athletes began wearing the garment and received mixed public reaction. Because Amelia Bloomer wore and publicly supported the outfit, people dubbed it "bloomers."

Students can observe Bloomer's birthday in several ways. First, they can examine the issue of women's rights. In particular, focus on how a woman was discouraged from owning and operating certain businesses and how she was regarded as her husband's property. Discuss voting rights and the amendment that granted women the right to vote. Students can make time lines to chronicle the suffrage movement and its main spokespeople.

In a lighter vein, students can explore fashion and how it has changed over time. One exercise might be to imagine that bloomers (actually the pants that followed them) had not become an accepted mode of dress. How might the activities girls participate in today be different? Students could design and draw what they think future fashions will be like. Bloomer's birthday might be designated as a classroom "dress crazy day."

A look at "foreign" fashions is an interesting way to bring multiculturalism into the classroom. Many cultures have ceremonial dress that reflects a variety of artistic styles. In some cultures the women wear what we would see as pants while the men wear "skirts."

Students may enjoy looking at unusual fashion trends and fads, too. Frequently these relate to the subject of beauty. Some suggestions are corsets, the nineteenth-century European custom of surgically removing a rib for slimmer waists, the custom of foot binding, the elaborate hairstyles of the seventeen hundreds, neck rings worn by certain African women, tattoos, and the modern American fascination with body piercing.

Literature connections include: *You Forgot Your Skirt, Amelia Bloomer!*, by Shana Corey (Scholastic, 0-439-07819-9, grades 3 to 6); *Bloomers!*, by Rhoda Blumberg (Simon and Schuster, 0-689-80455-5, grades K to 3); *Dressed for the Occasion: What Americans Wore 1620–1970*, by Brandon Miller (Lerner, 0-8225-1738-8, grades 6 to 9); and *Ballot Box Battle*, by Emily McCully (Knopf, 0-679-87938-2, grades 1 to 4). There are also many individual biographies about prominent leaders in the suffrage movement.

(166)

Top of the World

Mount Everest Summit Reached, May 29, 1953

On May 29, 1953, Edmund Hillary, a New Zealander, and his Sherpa guide, Tensing Norgay, became the first people to reach the summit of Mount Everest, the world's highest mountain. Hearing about braving icy temperatures and crossing treacherous crevasses fascinates children greatly (adults, too!). Learning about Hillary's adventure is exciting and informative. And readers will want to follow up with additional books about more recent summit adventures.

For geography, students could make a list of the world's ten highest mountains. Locate them on a map and calculate the distance your school is from each mountain. More in-depth research could include locating satellite images of the appropriate mountain ranges and pinpointing each mountain's location in the range. Students could look for photographs that show the specific routes used while attempting to reach each summit. For a height comparison, graph the elevation of your town against that of each mountain. How many times would you have to "stack up" your town to reach the height of the world's top ten mountains?

For science, students could find information about the specific dangers on Mount Everest. This could include finding out how oxygen levels change at higher elevations and how low oxygen levels affect the human body. Check out what happens to people when they experience hypothermia. Nighttime wind velocity is high on top of Mount Everest. How does it compare with that of Mount Washington in New Hampshire? With those of thunderstorms and hurricanes? Researching terms such as *glacier, crevasse,* and *icefalls* will help to illustrate the dangers involved in mountain climbing.

In language arts, students could try to put themselves in the shoes of Hillary and Norgay once they had reached the summit. Write a short paragraph to answer, How would you feel if you were standing on the top of the world? or What things in your life make you feel as if you are standing on top of the world?

There are several recently published books that complement Hillary's historic achievement. *Triumph on Everest,* by Broughton Coburn (National Geographic Society, 0-7922-7114-9, ages nine and up), is a photobiography of Hillary's life. *Mystery on Everest,* by Audrey Salkeld (0-7922-72222-6, ages nine and up), is the riveting story of George Mallory, who died in 1924 while attempting to reach Mount Everest's summit. Middle school and junior high readers will enjoy *Within Reach: My Everest Story,* by Mark Pfetzer and Jack Galvin (Penguin, 0-14-130497-9, ages ten and up), the autobiography of the teenager who ascended Mount Everest.

(167)

Fun in the Sun

As the weather gets warmer, summer vacation approaches, and attention spans grow shorter, a change of pace during recess is in order. Team sports may be beyond the scope of some neighborhoods, so focusing on smaller group activities may be the route you want to take. These kinds of games foster neighbor involvement and family fun. Students could ask parents and grandparents what games they played as children. These can be shared and played during recess.

Wildly popular years ago, marbles is making a comeback. It's versatile, since it can be played on pavement or dirt. Jacks is another old game now regaining popularity, although for safety's sake it needs to be played on a smooth floor. Hopscotch has never lost its appeal, and chalk, a pebble, and pavement are all you need to play. *Jacks Around the World*, by Mary D. Lankford (Morrow, 0-688-13707-5, grades K to 6), and *Hopscotch Around the World*, also by Lankford (Morrow, 0-688-147453, grades K to 6), contain instructions on how to play international versions of the two games.

Jumping rope is still popular, including the elastic-around-the-ankles version, often referred to as Chinese jump rope. *Miss Mary Mack*, by Johanna Cole and Stephanie Calmenson (Morrow, 0-688-09749-9, grades K to 5), contains good jump rope rhymes.

Bocce and horseshoes are games of skill. Ingenuity with materials gets you around purchasing a set. For example, use a golf ball as the target and tennis balls marked with *X*s and *O*s as the players' balls. Aluminum foil horseshoes are lightweight, but OK for preschoolers and kindergartners who can only toss a short distance accurately.

School and public libraries have many game books that explain rules and offer other game and activity suggestions. You can also look for books on outdoor cooperative games that tell the rules for fun variations on old favorites.

Résumés for Kids

Perhaps you recall building your first résumé. Was it hard work? Was it stressful? If so, keep your past experiences under wraps, 'cause kids often find this project fun and interesting. First of all the topic is very personal and engaging because it is all about them: their experiences, their goals, their lives. Second, this project is perfect for the buddy system. We all know the rule about never sending out a résumé until many eyes have screened it.

You may be wondering at this point why your kids would need a résumé. Chances are if you have children younger than about fifth grade this exercise is probably not for you. June is a good time to build a résumé because older elementary to middle schoolers (and up of course) can often use a simple résumé in applying for volunteer positions, special summer camps or schools, and paid work. Not that these require a résumé, but a child providing one is sure to get noticed!

The first thing students will need is scratch paper and some time to think. To help focus you can put the main elements of a résumé on the board. Kids will need: Name, Address, Phone, E-mail (if they like), Objective (also optional, especially on kid résumés), Experience, School, and Talents or Skills. The data parts are pretty easy. Then comes the dreaded "objective." Explain this in real-life terms. Say Sam wants to help out at a homeless shelter where his mom sometimes volunteers. He knows what volunteers are likely to help with, so he will put that in his objective: "To assist other volunteers with duties such as preparing and serving meals, putting together care packages, playing with young children, helping in the garden, or other tasks as assigned." Rosita wants to get into a space camp. She knows that it is hard to get in, so she will include a résumé with her application. Her objective might be really simple: "To attend Super Space Sendoff Week at Camp of the Stars."

Experience can be anything that helped build skills. Brainstorm this category and write all suggestions on the board. Obviously paid work is experience, but helping at home can be experience, as can travel, volunteer work, church activities, school activities, time spent in Scouts or similar organizations, and even tough life experiences can have a place.

School can be a simple or more elaborate section. Students should list the name of their school and the last grade they completed. If a graduation is coming up (say from sixth grade), that date and anticipated grade completed can be listed. School activities can have a special section if there are many.

Talents and skills may require another brainstorming session. Read a dictionary definition of each word. Work to name as many talents and skills you can think of as a group. Remember to include any languages spoken. Take time to come up with a big list. This will help students see their own talents, but a friendly reminder of what *you* know they possess is a good ego booster and will assist students who seem stumped here.

All these categories are available in a fill-in-the-blank, kid-friendly résumé work sheet online at careerkids.com/1152x864/resume.html. Students can work from their rough draft at a computer or you can print out a blank for them to use in class. After several drafts, each student will need to show his or her almost-final version to a partner and then to you. Make suggestions freely, because that is how the process should go for adults too! Return the draft and tell students to work to make it easy to read (pick an uncomplicated font and use at least 12 point size). Because they are kids they should not be faced with the chore of trying to squeeze too much in, so all kids' résumés should end up with lots of pleasant white space.

There are many kinds of résumés, and you may want to show your students some that you can collect from friends or colleagues, or a book of résumés like *McGraw-Hill's Big Red Book of Resumes* (0-07-140195-4, adult) so they can see the diversity. Students can line up their categories on the left or centered as it pleases them. They can capitalize, underline, use italics, or bold some section headings, but be sure they are consistent in how they use these highlighting techniques. In résumé building the writer aims to get across the main points, using very few words. In fact, observant kids may notice that many résumés don't even use real sentences. Students may use lists with bullets, or short sentences in a block paragraph, to explain skills or experiences.

Encourage those students with access to nice paper and printers at home to do their final draft at home and bring in the finished version. Remind them to save the résumé on a labeled disk in case they need to make changes either for this project or perhaps next year when they suddenly need a résumé. For students without access, see if you can get your hands on good quality paper and printer at school (perhaps your school office?) and print out the rest of the class's résumés.

Children will be justly proud of their efforts, and perhaps you will want to display the finished products in a school or classroom display. This exercise can be used as a warm-up to career units, or as a follow-up. If you wish to extend the unit, check out the career inventories and games at web.utk.edu/~amiser/career%20page.html. These can prove an insightful way to get children thinking ahead to what they might be interested in pursuing. Quintessential Careers' award-winning website is worth a visit for teens: quintcareers.com.html. Among other things this site offers a cover letter tutorial.

Two books to recommend to students who are interested in thinking about career preparation are: Sean Covey's (son of the famous time-management Coveys) *The Seven Habits of Highly Effective Teens* (Simon and Schuster, 0684856093, young adult), which includes cartoons, cool ideas, and great real-life stories about teens; *Writing a Resume*, by Stuart Schwartz (Capstone, 07368012, ages nine to twelve reading level but interest level to middle school).

June and July

---

(169)

Take 'em to the River

National Rivers Month, June

Since the Clean Water Act was enacted in 1972, river cleanup projects have become popular and are annual events in some communities. Why not observe National Rivers Month by investigating the rivers in your area?

First, focus on the largest river in your state. During geography, students can highlight the river on a state map and determine how far it is from your school. Note the big towns along the river's route. In what years were they incorporated? Do the dates reflect any sequences or settlement patterns?

For science, let them do some research on the Internet and locate facts about the river's health, past and present. A helpful search term when investigating rivers is a phrase such as "Mississippi River Basin." What kinds of fishes, birds, mammals, and plants live in or near the river? Have there been major concerns about pollution? Often high school biology teachers can serve as a resource to point you toward local experts. There may even be a local nonprofit group whose focus is your watershed. If so, ask for a speaker or at the least some handouts.

Make your river studies more local by doing the same sort of activities for the rivers and streams within one to ten miles of the school. Make a time line for your local river and see how the community and its inhabitants have changed throughout history. What kinds of commerce have used the river in the past and in the present? It might be fun for language arts to write a first-person narrative from the river's perspective.

Contact the state geological survey in your area and see if they have any hydrologic information about the water and its analysis. They may also be able to provide a map showing the watershed area that drains into your local river. Students can chart which creeks and streams are the tributaries that flow into the larger river. For hands-on water studies, students can measure turbidity of the river and do other simple tests that don't require a great deal of materials. Ask for information from your state's geological survey society or environmental agency.

Interested students might wish to join a river cleanup project, if one is planned. Local environmental organizations should be able to give you dates. Visit the Susquehanna River Watch website at tier.net/riverwatch. This site was created by teachers, students, and community volunteers and describes student monitoring projects of the Susquehanna River. It provides good ideas for local projects.

Students can design posters about things community members can do to preserve the river's health. Not dumping garbage into the water and reducing the use of pesticides and fertilizers on lawns are two examples. See if local businesses would post them during the month.

A number of schools in the Midwest take time every spring to make stencils and spray "Drains to River" on local street drains. This simple effort results in more awareness about the importance of not draining engine oil onto the street, and not pouring chemicals down those convenient drains. It is very satisfying work that can be done as a classroom or with a whole school.

There are several books that students might find interesting that chronicle river stories. *A River Ran Wild*, by Lynne Cherry (Harcourt, 0-15-200542-0, ages six to ten), tells the story of a river from prehistoric times to the present. Pollution cleanup is featured. *River Story*, by Meredith Hooper (Candlewick, 0-7636-0792-4, ages four to seven), is an introduction to the hydrologic cycle. It follows one river's journey to the sea.

The "Rivers of Life" website (cgee.hamline.edu/rivers) has projects and resources for K–12 students. Ask your reference librarian for assistance locating recent back issues of newsmagazines like *Time* or

Newsweek that will have articles on rivers in the news. *National Geographic* features rivers almost every month. Older students will enjoy the news pieces, and you can assign them to write a précis (a short summation), which is a very important tool for students to have in their writer's kit and makes it easy to share information with the rest of the class.

(170)

Back to the Farm

June Is National Dairy Month

The United States has deep agricultural roots. Although larger numbers of people now live and work in cities, if you ask around you will find many people who remember visiting relatives on the family farm. Cows have always been an important creature to cities and farms alike, because everyone needs dairy products. Even ranchers and crop farmers usually kept at least one or two cows to make dairy products for their family to eat.

Making butter or yogurt are fun activities for this month. Butter can be made if you have an energetic bunch of kids willing to shake a zippered plastic bag with cold heavy whipping cream until it starts making butter lumps. This is a fun activity to do with music that has a good beat. It will take a long time, so is not a good project for the really young primary students. For this age group, where patience is in shorter supply, use electric beaters or a blender. After large clumps of butter form, you remove the mess into a flat pan and lean the pan so that the buttermilk runs away from the butter.

Students can press the butter into a big clump and use a rubber spatula or the back of a spoon to squeeze more water out. The resulting buttermilk can be poured into Dixie cups to sample. Ice-cold buttermilk was a refreshing favorite of generations past. After the butter is well squeezed and looks like butter you can add a light sprinkle of salt and mix it in well. The lumps of butter can be shaped onto a plate or squished into bowls and served with crackers.

Yogurt making requires starting early in the day—perhaps first thing in the morning. You will need hot scalded milk (brought just to a boil then turned off), a little yogurt with live cultures for "starter," a slow cooker with a low setting, and a couple of sterile containers or jars. Milk should be at about 90 to 120 degrees. This temperature kills ordinary bacteria that makes milk sour, but encourages the yogurt cultures. You can cool scalded milk by pouring it back and forth between sterile jars or pans. Keep track of the temperature. When the milk is cool enough add about a half cup of yogurt with active cultures (from any store) to two quarts of milk (the amounts are not too important) in the warm slow cooker and stir gently.

If you have a sunny window you could skip the slow cooker and make solar yogurt by wrapping the sterile containers in black fabric and turning them occasionally. Old country yogurt was just set at the back of the wood stove for a few days! Either way you should have yogurt in about three to six hours, depending upon conditions. Flavor with a little honey or jam or maple syrup. Yogurt's flavor changes (for the worse) after refrigeration, so enjoy the treat right from the pot if possible. Beneficial cultures are great for humans' digestive and immune systems, so they have made yogurt a health food around the world for thousands of years.

Here are some fun, informative, and cute books for dairy month for the four- to eight-year-olds. *Extra Cheese Please: Mozzarella's Journey from Cow to Pizza*, by Chris Peterson (Boyds Mills Press, 1563971771), tells the story from the author's own farm to a pizza. It includes great facts—for example, one cow in one year can create forty thousand glasses of milk—and also features a bibliography, glossary, and pizza recipe. *The Milk Makers* (Reading Rainbow), by Gail Gibbons (Aladdin Paperbacks, 068971116), shows how milk gets from the cow to your glass in easy-to-read language with good illustrations to support the text. *Hooray for Dairy Farming*, by Bobbie Kalman (Crabtree, 0865056501), gives readers clear photos and text to compare agricultural practices then and now.

171

National Candy Month

Candy lovers stand up and be counted! Sweeten student attitudes with curriculum treats. The United States is a nation of candy lovers. We eat an average of twenty pounds of candy a year per person. The kinds of candy we eat vary widely from chocolate bars, to chewy treats, to brittle nutty nibbles. You can have classroom candy fun—without the calories or cavities—in lots of ways.

Sugar is the primary component in most candies. In science, older students can experiment with melting sugar crystals. Use candy thermometers to record melting points and how they vary according to the addition of other ingredients. Experiments for younger students that don't require heat are easy, too. Teach the concepts of solutions, saturation, and supersaturated liquids by stirring varying amounts of sugar into water. To supersaturate, students will have to use hot tap water. Students can read about making gum in *Bubble Gum*, by Arlene Erlbach (Lerner, 0-8225-2391-4, grades 2 to 5).

Math problems don't seem like work when students are graphing candy preferences. Conduct surveys to find out which types of candy are most popular. Make bar graphs to record results. Survey for monthly candy consumption. Ask students to estimate on a scale of 1 to 10 how much candy they eat in a given month. October, December, and the month Easter occurs in are likely to approach 10. Use line graphs to reflect consumption. Take the fear out of word problems with *The Candy Counting Book*, by Lisa McCourt (Bridgewater, 0-8167-6329-1, grades K to 3), a yummy collection of word problems. After learning how to decipher and solve these problems, students can write their own candy word problems. Barbara McGrath has written several M&M math counting books (Charlesbridge).

Each student can invent his or her own candy. Students can list ingredients, test-market names in the classroom and at home, design a wrapper, and create an advertising poster or commercial.

Find "candy" music and play it in the room. An example is the music for the "Dance of the Sugar Plum Fairy" from the *Nutcracker* ballet by Tchaikovsky. There are several silly chewing gum "pop" songs, too.

For social studies, students can research candies that were popular when their parents and grandparents were little. Does anyone have a grandma willing to come in and demonstrate taffy making or maple sugar making? Investigate biographies of famous candy makers such as Milton S. Hershey. Students can research prices and sizes of candy bars from the past and compare them to today's bars.

Encourage students to look into the favorite candies of children in different countries. Visiting students and recent immigrants may have fond memories of candy from their birth country. Many Middle Eastern nations favor candy made with sesame seeds, a flavor we tend to associate with savory foods, not deserts. See if you can find some unusual flavors of candy to sample. Ask students to share candy names and descriptions. The Internet may be a source for the names of candy manufacturers in foreign countries. Local health food, gourmet food, or international specialty stores can be the source of interesting candies. Chocolate, a perennial favorite in the United States, can be a unit all its own since it not only has a rich history but scientists have now discovered that it possesses healthy phytochemicals.

Fireworks!

Fireworks Safety Months, June and July

June may seem a bit early for talking about this, but children need to start thinking about the dangers presented by improper use of fireworks. Too many avoidable accidents occur on the Fourth of July.

Fireworks get their explosive power from gunpowder. The colorful fireworks that we see on the Fourth of July and other special occasions are a combination of gunpowder and chemicals such as sodium, copper, and barium and strontium compounds. When mixed, they produce the dazzling yellow, blue, green, and red color bursts. As a science-related writing project, have students contact the organization in your town responsible for arranging fireworks displays. Ask for the name of the manufacturer or distributor. Students can write to the company for information on how the umbrella shapes, twirly patterns, and sizzlers are controlled.

Invite one of the people responsible for igniting your town's fireworks to visit your classroom or school and give a demonstration of the safety practices they use while setting off the fireworks. He or she can also discuss firecracker and sparkler danger, and if appropriate to your area, the illegality of possessing explosive devices. *Follow My Leader*, by James Garfield (Puffin, 0-14-036485-4, grades 3 to 7), is a novel about a boy blinded by a firecracker. His adjustment to blindness and the use of a guide dog are particularly appealing.

Fireworks have been used as part of celebrations for hundreds of years. *The Firework-Maker's Daughter*, by Philip Pullman (Scholastic, 0-590-18719-8, grades 3 to 7), set in ancient times, is an entertaining novel about Lila, a headstrong heroine, determined to become a "firework-maker," a title traditionally bestowed only on men.

Children can have fun making their own fireworks art displays. Bring in picture books with scratchboard illustrations (Brian Pinkney has done many) to provide examples of finished products. Students can use crayons to cover paper with colors, scribble over the colorful pattern with black crayon, and scratch fireworks display patterns into the black crayon with an unbent paper clip or scissors edge. Three-dimensional fireworks can be made with curly ribbon, metallic streamers, and other items. Hang them from the ceiling.

Talk about fireworks music. The *1812 Overture*, by Peter Tchaikovsky, written to commemorate the withdrawal of Napoleon I and his troops from Moscow, is a stirring piece that resounds with fireworks-like booms. Look for a recording that includes cannons. Play the piece while students are creating their fireworks art displays.

Since fireworks have been used mostly for celebrations and religious rites in China, where gunpowder likely originated, since about the second century B.C., you can choose to focus on Asia. It is thought that what the Chinese called "gung pow" spread to Islamic Asia where it was developed into weaponry used in battles against Europeans.

The use of gunpowder for rocketry was then reintroduced into China. The original skyrocket was just a long stick.

Children may enjoy learning more about how fireworks work. To focus on science you need only get on the Internet, as many teachers have pulled this information together for you already. For the science behind the boom and bright lights start with tlc.discovery.com /tlcpages/fireworks, which offers links to a number of fireworks-related sites. If you are familiar with Big Chalk, you may want to send students there (bigchalk.com) for more science information.

(173)

Charles Drew

Birth, June 3, 1904

Charles Drew was an African American doctor who gained fame for his pioneering work on the study of blood plasma. During World War II he directed the Red Cross program to organize blood banks and ship plasma overseas for wounded American soldiers. He was killed in an automobile crash in 1950.

Celebrate Dr. Drew's birthday by drawing students' attention to the importance of your community's blood bank. Invite a hospital employee who can speak about donating blood and its many uses. Specific topics could include trauma and emergency room usage, autotransfusions, procedures for storing blood, and the necessity of maintaining a sufficient on-hand quantity. A representative of the local chapter of the Red Cross could focus on the organization's work in disaster relief and blood supply to war zones. Parents who have donated blood can share their experiences, emphasizing that this is one way students can help the community when they get older. Some high school students have organized blood donor days in their districts.

As part of the science curriculum, students can research blood types, the circulatory system, blood cells, and the importance of vitamins and diet for healthy blood. Projects could include making graphs to compare the percentages of people with various blood types, the increase in demand for blood, and how much was used during the past ten years. How much blood was used in WWII, the Korean War, and the Vietnam War? For a disgusting project, research the use of leeches in early medicine and how they are being used today in modern hospitals!

Books on these subjects include: *Charles Drew: A Life-Saving Doctor*, by Miles Shapiro (Raintree Steck-Vaughn, 0-8172-4403-4, grades 5 to 12); *The Heart*, by Seymour Simon (Morrow, 0-688-11407-5, grades 3 to 6); *Blood and Gore*, by Vicki Cobb (Scholastic, 0-590-92665-9, grades 2 to 6.); *The Circulatory System*, by Darlene R. Stille (Children's Press, 0-516-26261-0, grades 2 to 5).

D-Day

Anniversary, June 6, 1944

The term *D-day* is actually a military term for a date upon which a secret military action is scheduled. The most famous D-Day is probably June 6, 1944. Allied forces comprised of troops from the United States, Great Britain, Canada, and France crossed the English Channel and stormed the beaches of Normandy. It was the largest sea invasion in history.

World War II studies are an important focus of middle and junior high school social studies curriculum. Fortunately, there are a number of excellent books for young readers that focus on World War II.

One of the best is *The Good Fight: How World War II Was Won*, by Stephen Ambrose (Atheneum, 0-689-84361-5, ages nine and up). The book is full of photographs, maps, and diagrams. The photographs are well chosen, some are heartrending, and sidebars filled with "Quick Facts" about war-related topics are great eye-catchers. Readers will be gripped from the riveting first paragraph, which begins "World War II (1939–1945) was the greatest catastrophe in history." Manageable blocks of text describe important events of the war, such as D-Day, Iwo Jima, Guadalcanal, and the dropping of the atomic bomb. This honest, straightforward account of life and death during World War II should not be missed.

Children of the World War II Home Front, by Sylvia Whitman (Carolrhoda, 1-57505-484-1, ages seven to ten), looks at how children coped with the war and the efforts they made to "do their part," which included scrap-metal drives, buying war bonds, and planting victory gardens.

There are many novels set during WW II that make good literature circle choices. *Foster's War*, by Carolyn Reeder (Scholastic, 0-590-09846-2, ages ten and up); *Don't You Know There's a War On?*, by Avi (Avon, 0-380-97863-6, ages nine to twelve); and *Lily's Crossing*, by Patricia Giff (Bantam, 0-440-41453-9, ages twelve and up), all deal with living on the home front during the war. *When the Soldiers Were Gone*, by Vera Propp (Penguin, 0-399-23325-3, ages seven to eleven), is set in Holland immediately after the war. The protagonist is a young boy who has been living with what he thinks is his family during the war. His world turns upside down when another family comes and "reclaims" him. This is based on a true story of a Jewish boy whose parents placed him in a home with a Dutch family to save him from persecution.

PBS's "The American Experience" had a program about D-Day. Find supplementary information for older students at pbs.org/wgbh /amex/dday.

(175)

Verna Aardema

Birth, June 6, 1911

Children and adults have been enchanted by Verna Aardema's many folktales and stories, which are appropriate and fun for all ages. Well known for retelling African tales, Aardema wrote more than twenty-five books before she died in May 2000.

Why Mosquitos Buzz in People's Ears, one of her best known (and widely loved) tales, received the 1976 Caldecott Medal for the abstract illustrations by Leo and Diane Dillon and was the first Caldecott Medal awarded to an African American illustrator. The story, considering the topic, has one of the most logical and satisfying ends a folktale could have.

Bringing the Rain to Kapiti Plain (a Nandi tale) is a delightful cumulative tale about a drought. As each animal, and a shepherd boy, does its own part trying to end the drought, they begin a chain of events that restore lush greenery to the parched land. Young listeners will love chiming in for the text repetitions. It would also make a great felt-board story if you made animal cutouts. In addition to reading this story just because it's a great book, you can use it to complement weather or geography units.

Koi and the Kola Nuts (a Liberian tale) underscores the use of the magic number three in folktales. The lush illustrations perfectly depict the jungle areas where Koi attempts to complete the three impossible tasks set for him by a demanding king. The tale concludes with a succinctly stated moral that reflects the Golden Rule ("Do to others as you would have them do to you"), which is found in many cultures.

Anansi Does the Impossible (an Ashanti tale) adds to the collection of spider tales that fascinate readers. The tricky Anansi always manages to cleverly attain his goals. Compare the adventures in Aardema's Anansi story with those in *A Story, A Story*, by Gail Haley

(Simon and Schuster, 0-689-71201-4, all ages). Again, these stories stand on their own, but if you wish to use them to complement units on spiders or make art projects that feature spiders, go ahead.

Ever wonder how much your children really understand about the size and diversity of the continent of Africa? Why not honor Aardema by cutting out a bulletin board–size shape of the African continent, superimpose a spider's web on it, and then connect each of Aardema's African tales to its appropriate geographical location, with pictures and/or book reviews written by students.

Aardema wrote many more books your students will love. All are readily available in school and public libraries (bookstores, too).

(176)

Maurice Sendak

Birth, June 10, 1928

For decades children have thrilled to the adventures Max found after sailing in and out of a day to "where the wild things are." Max and his wolf suit, from the Caldecott Medal book *Where the Wild Things Are*, are instantly recognized by many children (adults, too). Celebrate the author/illustrator Sendak's birthday with a Sendak Fest.

Young children may want to dress as a favorite character from a Sendak story. Max, Pierre, the Wolf from Swine Lake, and Little Bear are a few possibilities. You can welcome parents to the classroom for the Fest. Let the children write and illustrate invitations to the party.

Max made mischief of "one kind or another." Have students look at the illustrations in the book and try to imagine what mischief Max might have done that would warrant being sent to his room. They can also write a story featuring themselves as Max and draw what they would do if they were King of the Wild Things.

Hold a Sendak Scavenger Hunt. Create a list of pictures, words, and phrases from books illustrated by Sendak. You might use words like *rumpus, kitchen, Grisly-Beard, rice*, and *higglety*. Divide students into teams and let them hunt through Sendak books in the learning center for the items. Older students could look for visual puns in Sendak books. *Swine Lake*, by James Marshall (Harper, 0-06-204171-7, grades 2 and up), is loaded with slyly humorous illustrations by Sendak.

Weston Woods Studios produced an excellent (and unusual) animated video of *Where the Wild Things Are* that students may enjoy. See if it is available in your learning center. Read *Swine Lake*, Marshall and Sendak's piggy parody of *Swan Lake*. Bring music and dance into the room with a recording of *Swan Lake*, by Peter Tchaikovsky. Students can address the book's theme: music tames the savage beast. Ask what music they would use to bring out the artist in themselves.

Some of Sendak's works have a more serious side. *We Are All in the Dumps with Jack and Guy* deals with homelessness. Both *Where the Wild Things Are* and *Outside Over There* represent how children handle their emotions. Middle school students might explore and compare these and other picture books, such as *Elizabeth Imagined an Iceberg*, by Chris Raschka (Orchard, 0-531-06817-X), that feature children dealing with difficult topics.

177

The Stars and Stripes

National Flag Week June 11-17;
Flag Day, June 14

There are many flag-oriented projects that will help students understand and appreciate the American flag. This is a good week to write out and discuss the Pledge of Allegiance. Put poor "Richard Stands"

to rest in the minds of primary students. Discussion of ways to honor and display the flag are appropriate this week.

All students will recognize today's flag, but many will be unfamiliar with historic American flags. Research projects could include locating pictures of early versions of the flag. Discuss the significance of the thirteen stripes, the stars, and why the colors red, white, and blue were chosen. The Continental Congress left no record of why they chose these colors, but if students investigate the creation of the Great Seal of the United States in 1782, they will find that the Congress of Confederation passed a resolution stating the choice of red, white, and blue for the Great Seal and their significance. Students might wish to draw and display early versions of the flag.

Students may wish to read about Francis Hopkinson, a signer of the Declaration of Independence and the man most scholars credit with designing the first flag. They may also want to learn about Betsy Ross, who may or may not have sewn the first flag.

Flag etiquette—under what conditions the flag should be flown, how to dispose of an old flag, and other issues—could be a discussion topic. Older students could research and debate flag desecration (burning, hanging upside down) and freedom of speech, a hotly debated current events issue. Research and discussion will help students decide where they stand on this issue.

For a musical tie-in, play a recording of John Philip Sousa's march "The Stars and Stripes Forever."

The website at usflag.org has information on every aspect of our flag and on Flag Day.

(178)

Helen Keller

Birth, June 27, 1880

Children are always captivated by the story of this inspiring woman, who achieved so much before her death in 1968. Scarlet fever left her blind and deaf at eighteen months of age. She grew up a wild child until teacher Anne Sullivan (who herself battled eye problems) reached her and helped her reenter the world. Keller went on to graduate from college and become an author and lecturer.

There are a number of books about Helen Keller, including her adult-level autobiography. Children's books include: *A Picture Book of Helen Keller*, by David Adler (Holiday House, 0-8234-0818-3, preschool to grade 3); *A Girl Named Helen Keller*, by Margo Lundell (Scholastic, 0-590-47963-6, grades 1 to 3); *Helen Keller*, by Johanna Hurwitz (Random House, 0-679-87705-3, grades 2 to 4); and *Helen Keller*, by Lois Nicholson (Chelsea House, 0-7910-2086-X, grades 5 and up).

Videos available movies about Helen Keller's life include two versions of *The Miracle Worker*. The 1962 movie, starring Anne Bancroft and Patty Duke, is in black and white. The 1979 TV remake stars Patty Duke and Melissa Gilbert.

Students can first be asked to imagine that they are blind. Have them list ways they could communicate. Then, ask them to do the same activity as though they are deaf. Finally, compare the lists and strike out ways of communication not possible if they were both blind and deaf. Now how would they communicate?

Older students could research how, in the last hundred years, educating blind and deaf people has changed. Key figures include Louis Braille (see Idea 86 in January) and Thomas Gallaudet and his two sons Thomas and Edward. Before their time it was common to simply keep blind or deaf children at home, hidden from the world, or worse, children were condemned to horrific institutions where life expectancy was very short.

(179)

Last Great Buffalo Hunt

Anniversary, June 25-27, 1882

Although most Americans call this shaggy, hump-shouldered animal a buffalo, zoologists consider them bison. Bison differ from true buffalo in shape and in skeleton. Gigantic herds of bison once roamed the North American prairies. In the mid–eighteen hundreds, as many as twenty million bison lived in America. Observers said the ground shook when the herds ran and the thundering of their hoofs could be heard more than a mile away.

Native Americans hunted bison and used all parts of the body for food, clothing, tools, and shelter. When white settlers came from the east in the late eighteen hundreds, they conducted huge hunts, often removing only the head as a trophy. Carcasses were left to rot on the prairie. On June 25–27, 1882, some two thousand Teton Sioux in full hunting regalia killed five thousand buffalo on reservation lands near Hettinger, North Dakota. This event came to be known as "The Last Great Buffalo Hunt." By 1890, fewer than six hundred bison were found in a free-range head count.

Social studies units can focus on the Plains Indian cultures whose societies revolved around the buffalo hunt. Cultural connections could include researching preparations for the hunt, such as tribal buffalo dances. *The Song of the Buffalo*, by Joseph Bruchac (Harcourt, 0-150200044-5, grades 1 to 4), and *Buffalo Jump*, by Peter Roop (Northland, 0-87358616-6, grades K to 3), are two picture books with a Native American perspective on the importance of the buffalo hunt. *Buffalo Hunt*, by Russell Freedman (Holiday House, 0-8234-0702-0, grades 3 to 7), is a nonfiction examination of the history of buffalo hunting. *Buffalo Days*, by Diane Hoyt-Goldsmith (Holiday, 0-8234-1327-6, grades 3 to 6), is a modern perspective on buffalo and the Crow Indians.

Students can research the home construction of Indians who hunted buffalo as a mainstay and compare it to the homes of more sedentary Indians. Discuss how mobility was an important factor in the lives of buffalo-hunting societies.

All parts of the buffalo were used by Indians. Students can investigate how meat and hides were preserved, the kind of clothing and shelters that were made, and how bones and sinew were used to make tools.

A science aspect of buffalo/bison could focus around reports on the bison life cycle and conservation efforts to prevent the species from becoming extinct. *American Bison*, by Ruth Berman (Carolrhoda, 0-87614-697-3, grades 2 to 5), is an excellent presentation of physical characteristics, life cycle, traditional history, and conservation.

In the last dozen years a number of white buffalo calves have been born. The first one was named Miracle and was born on a farm in Wisconsin. (See Web page at homestead.com/WhiteBuffaloMiracle for details). This is a very rare genetic oddity from a science perspective, and a sacred happening from the Native tradition. In fact, there is a very important story that tells how the sacred pipe was given to the Native Americans by White Buffalo Woman. White buffalo are so special that when word spread that a calf was born, people traveled hundreds of miles to leave offerings and to sing sacred songs to the calf. If you live someplace with a Native American population you might be able to find a storyteller to retell this important tale. Be sure your class understands that this is a sacred story, and should be respected as such. It might help to tell them that for Christians the tales from the Bible are considered sacred and that many people believe them to be very true and not at all myth. This comparison might help dispel the idea that the story of White Buffalo Woman should be seen as a tall tale.

A language arts project might be to write newspaper articles describing two scenes: a Native American buffalo hunt and that of the white hunters, who sometimes rode trains to a buffalo herd, got off, hunted, took souvenirs like skulls or tails, and then reentered the train and left. Students may want to take a look at the way buffalo and native people lived together for centuries on the plains, but buffalo were driven almost to extinction in a matter of years once they were targeted by settlers.

(180)

Celebrate the Declaration of Independence

Anniversary, July 8, 1776

After weeks of arguing, haggling and concessions, the Declaration of Independence was finally approved by the Continental Congress on July 4, 1776. However, it wasn't until the eighth of July that the document was publicly read. John Nixon gave the Declaration of Independence its first public reading before a crowd of Philadelphians who had gathered in Independence Square.

Why not have your students present a reenactment of that historic event? Designate one student to be John Nixon and several others to represent the crowd. Because of the length and complex language, reading only the Preamble and the Declaration of Rights may be appropriate for elementary and middle school students. The most important thing is to breathe life into this historic document. Its words have power, and they deserve to be heard aloud.

Thomas Jefferson had been called upon to write the groundbreaking document, but when he presented it to the Continental Congress, the members had many suggestions and complaints. One of the most fiercely debated sections pertained to slavery. To ensure passage, Jefferson was forced to delete a passage denouncing the slave trade (placating slave owners). This is a good topic for junior high and high school students to discuss.

Middle school students, who often moan about the unfairness of revision and editing, would enjoy *The Hatmaker's Sign: A Story by Benjamin Franklin*, retold by Candace Fleming (Orchard, 0-531-30075-7, ages seven to eleven). Franklin tells a disheartened Jefferson a story about editing text as a result of public input. Information about the writing of the Declaration is included in an afterword.

Junior high and older students will find that Natalie S. Bober's *Countdown to Independence* (Simon, 0-689-81329-5, ages twelve and up) contains a wealth of information on the times leading up to the Declaration of Independence. High school students should not miss *John Adams*, a new biography of our second president written by David McCullough (Simon and Schuster, 0-684-81363-7, ages fourteen and up). Excerpts from this excellent book will bring the circumstances and negotiations behind the scenes of early American politics to vibrant life for today's students.

Appendix

Ideas for July and Summer School

Since some schools go year-round, and some will have summer classes, we thought we'd offer a few ideas to spark lazy-day summertime discussions or projects—all based on holidays or anniversaries occurring in July.

- July 1 is the anniversary of the Battle of Gettysburg (1883)—and a good time to read or reread Abraham Lincoln's stirring Gettysburg Address, given at the memorial of the battlefield on November 19, 1883. Have your class discuss why the speech is so enduring.
- July 1 is also Canada Day—Canada's national day much like our own July 4. Canada Day commemorates the confederation of Upper and Lower Canada and some of the Maritime Provinces into the Dominion of Canada in 1867. It is a good day to look at our good neighbor to the north.
- July 1 is also the anniversary of the first U.S. zoo—in Philadelphia in 1874. Have your class research which animals were housed in this zoo.
- July is National July Belongs to Blueberries Month—put a little blue in your class day! Help your class discover the health benefits of the blueberry.
- Koko the Gorilla celebrates her birthday on July 4. Koko, who has a sign-language vocabulary of one thousand signs, makes for a good classroom discussion topic on animal communication.

Explore the language of dolphins or whales—there are many interesting recordings out there.

- If your students are crazy about baseball, introduce them to Satchel Paige, the great African American pitcher who was born on July 7, 1906.
- And if they're fascinated by disasters and extreme earth phenomena, tell them about the highest tsunami in recorded history: at Lituya Bay, Alaska, on July 9, 1958, a landslide created a wave of 1,700 feet—which is taller than the Sears Tower in Chicago (at 1,450 feet). Explain how tsunamis are created.
- July 20 marks the anniversary of the first Special Olympics. If your class is unfamiliar with this great sporting event, introduce them to it and the concept of doing one's best.
- And last but not least, July 31 marks the birthday of J. K. Rowling and her fictional character—drumroll, please—Harry Potter. A little Harry Potter Day is always welcome to kids!

Index